AI-Powered Security: The Future of Cyber Defense

Alter Pérez

In the relentless war against cyber threats, a new era has dawned. Imagine a world where cyber defenses are not merely reactive but predictive, where attacks are anticipated and neutralized before they can inflict damage. This is the promise of artificial intelligence (AI) in cybersecurity—a promise that is swiftly becoming a reality.

For decades, cybersecurity has been locked in a game of cat and mouse, with cybercriminals constantly evolving their tactics to outsmart even the most sophisticated security measures. Traditional defenses, reliant on predefined rules and human vigilance, have struggled to keep pace with the dynamic and ever-growing threat landscape. However, the advent of AI and machine learning has introduced a powerful ally in this ongoing battle.

AI's ability to process vast amounts of data, recognize patterns, and make decisions at lightning speed has revolutionized industries across the board. In cybersecurity, these capabilities translate to unprecedented levels of protection. AI can analyze network traffic, detect anomalies, and respond to threats in real-time, far surpassing the capabilities of human analysts and traditional security systems.

This book, "**AI-Powered Security: The Future of Cyber Defense**," delves into the transformative impact of AI on cybersecurity. We will explore how AI-driven solutions are reshaping the way we protect our digital assets, from fortifying network defenses to enhancing endpoint security, and from automating incident response to driving innovative threat intelligence.

As we embark on this journey, we will uncover the fundamental principles of AI and machine learning, and how they are applied to tackle some of the most pressing challenges in cybersecurity. Through real-world case studies and expert insights, we will illuminate the successes and lessons learned from AI implementations across various industries.

However, with great power comes great responsibility. The integration of AI in cybersecurity also raises important ethical and legal considerations. We must navigate the complexities of data privacy, bias in AI models, and the ethical use of AI in cyber defense.

The future of cybersecurity is not just about technology but also about strategy, collaboration, and continual adaptation. This book aims to equip you with the knowledge and tools to harness the power of AI, transforming it from a buzzword into a robust and indispensable component of your cyber defense strategy.

Welcome to the frontier of AI-powered security, where the future of cyber defense is being forged today. Let us embark on this exciting journey together, exploring the innovations that will define the next generation of cybersecurity and empower us to stay one step ahead in the digital arms race.

Chapter 1: Introduction to AI in Cybersecurity

In an era where digital landscapes are constantly under threat, the fusion of artificial intelligence (AI) with cybersecurity marks a pivotal advancement. Chapter 1 serves as your gateway to understanding this revolutionary convergence. We begin by exploring the fundamentals of AI and tracing its historical roots. This foundation is crucial to appreciating how AI has evolved to become a cornerstone of modern cyber defense.

The chapter also delves into the dynamic nature of cyber threats, highlighting why traditional defense mechanisms often fall short. As cybercriminals employ increasingly sophisticated tactics, the need for adaptive, intelligent security solutions has never been more pressing. Here, AI steps in, offering the ability to anticipate, detect, and mitigate threats with unprecedented speed and accuracy.

By the end of this chapter, you will have a solid grasp of the basic concepts of AI and its indispensable role in transforming cybersecurity. This understanding sets the stage for the more detailed explorations that follow, as we uncover how AI-driven technologies are reshaping the fight against cybercrime. Welcome to the dawn of AI-powered cyber defense, where innovation meets necessity, and the future of security is being forged today.

1.1 Definition and History of AI

Artificial Intelligence (AI) is a branch of computer science focused on creating systems capable of performing tasks that typically require human intelligence. These tasks include learning from experience, reasoning, problem-solving, understanding natural language, and perception. AI encompasses various subfields, including machine learning (ML), natural language processing (NLP), robotics, and computer vision, each contributing to the broader goal of developing intelligent machines.

AI systems are designed to mimic human cognitive processes. They can analyze large datasets, recognize patterns, and make decisions with varying degrees of autonomy. The intelligence exhibited by AI can be classified into two categories:

Narrow AI (Weak AI): This form of AI is designed for specific tasks or applications. Examples include voice assistants like Siri and Alexa, recommendation systems on streaming platforms, and automated email filtering. Narrow AI operates within predefined parameters and excels in its specific domain but lacks generalization across different tasks.

General AI (Strong AI): General AI refers to a hypothetical level of intelligence that can perform any intellectual task that a human can. It possesses cognitive abilities comparable to those of humans and can understand, learn, and apply knowledge in a general manner. As of now, General AI remains a theoretical concept and has not yet been achieved.

History of AI

The history of AI is a fascinating journey of innovation, exploration, and discovery. It can be divided into several key phases, each marked by significant developments and milestones.

Early Foundations (Pre-1950s)

The concept of artificial intelligence can be traced back to ancient myths and legends. Early thinkers envisioned the possibility of creating intelligent machines, but it wasn't until the 20th century that these ideas began to take shape in a scientific context. Notable contributions from this era include:

Al-Khwarizmi (9th Century): The Persian mathematician's work on algorithms laid the groundwork for computational methods.

Ada Lovelace (19th Century): Often regarded as the first computer programmer, Lovelace recognized the potential of machines to perform tasks beyond mere calculation.

The Birth of AI (1950s-1960s)

The formal field of AI began to take shape in the mid-20th century. Pioneering work during this period laid the foundation for modern AI research:

Alan Turing (1950): Turing, a British mathematician, proposed the "Turing Test" as a measure of a machine's ability to exhibit intelligent behavior indistinguishable from that of a human. His work was crucial in defining the goals of AI.

Dartmouth Conference (1956): The Dartmouth Conference, organized by John McCarthy, Marvin Minsky, Nathaniel Rochester, and Claude Shannon, is widely considered the birth of AI as a formal field of study. The term "Artificial Intelligence" was coined during this conference, and the attendees laid out ambitious goals for AI research.

Early AI Programs (1950s-1960s): During this period, researchers developed some of the first AI programs. Notable examples include the Logic Theorist, created by Allen Newell and Herbert A. Simon, which could prove mathematical theorems, and ELIZA, an early natural language processing program developed by Joseph Weizenbaum.

The First AI Winter (1970s)

The enthusiasm surrounding AI faced challenges during the 1970s, leading to a period known as the "AI Winter." The initial excitement about AI research was tempered by several factors:

Overestimation of Capabilities: Early AI research made grand promises that were difficult to achieve with the available technology. The limitations of computing power and the complexity of the problems posed significant challenges.

Funding and Interest Decline: As progress slowed and expectations were not met, funding for AI research decreased, and interest waned. This period was marked by reduced activity and skepticism about the feasibility of achieving AI's goals.

The Rise of Expert Systems (1980s)

Despite the setbacks of the AI Winter, the 1980s saw a resurgence of interest in AI, driven by the development of expert systems:

Expert Systems: Expert systems are AI programs designed to emulate the decision-making abilities of human experts in specific domains. They use knowledge bases and inference rules to solve complex problems. The success of expert systems, such as MYCIN (a medical diagnosis system), demonstrated the practical utility of AI and revitalized research in the field.

Expansion of AI Applications: The 1980s also saw the application of AI techniques in various domains, including finance, manufacturing, and logistics. These applications showcased the potential of AI to address real-world problems.

The Second AI Winter (1990s)

Another period of stagnation occurred in the 1990s, known as the "Second AI Winter." Several factors contributed to this slowdown:

Limitations of Expert Systems: While expert systems were successful in some areas, they had limitations, such as difficulty in handling uncertainty and adapting to new information. These limitations led to disillusionment with the potential of AI.

Advancements in Other Fields: During this period, advancements in other areas of computer science, such as database technology and networking, shifted attention away from AI research.

The Revival and Modern Era (2000s-Present)

The early 2000s marked the beginning of a new era of AI research and development, driven by significant advancements in technology:

Machine Learning and Big Data: The rise of machine learning algorithms, coupled with the availability of vast amounts of data and increased computing power, revitalized AI research. Machine learning, particularly deep learning, became a central focus, enabling significant progress in areas such as image recognition, natural language processing, and game playing.

AI Applications and Breakthroughs: AI achieved notable milestones, including the success of IBM's Watson in winning "Jeopardy!" and the development of self-driving cars. The practical applications of AI expanded across various industries, including healthcare, finance, and entertainment.

Ethical and Social Implications: As AI technologies became more integrated into society, discussions about their ethical and social implications grew. Issues such as privacy, bias, and the impact on employment became important areas of concern and debate.

The history of AI reflects a dynamic and evolving field characterized by periods of optimism, challenge, and innovation. From its early conceptualization to its current state of rapid advancement, AI has transformed the way we interact with technology and envision the future. As AI continues to evolve, it holds the promise of further revolutionizing industries, solving complex problems, and shaping the future of human-computer interactions.

1.2 Evolution of Cyber Threats

The evolution of cyber threats is a complex and ongoing process, reflecting changes in technology, tactics, and motives over time. As digital technology has advanced, so too have the methods and sophistication of cyber attacks. This section explores the development of cyber threats, from their early forms to the sophisticated threats seen today, providing insights into how the landscape has shifted and what that means for cybersecurity.

Early Cyber Threats (1980s-1990s)

1. Simple Viruses and Worms:

Early Malware: The 1980s and early 1990s saw the emergence of simple malware, including viruses and worms. These early threats often spread through infected floppy disks or email attachments and were primarily designed to cause disruption or damage to systems.

Notable Examples: The "Brain" virus (1986) is considered one of the first computer viruses, infecting floppy disks and damaging data. Similarly, the "Morris Worm" (1988) was one of the earliest worms to spread via the internet, causing widespread disruption.

2. Basic Phishing Attacks:

Initial Scams: Phishing attacks in this era were relatively straightforward, often involving fraudulent emails or messages designed to trick users into divulging personal information or login credentials. These early attacks were less sophisticated but laid the groundwork for future social engineering tactics.

3. Denial of Service (DoS) Attacks:

Network Disruption: Denial of Service attacks aimed to disrupt the availability of services by overwhelming them with excessive traffic. Early DoS attacks were relatively simple but demonstrated the potential for causing significant disruptions to online services.

Growth and Sophistication (2000s-2010s)

1. Advanced Malware and Trojans:

Complex Payloads: The 2000s saw the emergence of more advanced malware, including Trojans and rootkits. These threats were designed to stealthily gain control over systems, often for data theft or espionage. Unlike early viruses, modern malware often had complex payloads and could evade detection for extended periods.

Notable Examples: The "ILOVEYOU" virus (2000) was a highly successful Trojan that spread through email and caused significant damage globally. The "Stuxnet" worm (2010) targeted industrial control systems and was used for cyber-espionage and sabotage, demonstrating a new level of sophistication and state-sponsored activity.

2. Evolution of Phishing and Social Engineering:

Targeted Phishing (Spear Phishing): Phishing attacks became more targeted and sophisticated, with spear phishing focusing on specific individuals or organizations. Attackers used personal information to craft convincing messages, increasing the likelihood of success.

Business Email Compromise (BEC): BEC attacks involved impersonating executives or employees to execute fraudulent transactions or steal sensitive information. These attacks became more common and sophisticated, often involving detailed research and pretexting.

3. Ransomware Emergence:

Extortion Tactics: Ransomware attacks became increasingly prevalent, with attackers encrypting victims' data and demanding ransom payments for decryption. Ransomware evolved to include sophisticated techniques for evading detection and spreading across networks.

Notable Examples: The "WannaCry" ransomware attack (2017) exploited vulnerabilities in Windows to rapidly spread and encrypt files on infected systems. The "Ryuk" ransomware (2018) targeted large organizations, demanding high ransom payments and causing significant operational disruption.

4. State-Sponsored and Advanced Persistent Threats (APTs):

Sophisticated Espionage: State-sponsored actors and APT groups emerged, using advanced techniques and tools for cyber-espionage and intelligence gathering. These threats often targeted critical infrastructure, government agencies, and large corporations.

Notable Examples: The "APT28" group, also known as Fancy Bear, and the "APT29" group, or Cozy Bear, were linked to state-sponsored espionage campaigns, including attacks on political organizations and diplomatic institutions.

Modern Threats and Emerging Trends (2020s-Present)

1. Ransomware Evolution and Ransomware-as-a-Service (RaaS):

Ransomware-as-a-Service: The ransomware landscape has evolved to include Ransomware-as-a-Service, allowing less technically skilled attackers to deploy sophisticated ransomware tools. This model lowers the barrier to entry for launching ransomware attacks and has led to a surge in incidents.

Double Extortion Tactics: Modern ransomware attacks often involve double extortion, where attackers not only encrypt data but also steal sensitive information, threatening to release it unless a ransom is paid.

2. Supply Chain Attacks:

Compromising the Supply Chain: Supply chain attacks target the software and hardware supply chain, compromising legitimate products to infect end users. These attacks exploit the trust between suppliers and their customers, making them difficult to detect and mitigate.

Notable Examples: The "SolarWinds" attack (2020) involved compromising the SolarWinds Orion platform to gain access to numerous organizations, including government agencies and major corporations.

3. AI-Powered Attacks:

Sophisticated and Automated Threats: Attackers are increasingly using AI and machine learning to enhance their attack capabilities. AI-powered tools can automate phishing campaigns, develop more convincing social engineering tactics, and even identify vulnerabilities in systems.

Defensive AI: Similarly, AI is being employed defensively to improve threat detection, automate incident response, and enhance overall security posture. However, the use of AI by attackers presents new challenges and requires continuous adaptation by cybersecurity professionals.

4. Privacy and Data Breaches:

Increased Focus on Data: The frequency and severity of data breaches have risen, often involving the theft of large volumes of personal and sensitive information. Privacy regulations and data protection laws have become more stringent, with organizations facing significant legal and reputational consequences for breaches.

Notable Examples: The "Equifax" breach (2017) exposed sensitive information of millions of individuals, highlighting the risks associated with data breaches and the importance of robust security measures.

The evolution of cyber threats reflects a dynamic and continually shifting landscape. From early viruses and simple phishing attacks to sophisticated ransomware, APTs, and AI-powered threats, the nature of cyber threats has become increasingly complex and challenging. Understanding this evolution is crucial for developing effective cybersecurity strategies and staying ahead of emerging threats. As technology continues to advance, both attackers and defenders will adapt, requiring ongoing vigilance and innovation in the field of cybersecurity.

1.3 The Intersection of AI and Cybersecurity

The intersection of artificial intelligence (AI) and cybersecurity represents a crucial convergence of technology, where AI's capabilities are leveraged to enhance security measures, and cybersecurity principles are adapted to address the challenges posed by advanced AI technologies. This section explores how AI and cybersecurity intersect, the benefits and challenges of this integration, and the transformative impact it has on the security landscape.

1. AI Enhancing Cybersecurity

1.1. Threat Detection and Response:

Advanced Detection Techniques: AI significantly enhances threat detection by analyzing vast amounts of data to identify anomalies and patterns indicative of cyber threats. Machine learning algorithms can process network traffic, system logs, and user behavior to detect unusual activities that may signal an attack.

Behavioral Analysis: AI systems can learn from historical data to establish normal behavior patterns and detect deviations. For example, if an AI system identifies unusual login times or access patterns, it can trigger alerts or automated responses, improving the speed and accuracy of threat detection.

1.2. Automated Incident Response:

Rapid Reaction: AI-driven automation enables faster response to security incidents. Automated response systems can take predefined actions, such as isolating affected systems, blocking malicious IP addresses, or applying security patches, reducing the time between detection and mitigation.

Reducing Human Error: By automating routine and repetitive tasks, AI reduces the risk of human error and ensures that responses are consistent and timely, which is critical in high-pressure security situations.

1.3. Enhanced Security Analytics:

Data Analysis and Correlation: AI enhances security analytics by processing and correlating large volumes of data from diverse sources. This includes analyzing threat intelligence feeds, vulnerability databases, and incident reports to provide actionable insights and improve decision-making.

Predictive Capabilities: AI models can predict potential threats by analyzing trends and patterns in historical data. Predictive analytics help organizations anticipate and prepare for future attacks, enhancing their proactive security measures.

2. AI in Cybersecurity Applications

2.1. Intrusion Detection Systems (IDS):

Intelligent IDS: AI-powered IDS use machine learning algorithms to identify and respond to intrusions based on abnormal behavior and emerging threat patterns. Unlike traditional signature-based systems, AI-driven IDS can detect novel attacks by recognizing deviations from established norms.

2.2. Security Information and Event Management (SIEM):

Advanced SIEM Solutions: AI enhances SIEM systems by automating log analysis, event correlation, and alert generation. AI algorithms can identify complex attack vectors and reduce false positives, allowing security teams to focus on genuine threats and critical incidents.

2.3. Endpoint Protection:

Next-Generation Antivirus: AI-driven endpoint protection solutions use machine learning to detect and mitigate threats in real time. These solutions analyze file behaviors, process interactions, and network activities to identify and block malware, ransomware, and other malicious threats.

2.4. Threat Intelligence:

Automated Threat Analysis: AI enhances threat intelligence by automating the collection and analysis of threat data from multiple sources. Natural language processing (NLP) and machine learning techniques are used to extract relevant information, identify emerging threats, and provide actionable intelligence.

3. Challenges and Considerations

3.1. Data Privacy and Security:

Sensitive Data Handling: The use of AI in cybersecurity involves processing sensitive and personal data, raising concerns about data privacy and security. Organizations must ensure that AI systems comply with data protection regulations and implement measures to safeguard data integrity.

3.2. AI Bias and Accuracy:

Bias in Algorithms: AI systems can be susceptible to bias if trained on skewed or unrepresentative data. Bias in AI algorithms can lead to incorrect threat detection or discriminatory practices. Ensuring fairness and accuracy in AI-driven security solutions is crucial to maintaining trust and effectiveness.

3.3. Adversarial AI:

Exploiting AI: Attackers may use adversarial AI techniques to evade detection and manipulate security systems. For example, adversarial attacks can exploit vulnerabilities in AI models, leading to false negatives or misclassification of threats. Defenders must continuously update and refine AI models to address these challenges.

3.4. Complexity and Integration:

System Complexity: Integrating AI into existing cybersecurity infrastructure can be complex and resource-intensive. Organizations must ensure that AI solutions are compatible with their current systems and workflows, and that they provide value without introducing additional complexities or overhead.

4. The Future of AI and Cybersecurity

4.1. Evolution of AI Capabilities:

Advancing Technology: As AI technology continues to evolve, its applications in cybersecurity will become more sophisticated. Future advancements may include more accurate threat detection, enhanced automation, and improved predictive analytics, further strengthening security measures.

4.2. Collaborative Approaches:

Human-AI Collaboration: The future of cybersecurity will likely involve increased collaboration between human expertise and AI systems. While AI can handle routine tasks and analyze vast amounts of data, human judgment and oversight will remain essential for interpreting complex threats and making strategic decisions.

4.3. Ethical and Regulatory Considerations:

Governance and Compliance: The integration of AI in cybersecurity will require ongoing attention to ethical and regulatory considerations. Organizations must navigate privacy concerns, data protection regulations, and ethical implications to ensure responsible and effective use of AI technologies.

The intersection of AI and cybersecurity represents a dynamic and transformative area of technology. AI enhances cybersecurity by improving threat detection, automating responses, and providing advanced security analytics. However, it also presents challenges related to data privacy, algorithmic bias, and adversarial attacks. As AI continues to advance, its role in cybersecurity will become increasingly integral, shaping the future of how we protect digital assets and manage cyber threats. The successful integration of AI in cybersecurity will depend on addressing these challenges while leveraging its capabilities to build more resilient and adaptive security solutions.

1.4 Importance of AI in Modern Cyber Defense

In the ever-evolving landscape of cybersecurity, artificial intelligence (AI) has become a crucial component of modern cyber defense strategies. As cyber threats become increasingly sophisticated and pervasive, AI provides essential tools and capabilities to enhance the effectiveness of security measures. This section explores the importance of AI in modern cyber defense, highlighting its role in addressing contemporary challenges, improving security operations, and shaping the future of cybersecurity.

1. Addressing Complex Threats

1.1. Evolving Threat Landscape:

Advanced Threats: Modern cyber threats are more complex and diverse than ever before. Attackers use advanced techniques such as polymorphic malware, ransomware-as-a-service, and sophisticated phishing schemes. AI's ability to analyze and process vast amounts of data enables it to detect and respond to these advanced threats more effectively than traditional methods.

Real-Time Analysis: AI systems can analyze network traffic, system logs, and user behavior in real time to identify anomalies and potential threats. This capability is essential for detecting and mitigating threats that may otherwise go unnoticed by conventional security solutions.

1.2. Behavioral Analysis:

Pattern Recognition: AI excels at recognizing patterns and deviations from established norms. By learning from historical data, AI can identify unusual behavior that may indicate a cyber attack. For example, AI can detect abnormal login patterns, unauthorized access attempts, or unusual file activity, providing early warnings of potential security breaches.

Adaptive Defense: AI systems can adapt to evolving threats by continuously learning and updating their models. This adaptability allows AI to stay ahead of attackers who constantly refine their tactics and techniques.

2. Enhancing Efficiency and Effectiveness

2.1. Automation of Routine Tasks:

Operational Efficiency: AI-driven automation streamlines routine security tasks such as log analysis, threat hunting, and incident response. This automation reduces the workload on security teams, allowing them to focus on more strategic and complex tasks. For example, AI can automatically analyze thousands of security events, prioritize alerts, and execute predefined response actions.

Consistency and Accuracy: Automated systems eliminate human errors and ensure consistent application of security policies. AI-driven solutions apply rules and procedures uniformly, reducing the risk of oversight or misconfiguration.

2.2. Scalability:

Handling Large Volumes of Data: The exponential growth of data and network traffic presents challenges for traditional security tools. AI's scalability allows it to handle large volumes of data efficiently, providing comprehensive visibility and analysis across complex and distributed environments.

Expanding Coverage: AI can scale to address the needs of large and diverse organizations, adapting to various environments, including cloud, on-premises, and hybrid infrastructures. This scalability ensures that security measures remain effective as organizations grow and evolve.

3. Improving Threat Detection and Response

3.1. Advanced Threat Detection:

Machine Learning Models: AI leverages machine learning models to detect threats that may not be identifiable through signature-based detection alone. These models can identify previously unknown threats by analyzing behavioral patterns, anomalies, and deviations from expected norms.

Early Detection: AI's ability to detect threats early is crucial for preventing significant damage. By identifying indicators of compromise (IOCs) and tactics, techniques, and procedures (TTPs) associated with attacks, AI can provide early warnings and enable proactive measures.

3.2. Accelerated Incident Response:

Rapid Response: AI-powered systems can automate incident response actions, such as isolating affected systems, blocking malicious IP addresses, and applying security patches. This acceleration minimizes the time between detection and remediation, reducing the potential impact of cyber incidents.

Forensic Analysis: AI assists in forensic analysis by analyzing large volumes of data to identify the root cause of incidents, track the progression of attacks, and gather evidence for investigations. This capability supports effective post-incident analysis and improves future defenses.

4. Enhancing Threat Intelligence

4.1. Automated Threat Intelligence:

Data Collection and Analysis: AI automates the collection and analysis of threat intelligence from diverse sources, including dark web forums, social media, and threat feeds. By processing this data, AI identifies emerging threats, trends, and indicators of compromise.

Contextual Insights: AI provides contextual insights by correlating threat intelligence with internal security data. This correlation enhances the relevance and accuracy of threat information, enabling more informed decision-making and strategic planning.

4.2. Predictive Capabilities:

Predictive Analytics: AI's predictive analytics capabilities allow organizations to anticipate potential threats and vulnerabilities based on historical data and emerging trends. By forecasting potential attack vectors and vulnerabilities, AI helps organizations proactively address security risks and strengthen their defenses.

5. Supporting Human Expertise

5.1. Augmenting Security Teams:

Enhanced Decision-Making: AI augments the capabilities of security teams by providing actionable insights, prioritizing alerts, and automating routine tasks. This support enables security professionals to focus on complex and strategic aspects of cybersecurity, enhancing overall effectiveness.

Continuous Learning: AI systems continuously learn from new data and experiences, improving their accuracy and effectiveness over time. This continuous learning process supports security teams by providing up-to-date threat intelligence and adaptive defense mechanisms.

5.2. Collaboration and Integration:

Integrated Solutions: AI integrates with existing security tools and platforms to enhance their capabilities. For example, AI can be integrated into Security Information and Event Management (SIEM) systems, Intrusion Detection Systems (IDS), and Endpoint Protection Platforms (EPP) to provide a more comprehensive and effective security posture.

AI plays a pivotal role in modern cyber defense by addressing complex threats, enhancing efficiency, improving threat detection and response, and supporting human expertise. As the cyber threat landscape continues to evolve, AI provides essential tools and capabilities to stay ahead of attackers and safeguard digital assets. Its ability to analyze vast amounts of data, automate routine tasks, and adapt to new threats makes it a critical component of contemporary cybersecurity strategies. Embracing AI in cyber defense not only enhances security measures but also prepares organizations to navigate the challenges of an increasingly interconnected and vulnerable digital world.

Chapter 2: Understanding the Cyber Threat Landscape

As we delve into Chapter 2, we take a closer look at the ever-evolving cyber threat landscape. This chapter provides a comprehensive overview of the various types of cyber threats that organizations face today. From malware and ransomware to phishing attacks and advanced persistent threats (APTs), understanding these threats is crucial for building effective defenses.

We begin by categorizing and defining the different types of cyber threats, offering insights into their methods of operation and the damage they can cause. This foundational knowledge is essential for appreciating the complexity and sophistication of modern cyber attacks.

The chapter then explores the concept of Advanced Persistent Threats (APTs), detailing how these stealthy and prolonged attacks target specific entities. By examining real-world examples, we illustrate the tactics, techniques, and procedures (TTPs) employed by APT actors.

Next, we turn our attention to recent trends in cyber attacks, highlighting how cybercriminals continually adapt and innovate. Understanding these trends helps us anticipate future threats and adjust our defense strategies accordingly.

We also address the limitations of traditional cybersecurity measures in the face of these advanced threats. Static defenses, while necessary, often struggle to keep pace with the dynamic and evolving nature of cyber attacks. This sets the stage for the introduction of AI as a game-changing solution in subsequent chapters.

Finally, we discuss the critical role of AI in identifying and mitigating these emerging threats. AI's ability to analyze vast amounts of data and recognize patterns that elude human detection makes it a powerful tool in the fight against cybercrime.

By the end of this chapter, you will have a clear understanding of the current cyber threat landscape and the challenges it presents. This knowledge will underscore the necessity of adopting AI-driven solutions to enhance our cybersecurity posture.

2.1 Types of Cyber Threats: Malware, Phishing, Ransomware

In the realm of cybersecurity, understanding the various types of cyber threats is fundamental to developing effective defense strategies. This section delves into three prominent types of cyber threats: malware, phishing, and ransomware. Each of these threats poses unique risks and requires distinct approaches for detection, prevention, and mitigation.

Malware

1. Definition and Characteristics:

Malware (short for malicious software) encompasses a wide range of harmful software programs designed to infiltrate, damage, or exploit computer systems and networks. Common types of malware include viruses, worms, Trojans, and spyware.

Behavior: Malware can perform a variety of malicious actions, such as corrupting files, stealing sensitive data, or providing unauthorized access to attackers.

2. Common Types of Malware:

- **Viruses**: Malicious code that attaches itself to legitimate programs or files and spreads to other systems when the infected file is executed. Viruses often corrupt or delete data and can disrupt system operations.
- **Worms**: Standalone malicious programs that replicate themselves to spread across networks. Unlike viruses, worms do not require a host file and can exploit vulnerabilities to propagate.
- **Trojans**: Malware that disguises itself as legitimate software to gain unauthorized access to systems. Trojans often create backdoors for attackers to exploit and can facilitate further attacks.
- **Spyware**: Software designed to secretly monitor and collect user information, such as keystrokes, browsing habits, or personal data. Spyware can be used for identity theft and other malicious purposes.

3. Detection and Mitigation:

Antivirus Software: Regularly updated antivirus programs can detect and remove known malware signatures. Behavior-based detection can also identify suspicious activities that may indicate malware presence.

Regular Updates and Patches: Keeping software and systems updated with the latest security patches helps protect against known vulnerabilities exploited by malware.

Safe Browsing Practices: Users should avoid downloading software from untrusted sources and be cautious of email attachments and links from unknown senders.

Phishing

1. Definition and Characteristics:

Phishing is a social engineering attack where attackers deceive individuals into providing sensitive information, such as usernames, passwords, or financial details. Phishing typically involves fraudulent emails, messages, or websites that appear legitimate.

2. Common Phishing Techniques:

- **Email Phishing**: Attackers send emails that appear to be from legitimate sources, such as banks or online services, requesting users to click on malicious links or provide personal information. These emails often create a sense of urgency or use familiar branding to deceive recipients.
- **Spear Phishing**: A targeted form of phishing aimed at specific individuals or organizations. Spear phishing attacks are more personalized and often involve extensive research to craft convincing messages that exploit the recipient's trust.
- **Whaling**: A type of spear phishing that targets high-profile individuals, such as executives or senior managers, with highly sophisticated and convincing messages. Whaling attacks often involve significant financial or reputational risk.
- **Pharming**: An attack that redirects users from legitimate websites to fraudulent ones designed to capture sensitive information. Pharming often involves compromising DNS settings or exploiting vulnerabilities in web browsers.

3. Detection and Mitigation:

- **Email Filtering**: Implementing email filters can help detect and block phishing emails before they reach users' inboxes. Filters can analyze email content, sender reputation, and known phishing indicators.
- **User Education**: Training users to recognize phishing attempts and verify the authenticity of requests for sensitive information can reduce the risk of falling victim to phishing attacks.
- **Multi-Factor Authentication (MFA):** Enabling MFA adds an extra layer of security, making it more difficult for attackers to access accounts even if they obtain login credentials through phishing.

Ransomware

1. Definition and Characteristics:

Ransomware is a type of malicious software that encrypts the victim's files or locks them out of their system, demanding a ransom payment for the decryption key or to regain access. Ransomware attacks can cause significant operational disruption and data loss.

2. Common Ransomware Variants:

- **Cryptocurrency Ransomware**: Encrypts files and demands payment in cryptocurrency, such as Bitcoin, which is harder to trace and recover. This variant often targets individuals and organizations for financial gain.
- **Locker Ransomware**: Locks users out of their systems or devices entirely, preventing access to files or applications. Locker ransomware often displays threatening messages and demands a ransom for unlocking the system.
- **Doxware (or Leakware):** Steals sensitive information and threatens to release it publicly unless the ransom is paid. Doxware attacks can result in reputational damage and legal consequences, in addition to financial losses.

3. Detection and Mitigation:

- **Regular Backups**: Regularly backing up critical data and storing backups offline or in secure cloud environments can mitigate the impact of ransomware attacks. Backups enable organizations to restore data without paying the ransom.
- **Security Awareness Training**: Educating users about safe practices, such as avoiding suspicious email attachments and links, can reduce the likelihood of ransomware infections.
- **Endpoint Protection**: Using advanced endpoint protection solutions with real-time threat detection and response capabilities can help identify and block ransomware before it encrypts files.

Understanding the different types of cyber threats—malware, phishing, and ransomware—is essential for developing effective cybersecurity strategies. Each threat type presents unique challenges and requires tailored approaches for detection, prevention, and mitigation. By leveraging a combination of technological solutions, user education, and best practices, organizations can enhance their defenses and reduce the risk of falling victim to these pervasive cyber threats.

2.2 Advanced Persistent Threats (APTs)

Advanced Persistent Threats (APTs) represent a sophisticated category of cyber threats characterized by their stealth, persistence, and targeted approach. Unlike typical cyber attacks that may be opportunistic or random, APTs are deliberate and strategic, often conducted by well-resourced and skilled adversaries with specific objectives. This section explores the nature of APTs, their common tactics and techniques, and strategies for detection and mitigation.

1. Definition and Characteristics

1.1. Definition of APTs:

- **Advanced**: Refers to the use of advanced techniques and tools by the attackers. APTs involve sophisticated methods that bypass traditional security measures and are often designed to exploit specific vulnerabilities in targeted systems.
- **Persistent**: Indicates that the attackers maintain a long-term presence within the victim's network. They avoid detection by operating stealthily and often work to ensure their continued access over an extended period.
- **Threats**: Highlights the malicious intent behind these attacks, which usually involve stealing sensitive information, compromising systems, or causing disruption for strategic purposes.

1.2. Key Characteristics:

- **Targeted Attacks**: APTs are highly targeted and usually aimed at specific organizations or individuals, often based on strategic interests such as intellectual property, confidential information, or critical infrastructure.
- **Long-Term Engagement**: Attackers behind APTs establish and maintain persistent access to the target's network, often remaining undetected for months or even years.
- **Stealth and Evasion**: APT attackers employ advanced techniques to avoid detection and maintain their foothold. They use encryption, obfuscation, and sophisticated evasion tactics to bypass security defenses.

2. Common Tactics and Techniques

2.1. Initial Compromise:

- **Phishing**: A common entry vector for APTs is phishing, where attackers use deceptive emails or messages to trick users into revealing credentials or downloading malicious attachments. Phishing emails are often highly customized and tailored to the target.
- **Exploitation of Vulnerabilities**: APTs frequently exploit known or zero-day vulnerabilities in software, operating systems, or network services to gain initial access. Attackers may use exploit kits or custom malware to exploit these weaknesses.

2.2. Lateral Movement:

- **Network Scanning**: Once inside the network, APT attackers perform network scanning to identify additional systems and potential targets. They map out the network to understand its structure and identify critical assets.
- **Privilege Escalation**: Attackers seek to escalate their privileges to gain higher-level access within the network. This often involves exploiting vulnerabilities or using stolen credentials to gain administrative or root access.

2.3. Data Exfiltration:

- **Data Collection**: APT attackers methodically collect sensitive data over time, including intellectual property, financial information, and personal data. They use various tools and techniques to gather and organize this information.
- **Exfiltration Channels**: Data exfiltration is conducted through covert channels, such as encrypted communication or steganography, to avoid detection. Attackers may use command-and-control servers or legitimate cloud services to transmit the stolen data.

2.4. Maintaining Persistence:

- **Backdoors and Rootkits**: To maintain access, APT attackers often install backdoors or rootkits that provide persistent and stealthy access to the compromised systems. These tools are designed to evade detection by traditional security measures.
- **Regular Updates**: Attackers may update their tools and techniques regularly to adapt to changes in the target environment and avoid detection. This ongoing refinement helps them maintain their presence and effectiveness.

3. Detection and Mitigation Strategies

3.1. Detection Techniques:

- **Behavioral Analysis**: Monitoring network and system behavior for unusual activities can help detect APTs. Behavioral analysis focuses on identifying anomalies that may indicate the presence of an attacker, such as unusual network traffic patterns or abnormal access to sensitive data.
- **Threat Intelligence**: Leveraging threat intelligence feeds and services provides valuable insights into known APT actors, their tactics, and indicators of compromise (IOCs). This information helps organizations recognize and respond to APTs more effectively.
- **Advanced Threat Detection Tools**: Implementing advanced threat detection solutions, such as Endpoint Detection and Response (EDR) and Security Information and Event Management (SIEM) systems, enhances the ability to identify and respond to APTs. These tools analyze large volumes of data and provide real-time alerts on potential threats.

3.2. Mitigation Strategies:

- **Network Segmentation**: Segmenting the network into isolated zones can limit the spread of APTs and reduce the impact of an attack. Network segmentation helps contain breaches and prevents attackers from moving laterally across the entire network.
- **Regular Updates and Patching**: Keeping software, systems, and applications updated with the latest security patches reduces the risk of exploitation by APTs. Regular patch management addresses known vulnerabilities and strengthens defenses.
- **Security Awareness Training**: Educating employees about security best practices, including recognizing phishing attempts and avoiding risky behaviors, reduces the likelihood of initial compromise and enhances overall security posture.

3.3. Incident Response:

- **Preparedness**: Developing and maintaining a robust incident response plan ensures that organizations are prepared to respond to APTs effectively. The plan should include procedures for detecting, containing, eradicating, and recovering from APT incidents.
- **Forensic Analysis**: Conducting thorough forensic analysis following an APT attack helps identify the attack vectors, assess the extent of the breach, and

gather evidence for remediation and legal purposes. Forensic analysis also provides insights for improving future defenses.

4. Case Studies and Examples
4.1. Notable APT Campaigns:

- **Stuxnet**: A sophisticated APT attack that targeted Iran's nuclear program by disrupting industrial control systems. Stuxnet demonstrated the capability of APTs to target critical infrastructure with high precision.
- **APT28 (Fancy Bear):** A known APT group associated with Russian state-sponsored cyber espionage, which has been linked to various high-profile attacks on government and political entities.

4.2. Lessons Learned:

- **Adaptability**: APT attackers are highly adaptable and continually evolve their tactics. Organizations must remain vigilant and proactive in updating their security measures to address emerging threats.
- **Collaboration**: Collaboration between industry, government, and intelligence agencies enhances the collective ability to detect and respond to APTs. Sharing threat intelligence and best practices strengthens overall cyber defense.

Advanced Persistent Threats (APTs) represent a significant challenge in modern cybersecurity due to their sophisticated and persistent nature. Understanding the tactics, techniques, and characteristics of APTs is crucial for developing effective detection and mitigation strategies. By leveraging advanced threat detection tools, implementing robust security measures, and fostering collaboration, organizations can enhance their ability to defend against and respond to these complex and targeted cyber threats.

2.3 Recent Trends in Cyber Attacks

The cybersecurity landscape is dynamic, with attack vectors and techniques continually evolving. Staying abreast of recent trends in cyber attacks is crucial for organizations to adapt their defenses and mitigate risks effectively. This section explores some of the most significant trends in cyber attacks, highlighting their implications and the strategies needed to address them.

1. Ransomware Evolution

1.1. Ransomware-as-a-Service (RaaS):

- **Service Model**: Ransomware-as-a-Service has emerged as a business model where cybercriminals offer ransomware tools and services on a subscription basis. This model lowers the barrier to entry for attackers, allowing even those with limited technical skills to launch sophisticated ransomware attacks.
- **Revenue Sharing**: RaaS providers often operate on a revenue-sharing model, taking a cut of the ransom payments. This incentivizes widespread distribution and increased targeting of organizations.

1.2. Double Extortion Tactics:

- **Data Encryption and Theft**: Modern ransomware attacks often employ double extortion tactics. Attackers not only encrypt the victim's data but also steal sensitive information. They then threaten to release the stolen data publicly if the ransom is not paid.
- **Increased Pressure**: This tactic increases the pressure on victims to pay the ransom to prevent both operational disruption and reputational damage.

2. Supply Chain Attacks

2.1. Targeting Third-Party Vendors:

- **Indirect Attacks**: Supply chain attacks involve compromising a third-party vendor to gain access to the primary target. Attackers exploit the trust relationships between organizations and their suppliers or partners.
- **High-Profile Examples**: Notable examples include the SolarWinds attack, where malicious code was inserted into software updates, affecting thousands of organizations globally. These attacks can have widespread and severe impacts.

2.2. Compromising Software and Hardware:

- **Infiltration of Software Updates**: Attackers can insert malicious code into legitimate software updates or hardware components, compromising the integrity of widely used products. This method can be particularly challenging to detect and mitigate.
- **Long-Term Impact**: Supply chain attacks can lead to prolonged exposure and compromise of sensitive data, as the attackers gain persistent access through trusted channels.

3. Cloud Security Threats

3.1. Misconfigured Cloud Services:

- **Exposure Risks**: Misconfigurations in cloud services, such as improper access controls or exposed storage buckets, can lead to significant data breaches. These vulnerabilities often arise from insufficient understanding or oversight of cloud security settings.
- **Increased Attack Surface**: As organizations migrate more services to the cloud, the attack surface expands, creating new opportunities for cybercriminals to exploit misconfigurations.

3.2. Cloud-native Threats:

- **Container and Orchestration Vulnerabilities**: Threats targeting containerized environments and orchestration tools like Kubernetes are on the rise. Vulnerabilities in container configurations or orchestration settings can lead to unauthorized access and data breaches.
- **Account Compromise**: Attacks targeting cloud service provider accounts, including privilege escalation and unauthorized access, pose significant risks to cloud infrastructure and data.

4. Social Engineering and Phishing Sophistication

4.1. Personalized Phishing Attacks:

- **Spear Phishing**: Attackers are increasingly using spear phishing techniques, crafting highly personalized and convincing messages based on detailed information about the target. This personalization increases the likelihood of successful deception.
- **Deepfake Technology**: The use of deepfake technology to create realistic but fraudulent audio or video content adds another layer of sophistication to social engineering attacks. Attackers use deepfakes to impersonate trusted individuals and manipulate victims.

4.2. Business Email Compromise (BEC):

- **CEO Fraud**: Business Email Compromise attacks involve compromising executive email accounts to initiate fraudulent transactions or gather sensitive

information. These attacks often exploit social engineering to bypass traditional security measures.
- **Financial Losses**: BEC attacks can result in substantial financial losses for organizations, as attackers use compromised email accounts to execute fraudulent wire transfers or manipulate financial transactions.

5. IoT and Operational Technology Vulnerabilities

5.1. IoT Device Exploitation:

- **Insecure Devices**: Many Internet of Things (IoT) devices are designed with minimal security features, making them susceptible to exploitation. Attackers can compromise IoT devices to launch large-scale attacks, such as Distributed Denial of Service (DDoS) attacks.
- **Network Access:** Compromised IoT devices can provide attackers with entry points into corporate networks, leading to broader security breaches.

5.2. Attacks on Operational Technology (OT):

- **Industrial Control Systems (ICS):** Attacks targeting industrial control systems and operational technology can disrupt critical infrastructure and manufacturing processes. These attacks can have serious implications for safety and operational continuity.
- **Ransomware and Sabotage**: Ransomware and sabotage attacks on OT systems can cause physical damage or operational failures, impacting industrial operations and public safety.

6. Zero-Day Exploits

6.1. Exploitation of Unpatched Vulnerabilities:

- **Zero-Day Vulnerabilities**: Zero-day exploits involve attacks that target previously unknown vulnerabilities for which no patches or fixes are available. These exploits can be highly damaging due to the lack of defenses.
- **Market for Zero-Days**: A growing market for zero-day vulnerabilities, including underground marketplaces and state-sponsored actors, contributes to the increased risk of zero-day attacks.

6.2. High-Value Targets:

- **Strategic Use**: Zero-day exploits are often used in targeted attacks against high-value targets, including government agencies, financial institutions, and technology companies. These attacks leverage the element of surprise to maximize impact.

7. Increased Use of AI and Machine Learning by Attackers

7.1. Automation of Attack Techniques:

- **AI-Driven Attacks**: Cybercriminals are increasingly using AI and machine learning to automate and enhance their attack techniques. This includes automating phishing campaigns, crafting sophisticated malware, and evading detection.
- **Adversarial AI**: Attackers may employ adversarial AI to manipulate or bypass AI-driven security systems. This involves creating inputs designed to deceive or confuse machine learning models.

7.2. Enhanced Social Engineering:

- **AI-Powered Reconnaissance**: AI tools enable attackers to perform extensive reconnaissance and gather detailed information about targets, improving the effectiveness of social engineering attacks.

Recent trends in cyber attacks highlight the increasing sophistication and diversity of threats facing organizations today. Ransomware-as-a-Service, supply chain attacks, cloud security threats, and advanced social engineering techniques represent some of the most pressing challenges. By staying informed about these trends and implementing proactive security measures, organizations can better defend against emerging threats and strengthen their overall cybersecurity posture. Adapting to the evolving threat landscape requires continuous vigilance, advanced detection capabilities, and a comprehensive approach to risk management.

2.4 Challenges in Traditional Cyber Defense

Traditional cyber defense strategies, while foundational, face significant challenges in effectively mitigating modern cyber threats. As cyber threats evolve in sophistication and scale, these traditional approaches often fall short in addressing the complexities of contemporary cyber environments. This section explores the primary challenges faced by traditional cyber defense mechanisms and highlights the need for more advanced and adaptive security solutions.

1. Insufficient Threat Intelligence

1.1. Reactive Approach:

- **Delayed Detection**: Traditional cyber defense often relies on signature-based detection and known threat indicators, which can be reactive rather than proactive. This approach can lead to delayed detection of new and emerging threats that do not match existing signatures.
- **Limited Context**: Traditional methods may lack the context needed to fully understand and respond to advanced threats. Threat intelligence is often fragmented, providing only partial visibility into the threat landscape.

1.2. Challenges in Updating Intelligence:

- **Manual Updates**: Maintaining up-to-date threat intelligence requires constant manual updates and verification, which can be time-consuming and prone to errors.
- **Inadequate Sharing**: Limited collaboration and information sharing among organizations and industry sectors can hinder the effectiveness of threat intelligence, leaving gaps in defense.

2. Complexity and Fragmentation

2.1. Disparate Security Tools:

- **Tool Overload**: Many organizations use a multitude of security tools, each addressing specific aspects of the security posture. This can result in tool overload and challenges in integrating and managing these disparate solutions.
- **Inconsistent Coverage**: Different tools may offer varying levels of protection, leading to inconsistencies in coverage and leaving potential gaps in security.

2.2. Integration Issues:

- **Interoperability**: Integrating various security tools and platforms can be complex, and lack of interoperability may hinder effective communication and coordination between tools.

- **Complex Management**: Managing and correlating data from multiple sources can be challenging, requiring significant manual effort and expertise to maintain a coherent security posture.

3. Limited Visibility and Detection

3.1. Insufficient Monitoring:

- **Blind Spots**: Traditional defenses often struggle to provide comprehensive visibility across the entire IT environment, including cloud services, IoT devices, and remote endpoints. This can create blind spots where threats can go undetected.
- **Lack of Real-Time Analysis**: Many traditional systems rely on periodic scanning and log analysis, which may not provide real-time detection of active threats or anomalies.

3.2. Inadequate Incident Response:

- **Slow Response Times**: Traditional incident response mechanisms may not be equipped to handle the speed and complexity of modern cyber attacks. This can result in slow response times and prolonged exposure to threats.
- **Manual Processes**: Incident response processes often involve manual investigation and remediation, which can be time-consuming and less effective in rapidly evolving attack scenarios.

4. Difficulty in Adapting to New Threats

4.1. Evolving Threat Landscape:

- **Rapid Evolution**: Cyber threats and attack techniques evolve rapidly, and traditional defenses may struggle to keep pace with the latest threats. This includes new forms of malware, sophisticated phishing tactics, and advanced persistent threats (APTs).
- **Emerging Technologies**: The adoption of new technologies, such as cloud computing, IoT, and artificial intelligence, introduces new attack vectors that traditional defenses may not be fully equipped to handle.

4.2. Lack of Flexibility:

- **Static Defenses**: Many traditional security measures are static and may not adapt well to changing threat landscapes. This can result in outdated defenses that are ineffective against novel or adaptive attack techniques.

5. Resource and Cost Constraints

5.1. High Costs:

- **Expense of Tools**: The cost of acquiring, deploying, and maintaining a wide range of traditional security tools can be prohibitive for many organizations, especially smaller ones with limited budgets.
- **Resource Allocation**: Managing and maintaining traditional security defenses often requires significant personnel resources and expertise, which can strain organizational resources.

5.2. Complexity of Implementation:

- **Deployment Challenges**: Implementing and configuring traditional security solutions can be complex and time-consuming, requiring specialized knowledge and skills.
- **Ongoing Maintenance**: Regular updates, patch management, and tuning of security tools can be resource-intensive and may divert attention from other critical security tasks.

6. Human Factors and Skill Gaps

6.1. Skill Shortages:

- **Expertise Required**: Traditional cyber defense often relies heavily on skilled security professionals to manage and interpret security data. The shortage of cybersecurity talent can limit the effectiveness of these defenses.
- **Training Needs:** Ongoing training and development are necessary to keep security teams up-to-date with the latest threats and technologies. However, this can be challenging given the rapid pace of change in the cybersecurity field.

6.2. Human Error:

- **Misconfigurations**: Errors in configuring security tools or implementing security policies can create vulnerabilities and reduce the effectiveness of traditional defenses.

- **Inadequate Awareness**: Lack of awareness or understanding of cybersecurity best practices among employees can lead to risky behaviors and potential security breaches.

Traditional cyber defense mechanisms face numerous challenges in effectively addressing the complex and evolving threat landscape. Insufficient threat intelligence, complexity and fragmentation of security tools, limited visibility and detection capabilities, difficulty adapting to new threats, resource and cost constraints, and human factors all contribute to the limitations of traditional approaches. To enhance cybersecurity resilience, organizations must adopt more advanced and integrated security solutions, leverage threat intelligence and automation, and continually adapt to the changing threat environment. Embracing modern cybersecurity practices and technologies is essential for building a robust and adaptive defense posture capable of mitigating today's sophisticated cyber threats.

2.5 How AI Can Address These Challenges

Artificial Intelligence (AI) has emerged as a transformative force in cybersecurity, offering innovative solutions to the challenges faced by traditional cyber defense mechanisms. By leveraging AI technologies, organizations can enhance their ability to detect, respond to, and mitigate modern cyber threats more effectively. This section explores how AI can address the key challenges in traditional cyber defense.

1. Enhancing Threat Intelligence

1.1. Proactive Threat Detection:

- **Behavioral Analysis**: AI can analyze vast amounts of data to identify patterns and anomalies that indicate potential threats. By employing machine learning algorithms, AI systems can detect unusual behavior and predict emerging threats before they manifest.
- **Threat Intelligence Aggregation**: AI can aggregate and analyze data from multiple sources, including threat feeds, historical data, and real-time inputs, to provide a comprehensive view of the threat landscape. This aggregation helps in understanding and anticipating new attack vectors and tactics.

1.2. Real-Time Updates:

- **Automated Intelligence Updates**: AI systems can automatically update threat intelligence by continuously monitoring and analyzing new data. This automation reduces the reliance on manual updates and ensures that security measures are current with the latest threat information.
- **Adaptive Learning**: AI can adapt to evolving threats by learning from new data and incorporating new threat intelligence into its models. This adaptability helps in addressing emerging threats more effectively.

2. Reducing Complexity and Fragmentation

2.1. Integrated Security Platforms:

- **Unified Solutions**: AI-driven security platforms can integrate various security tools and functions into a unified solution. This integration reduces tool fragmentation and streamlines the management of security operations.
- **Centralized Management**: AI provides centralized management capabilities, allowing organizations to oversee and coordinate their security efforts from a single platform, improving efficiency and reducing complexity.

2.2. Automation and Orchestration:

- **Automated Threat Response**: AI can automate repetitive tasks such as threat detection, incident response, and system updates. Automation reduces the manual workload on security teams and accelerates response times.
- **Orchestration of Security Operations**: AI-driven orchestration tools can coordinate actions across different security systems, ensuring a cohesive response to threats and improving overall security posture.

3. Improving Visibility and Detection

3.1. Advanced Monitoring:

- **Deep Packet Inspection**: AI can perform deep packet inspection to analyze network traffic and identify hidden threats that traditional methods might miss. This level of scrutiny enhances visibility into network activities.
- **Enhanced Endpoint Detection**: AI enhances endpoint detection by continuously monitoring and analyzing activities on endpoints. AI models can detect anomalies and potential threats in real-time, providing improved visibility and early detection.

3.2. Real-Time Analytics:

- **Continuous Monitoring**: AI systems provide continuous monitoring of network and system activities, offering real-time analytics and alerts. This continuous oversight ensures that threats are detected and addressed promptly.
- **Anomaly Detection**: AI uses advanced algorithms to detect deviations from normal behavior, identifying potential threats and providing insights into their nature and scope.

4. Adapting to New Threats

4.1. Adaptive Threat Models:

- **Dynamic Learning**: AI can adapt to new threats by continuously learning from new data and evolving attack patterns. Machine learning models can update their algorithms to recognize and respond to emerging threats effectively.
- **Predictive Analysis**: AI can analyze historical data and current trends to predict future threats. This predictive capability helps organizations anticipate and prepare for potential attacks before they occur.

4.2. Threat Simulation:

- **AI-Driven Simulations**: AI can simulate various attack scenarios to test and refine security measures. These simulations help organizations understand potential vulnerabilities and improve their defenses against new attack techniques.

5. Addressing Resource and Cost Constraints

5.1. Cost Efficiency:

- **Reduced Operational Costs**: AI-driven automation and orchestration reduce the need for extensive manual intervention, leading to cost savings in operational expenses. By automating routine tasks, organizations can allocate resources more effectively.
- **Scalable Solutions**: AI solutions are often scalable, allowing organizations to expand their security capabilities without proportional increases in cost. Scalable AI systems can handle growing volumes of data and threats efficiently.

5.2. Efficient Resource Utilization:

- **Optimized Resource Allocation**: AI can optimize the allocation of resources by prioritizing threats and incidents based on their severity. This prioritization ensures that security teams focus on the most critical issues.
- **Streamlined Operations**: AI helps streamline security operations by providing actionable insights and automating repetitive tasks, allowing security teams to focus on strategic and high-impact activities.

6. Mitigating Human Factors and Skill Gaps

6.1. Augmented Decision-Making:

- **AI-Assisted Analysis**: AI tools assist security professionals by providing actionable insights and recommendations based on data analysis. This support enhances decision-making and reduces the reliance on extensive human expertise.
- **Skill Enhancement**: AI-driven systems can help bridge skill gaps by providing advanced analytics and guidance, enabling less experienced staff to manage complex security tasks more effectively.

6.2. Error Reduction:

- **Automated Configuration**: AI can automate the configuration and management of security tools, reducing the risk of misconfigurations and human errors.
- **Enhanced Training**: AI can be used to create realistic training scenarios and simulations, helping security teams improve their skills and readiness for handling various types of attacks.

AI offers powerful solutions to the challenges faced by traditional cyber defense mechanisms. By enhancing threat intelligence, reducing complexity, improving visibility, adapting to new threats, addressing resource constraints, and mitigating human factors, AI helps organizations build more effective and resilient cybersecurity defenses. Embracing AI technologies enables organizations to stay ahead of evolving threats, streamline security operations, and enhance their overall security posture in an increasingly complex cyber landscape.

Chapter 3: Machine Learning Fundamentals for Cybersecurity

As the digital landscape becomes increasingly complex, traditional cybersecurity measures often fall short in addressing the sophisticated nature of modern cyber threats. Enter machine learning (ML)—a game-changer in the field of cybersecurity. Chapter 3 introduces you to the fundamentals of machine learning, highlighting its transformative potential in detecting, preventing, and responding to cyber attacks.

We begin by exploring the basic concepts of ML, laying the groundwork for understanding its varied applications in cybersecurity. Through a detailed examination of supervised, unsupervised, and reinforcement learning techniques, we will uncover how these methods enable advanced threat detection and mitigation. By the end of this chapter, you will have a solid grasp of machine learning principles and their critical role in fortifying our cyber defenses against an ever-evolving threat landscape. Welcome to the intersection of artificial intelligence and cybersecurity, where the power of machine learning is harnessed to protect our digital world.

3.1 Basics of Machine Learning

Machine Learning (ML) is a subset of artificial intelligence that enables systems to learn and improve from experience without being explicitly programmed. By using algorithms and statistical models, machine learning can analyze data, identify patterns, and make predictions or decisions based on that data. Understanding the basics of machine learning is essential for leveraging its capabilities in cybersecurity applications.

1. Overview of Machine Learning

1.1. Definition:

Machine Learning (ML): Machine learning is a field of computer science that focuses on the development of algorithms that allow computers to learn from and make decisions based on data. Unlike traditional programming, where explicit instructions are given for every task, machine learning algorithms improve their performance as they are exposed to more data.

1.2. Types of Machine Learning:

Supervised Learning: In supervised learning, the algorithm is trained on labeled data, where the correct output is provided for each input. The goal is for the model to learn the mapping from inputs to outputs so it can make accurate predictions on new, unseen data. Common supervised learning tasks include classification (e.g., spam detection) and regression (e.g., predicting sales).

Unsupervised Learning: Unsupervised learning involves training the algorithm on unlabeled data, where the goal is to identify patterns or structures in the data. Techniques include clustering (e.g., customer segmentation) and dimensionality reduction (e.g., principal component analysis).

Reinforcement Learning: Reinforcement learning involves training an agent to make decisions by rewarding desired behaviors and penalizing undesired ones. The agent learns to maximize cumulative rewards through trial and error. This type of learning is commonly used in robotics and game playing.

2. Key Concepts in Machine Learning

2.1. Algorithms and Models:

Algorithms: Machine learning algorithms are mathematical procedures that process data to identify patterns and make predictions. Examples include decision trees, neural networks, and support vector machines.

Models: A model is the output of a machine learning algorithm after it has been trained on data. The model is used to make predictions or decisions based on new data. For instance, a trained model might predict whether an email is spam based on its content.

2.2. Training and Testing:

Training: Training involves feeding the machine learning algorithm with a dataset (training data) that includes both inputs and the corresponding correct outputs. The algorithm uses this data to learn and adjust its parameters to improve accuracy.

Testing: Testing involves evaluating the performance of the trained model on a separate dataset (testing data) that was not used during training. This helps assess how well the model generalizes to new, unseen data.

2.3. Overfitting and Underfitting:

Overfitting: Overfitting occurs when a model learns the details and noise in the training data to the extent that it negatively impacts the model's performance on new data. An overfitted model performs well on training data but poorly on testing data.

Underfitting: Underfitting occurs when a model is too simple to capture the underlying patterns in the data. An underfitted model performs poorly on both training and testing data.

2.4. Evaluation Metrics:

Accuracy: Accuracy measures the proportion of correctly predicted instances out of the total instances. It is commonly used for classification tasks.

Precision and Recall: Precision measures the proportion of true positive predictions out of all positive predictions made by the model. Recall measures the proportion of true positive predictions out of all actual positives. These metrics are important for evaluating the performance of classification models, especially in cases where class imbalances exist.

F1 Score: The F1 score is the harmonic mean of precision and recall, providing a single metric to evaluate model performance when dealing with imbalanced datasets.

3. Practical Applications in Cybersecurity

3.1. Threat Detection:

Anomaly Detection: Machine learning can be used to identify unusual patterns in network traffic or user behavior that may indicate potential threats. Anomaly detection algorithms can help in spotting deviations from normal activity that could signify a security breach.

3.2. Malware Analysis:

Malware Classification: Machine learning algorithms can analyze and classify malware based on features extracted from executable files. This helps in identifying new and previously unknown malware strains.

3.3. Phishing Detection:

Email Filtering: Machine learning can be employed to analyze email content and detect phishing attempts. By learning from past phishing emails, models can identify similar patterns in new emails and flag them as potential threats.

3.4. User Authentication:

Behavioral Biometrics: Machine learning can enhance user authentication by analyzing behavioral biometrics, such as typing patterns and mouse movements, to detect anomalies that might indicate unauthorized access.

3.5. Incident Response:

Automated Response: Machine learning models can automate responses to certain types of security incidents, such as isolating affected systems or blocking malicious IP addresses, based on learned patterns of attack behavior.

4. Challenges and Considerations

4.1. Data Quality and Quantity:

Data Requirements: Machine learning models require large amounts of high-quality data to perform well. Inadequate or poor-quality data can lead to inaccurate models and unreliable results.

4.2. Interpretability:

Model Interpretability: Some machine learning models, particularly complex ones like deep neural networks, can be challenging to interpret. Understanding how a model makes decisions is crucial for ensuring trust and accountability in cybersecurity applications.

4.3. Bias and Fairness:

Bias in Data: Machine learning models can inherit biases present in the training data. Ensuring that models are fair and unbiased is important for maintaining equitable and effective cybersecurity measures.

Understanding the basics of machine learning provides a foundation for leveraging its capabilities in cybersecurity. By grasping key concepts such as algorithms, models, and evaluation metrics, and recognizing the practical applications and challenges, organizations can effectively utilize machine learning to enhance their security posture. As machine learning technologies continue to advance, their integration into cybersecurity practices will play a critical role in addressing the complexities of modern cyber threats.

3.2 Supervised Learning Techniques

Supervised learning is a fundamental machine learning approach where algorithms are trained on labeled data. In supervised learning, the algorithm learns from input-output pairs, with the goal of making predictions or decisions based on new, unseen data. This section explores key supervised learning techniques, including their methodologies, applications, and considerations.

1. Linear Regression

1.1. Overview:

Definition: Linear regression is a statistical method used to model the relationship between a dependent variable and one or more independent variables. The goal is to find the linear relationship that best fits the data.

1.2. Applications:

- **Predictive Modeling**: Used to predict continuous outcomes, such as sales forecasts or temperature predictions.
- **Trend Analysis**: Helps in understanding trends and relationships in data.

1.3. Considerations:

- **Assumptions**: Assumes linear relationships between variables, normal distribution of errors, and homoscedasticity (constant variance of errors).
- **Limitations**: May not perform well with non-linear relationships or when there are multiple interacting variables.

2. Logistic Regression

2.1. Overview:

Definition: Logistic regression is used for binary classification problems, where the goal is to predict the probability of a binary outcome (e.g., yes/no, spam/ham).

2.2. Applications:

- **Classification**: Commonly used in scenarios such as email spam detection, disease diagnosis, and credit scoring.
- **Probability** Estimation: Provides probabilities for classification decisions, useful for risk assessment.

2.3. Considerations:

- **Assumptions**: Assumes a linear relationship between the input variables and the log odds of the outcome.
- **Limitations**: Limited to binary classification; extensions like multinomial logistic regression are needed for multi-class problems.

3. Decision Trees

3.1. Overview:

- **Definition**: Decision trees are a model that splits data into subsets based on feature values, forming a tree-like structure with decision nodes and leaf nodes.
- **Algorithm**: The decision tree algorithm recursively splits the data to maximize information gain or minimize impurity (e.g., Gini index or entropy).

3.2. Applications:

- **Classification and Regression**: Used for both classification (e.g., categorizing customer segments) and regression (e.g., predicting house prices).
- **Interpretability**: Provides an intuitive and easily interpretable model structure.

3.3. Considerations:

- **Overfitting**: Decision trees can overfit the training data, leading to poor generalization on unseen data. Pruning techniques can help mitigate this.
- **Complexity**: Large trees can become complex and less interpretable.

4. Random Forests

4.1. Overview:

- **Definition**: Random forests are an ensemble method that combines multiple decision trees to improve predictive performance and control overfitting.
- **Algorithm**: Uses bagging (bootstrap aggregating) to create multiple decision trees from random subsets of the data, and aggregates their predictions (e.g., by majority voting for classification or averaging for regression).

4.2. Applications:

- **Improved Accuracy**: Often used in scenarios requiring high accuracy and robustness, such as financial forecasting and medical diagnostics.
- **Feature Importance**: Can be used to determine the importance of different features in the model.

4.3. Considerations:

- **Complexity**: Random forests can be computationally intensive and less interpretable than single decision trees.
- **Performance**: Generally provides better performance and generalization than individual decision trees.

5. Support Vector Machines (SVM)

5.1. Overview:

- **Definition**: Support Vector Machines are a classification technique that finds the hyperplane that best separates different classes in the feature space.
- **Algorithm**: SVMs maximize the margin between classes by finding the optimal hyperplane. For non-linear problems, kernel functions (e.g., polynomial or radial basis function) are used to map data into higher dimensions.

5.2. Applications:

- **Binary and Multi-Class Classification**: Used for image recognition, text classification, and bioinformatics.
- **Effective in High-Dimensional Spaces**: Performs well in scenarios with many features.

5.3. Considerations:

- **Parameter Tuning**: Requires careful tuning of parameters such as the regularization parameter and kernel parameters.
- **Scalability**: May become computationally expensive with large datasets.

6. k-Nearest Neighbors (k-NN)

6.1. Overview:

- **Definition**: k-Nearest Neighbors is a simple, instance-based learning algorithm that classifies a data point based on the majority class among its k nearest neighbors in the feature space.
- **Algorithm**: Computes the distance between data points (e.g., using Euclidean distance) and assigns the class based on the majority vote of the k nearest neighbors.

6.2. Applications:

- **Classification and Regression**: Used for pattern recognition, recommendation systems, and anomaly detection.
- **Simplicity**: Easy to implement and understand.

6.3. Considerations:

- **Computational Cost**: Can be slow and computationally expensive for large datasets, as it requires calculating distances for every prediction.
- **Choice of k**: The choice of k (number of neighbors) and distance metric can significantly affect performance.

7. Neural Networks

7.1. Overview:

- **Definition**: Neural networks are a set of algorithms modeled after the human brain, designed to recognize patterns and learn from data through layers of interconnected nodes (neurons).
- **Architecture**: Consists of an input layer, one or more hidden layers, and an output layer. Each layer performs transformations on the data through learned weights.

7.2. Applications:

- **Complex Tasks**: Used in complex tasks such as image and speech recognition, natural language processing, and game playing.
- **Deep Learning**: Deep neural networks (DNNs) with many hidden layers are used for more advanced applications.

7.3. Considerations:

- **Training Time**: Neural networks, especially deep networks, can require significant computational resources and time for training.
- **Interpretability**: Neural networks are often considered "black boxes" and can be challenging to interpret.

Supervised learning techniques provide a range of methods for solving classification and regression problems. From linear and logistic regression to more complex methods like random forests and neural networks, each technique has its own strengths and limitations. Understanding these techniques and their applications helps in selecting the appropriate method for a given problem and leveraging machine learning effectively in cybersecurity and other domains.

3.3 Unsupervised Learning Techniques

Unsupervised learning involves training algorithms on data that is not labeled, meaning the model learns to identify patterns and relationships within the data without explicit guidance. This approach is valuable for exploring data, discovering hidden structures, and identifying patterns that were not previously known. This section covers key unsupervised learning techniques, their methodologies, applications, and considerations.

1. Clustering

1.1. Overview:

- **Definition**: Clustering is the process of grouping similar data points together based on their features. The goal is to create clusters where data points within each cluster are more similar to each other than to those in other clusters.
- **Algorithms**: Common clustering algorithms include K-Means, Hierarchical Clustering, and DBSCAN.

1.2. Key Algorithms:

K-Means Clustering:

- **Algorithm**: K-Means partitions data into k clusters by iteratively assigning data points to the nearest cluster center (centroid) and updating the centroids based on the mean of the assigned points.
- **Applications**: Used in customer segmentation, image compression, and market research.

Hierarchical Clustering:

- **Algorithm**: Hierarchical clustering builds a hierarchy of clusters by either agglomerating (bottom-up) or dividing (top-down) data points. Dendrograms are used to visualize the hierarchy.
- **Applications**: Useful in taxonomy, genetic data analysis, and organizational structures.

DBSCAN (Density-Based Spatial Clustering of Applications with Noise):

- **Algorithm**: DBSCAN clusters data based on density, identifying dense regions separated by sparser areas. It can handle noise and discover clusters of varying shapes.
- **Applications**: Suitable for spatial data analysis, anomaly detection, and image segmentation.

1.3. Considerations:

- **Choosing the Number of Clusters**: In methods like K-Means, determining the optimal number of clusters (k) can be challenging. Techniques like the Elbow Method or Silhouette Score can assist in choosing □.
- **Scalability**: Some clustering algorithms may not scale well with large datasets or high-dimensional data.

2. Dimensionality Reduction

2.1. Overview:

- **Definition**: Dimensionality reduction involves reducing the number of features or dimensions in a dataset while retaining as much information as possible. This technique helps in visualizing data, reducing noise, and improving the efficiency of other machine learning algorithms.
- **Techniques**: Common dimensionality reduction techniques include Principal Component Analysis (PCA) and t-Distributed Stochastic Neighbor Embedding (t-SNE).

2.2. Key Techniques:

Principal Component Analysis (PCA):

- **Algorithm**: PCA transforms data into a new coordinate system where the greatest variances are on the first few coordinates (principal components). It reduces dimensionality by selecting the top principal components.
- **Applications**: Used in exploratory data analysis, image compression, and feature reduction.

t-Distributed Stochastic Neighbor Embedding (t-SNE):

- **Algorithm**: t-SNE is a technique for visualizing high-dimensional data by mapping it to a lower-dimensional space while preserving local relationships. It is particularly useful for visualizing clusters and patterns.
- **Applications**: Commonly used in data visualization, exploratory data analysis, and understanding complex data structures.

2.3. Considerations:

- **Interpretability**: Dimensionality reduction can make the data more interpretable, but some techniques, like t-SNE, may make it challenging to understand the exact relationships between features.
- **Computational** Complexity: Some techniques, especially t-SNE, can be **computationally intensive** and may require careful parameter tuning.

3. Anomaly Detection

3.1. Overview:

- **Definition**: Anomaly detection involves identifying data points that deviate significantly from the norm. These outliers or anomalies may indicate rare events, fraud, or errors.
- **Techniques**: Common techniques for anomaly detection include Isolation Forest, One-Class SVM, and Autoencoders.

3.2. Key Techniques:

Isolation Forest:

- **Algorithm**: Isolation Forest isolates anomalies by randomly selecting features and splitting values. Anomalies are isolated more quickly than normal data points, making them easier to detect.
- **Applications**: Used in fraud detection, network security, and quality control.

One-Class SVM:

- **Algorithm**: One-Class SVM is a variant of SVM used for anomaly detection. It models the distribution of normal data and identifies points that do not fit this distribution as anomalies.
- **Applications**: Useful in industrial monitoring, financial fraud detection, and fault detection.

Autoencoders:

- **Algorithm**: Autoencoders are neural networks trained to reconstruct input data. Anomalies are detected by measuring reconstruction errors; data points with high reconstruction errors are considered anomalies.
- **Applications**: Applied in image anomaly detection, network intrusion detection, and system fault detection.

3.3. Considerations:

- **False Positives**: Anomaly detection algorithms may produce false positives, identifying normal data points as anomalies. Careful tuning and validation are required to minimize this issue.
- **Scalability**: Some anomaly detection methods may struggle with large datasets or high-dimensional data.

4. Association Rule Learning

4.1. Overview:

- **Definition**: Association rule learning is used to discover interesting relationships between variables in large datasets. It identifies patterns or associations between items based on their co-occurrence.
- **Algorithms**: The most well-known algorithm for association rule learning is the Apriori algorithm.

4.2. Key Algorithms:

Apriori Algorithm:

- **Algorithm**: The Apriori algorithm identifies frequent itemsets by iteratively generating candidate itemsets and pruning those that do not meet a minimum support threshold. It then generates association rules based on these frequent itemsets.
- **Applications**: Commonly used in market basket analysis, recommendation systems, and cross-selling strategies.

4.3. Considerations:

- **Support, Confidence, and Lift**: Key metrics used in association rule learning include support (frequency of itemset), confidence (reliability of rule), and lift (measure of rule's strength compared to random occurrence).
- **Scalability**: The Apriori algorithm can be computationally expensive with large datasets, leading to the development of more efficient algorithms like FP-Growth.

5. Self-Organizing Maps (SOMs)

5.1. Overview:

- **Definition**: Self-Organizing Maps (SOMs) are a type of artificial neural network used for clustering and visualizing high-dimensional data. SOMs map data points onto a lower-dimensional grid while preserving the topological structure.
- **Algorithm**: SOMs use unsupervised learning to adjust the weights of neurons in the grid to represent data patterns. The output is a map where similar data points are grouped together.

5.2. Applications:

- **Data Visualization**: Helps in visualizing and interpreting complex data by mapping it to a 2D grid.
- **Clustering and Pattern Recognition**: Used for exploratory data analysis, pattern recognition, and feature extraction.

5.3. Considerations:

- **Training Time**: Training SOMs can be time-consuming, especially with large datasets or complex data structures.
- **Grid Size**: The size and shape of the grid can impact the quality and usefulness of the resulting map.

Unsupervised learning techniques provide powerful methods for exploring and understanding data without labeled examples. Clustering, dimensionality reduction, anomaly detection, association rule learning, and self-organizing maps each offer unique capabilities for discovering patterns, relationships, and anomalies in data. By applying these techniques, organizations can gain valuable insights, improve decision-making, and uncover hidden structures in their data. As with any machine learning approach, careful consideration of the algorithm's strengths and limitations is essential for achieving effective and meaningful results.

3.4 Reinforcement Learning

Reinforcement Learning (RL) is a type of machine learning where an agent learns to make decisions by performing actions in an environment to maximize a cumulative reward. Unlike supervised learning, where the model is trained on labeled input-output pairs, reinforcement learning involves learning through interaction, feedback, and trial-and-error.

1. Fundamentals of Reinforcement Learning

1.1. Key Concepts:

- **Agent**: The entity that makes decisions and performs actions within an environment.
- **Environment**: The external system or context in which the agent operates and interacts.
- **Action**: Choices made by the agent that affect the state of the environment.

- **State**: A representation of the current situation or context within the environment.
- **Reward**: A feedback signal received by the agent after performing an action, indicating the immediate benefit or cost of the action.
- **Policy**: A strategy or rule that the agent follows to determine which actions to take in various states.
- **Value Function**: A function that estimates the expected cumulative reward that can be obtained from a given state or state-action pair.

1.2. Goals:

- **Exploration vs. Exploitation**: Balancing the exploration of new actions and states with the exploitation of known actions that yield high rewards.
- **Optimal Policy**: Finding a policy that maximizes the cumulative reward over time.

2. Key Algorithms in Reinforcement Learning

2.1. Q-Learning:

Overview: Q-Learning is a model-free algorithm that aims to learn the value of state-action pairs. The Q-function (or action-value function) is updated based on the rewards received and the maximum estimated future rewards.

Applications: Used in various tasks, including game playing (e.g., chess, Go) and robotics.

2.2. SARSA (State-Action-Reward-State-Action):

Overview: SARSA is an on-policy algorithm that updates the Q-values based on the action taken by the agent in the current policy, rather than the maximum estimated future reward.

Applications: Used in tasks where policy improvement is more important than exploring new strategies, such as in real-time systems.

2.3. Deep Q-Networks (DQN):

Overview: Deep Q-Networks extend Q-Learning by using neural networks to approximate the Q-function, allowing for the handling of high-dimensional state spaces.

Algorithm: DQN combines Q-Learning with experience replay and target networks to stabilize training and improve performance.

Applications: Applied in complex environments such as video games (e.g., Atari games) and robotics.

2.4. Policy Gradient Methods:

Overview: Policy Gradient methods directly optimize the policy by estimating the gradient of the expected reward with respect to the policy parameters. These methods are suitable for problems with large or continuous action spaces.

Applications: Used in scenarios such as robotic control, natural language processing, and autonomous vehicles.

2.5. Actor-Critic Methods:

- **Overview**: Actor-Critic methods combine value-based and policy-based approaches by having two components: the actor (which updates the policy) and the critic (which evaluates the policy by estimating the value function).
- **Algorithm**: The critic evaluates the actions taken by the actor by estimating the value function, and the actor updates the policy based on the feedback from the critic.
- **Applications**: Applied in continuous control tasks, game playing, and reinforcement learning in complex environments.

3. Applications of Reinforcement Learning

3.1. Game Playing:

- **Overview**: RL has achieved remarkable success in game playing, where agents learn to master games like chess, Go, and video games through self-play and interaction with the environment.
- **Example**: AlphaGo by DeepMind demonstrated the power of RL by defeating world champions in the game of Go.

3.2. Robotics:

- **Overview**: RL is used in robotics for tasks such as robot control, manipulation, and navigation. Agents learn to perform complex tasks by interacting with their environment and receiving feedback.
- **Example**: RL has been applied to teaching robots to walk, grasp objects, and navigate in dynamic environments.

3.3. Autonomous Vehicles:

- **Overview**: RL plays a crucial role in the development of autonomous vehicles by enabling vehicles to learn driving strategies and make decisions based on real-time sensor data and environment interactions.
- **Example**: RL algorithms help autonomous vehicles in tasks such as lane keeping, obstacle avoidance, and traffic light recognition.

3.4. Finance:

- **Overview**: RL is used in financial markets for portfolio management, trading strategies, and risk management. Agents learn to optimize investment strategies based on historical data and market conditions.
- **Example**: RL algorithms have been applied to develop trading strategies that adapt to changing market conditions and maximize returns.

3.5. Healthcare:

- **Overview**: RL is used in healthcare for personalized treatment planning, drug discovery, and patient management. Agents learn to optimize treatment protocols based on patient responses and outcomes.
- **Example**: RL has been applied to optimize dosage regimens for chronic diseases and develop personalized treatment plans.

4. Challenges and Considerations

4.1. Exploration vs. Exploitation:

Challenge: Balancing exploration (trying new actions) and exploitation (choosing the best-known actions) is a critical challenge in RL. Strategies such as epsilon-greedy and softmax policies help manage this balance.

4.2. Reward Design:

Challenge: Designing appropriate reward functions that accurately reflect the desired outcomes is essential. Poor reward design can lead to unintended behaviors or suboptimal performance.

4.3. Sample Efficiency:

Challenge: RL algorithms can require a large number of interactions with the environment to learn effectively. Techniques such as experience replay and transfer learning can improve sample efficiency.

4.4. Stability and Convergence:

Challenge: Ensuring the stability and convergence of RL algorithms, especially in high-dimensional or continuous environments, can be challenging. Methods such as target networks and normalization techniques help address these issues.

4.5. Real-World Deployment:

Challenge: Deploying RL models in real-world scenarios requires careful consideration of safety, reliability, and generalization. Real-world environments often have complex dynamics and constraints that need to be addressed.

Reinforcement Learning is a powerful and versatile approach to training agents to make decisions and learn from their interactions with the environment. By leveraging key algorithms such as Q-Learning, SARSA, Deep Q-Networks, and Policy Gradient methods, RL can be applied to a wide range of domains including game playing, robotics, autonomous vehicles, finance, and healthcare. Despite its challenges, such as balancing exploration and exploitation and ensuring stability, RL continues to advance and provide innovative solutions to complex problems. Understanding these techniques and their applications is crucial for leveraging reinforcement learning effectively in various fields.

3.5 Applications of ML in Cybersecurity

Machine Learning (ML) has become a transformative force in cybersecurity, offering innovative solutions to traditional challenges and enhancing the ability to detect, respond to, and mitigate cyber threats. By leveraging advanced algorithms and data-driven insights, ML can significantly improve the effectiveness and efficiency of cybersecurity measures. This section explores key applications of ML in cybersecurity, detailing their methodologies, benefits, and considerations.

1. Threat Detection and Prevention

1.1. Intrusion Detection Systems (IDS):

- **Overview**: ML-powered IDS can analyze network traffic and system behaviors to identify suspicious activities or potential intrusions. Unlike traditional rule-based systems, ML models learn from patterns in data to detect anomalies and emerging threats.
- **Techniques**: Supervised learning algorithms, such as Random Forests and Support Vector Machines, and unsupervised methods, like clustering, are used to classify normal and anomalous behavior.
- **Applications**: Detecting network intrusions, identifying malware, and monitoring user behavior.

1.2. Malware Detection:

- **Overview**: ML algorithms analyze files, processes, and system behaviors to identify malware. By learning from known malware samples and benign files, ML models can recognize new or variant malware with high accuracy.
- **Techniques**: Feature extraction from files, dynamic analysis of processes, and behavioral analysis using algorithms like Neural Networks and Decision Trees.
- **Applications**: Detecting and classifying viruses, trojans, worms, and ransomware.

1.3. Phishing Detection:

- **Overview**: ML can be used to identify phishing emails and websites by analyzing features such as URL patterns, email content, and sender information. By training on known phishing and legitimate samples, ML models can detect deceptive schemes.
- **Techniques**: Natural Language Processing (NLP) for analyzing email content, and classification algorithms like Naive Bayes and Deep Learning.
- **Applications**: Preventing phishing attacks by filtering malicious emails and blocking fraudulent websites.

2. Threat Intelligence and Analysis

2.1. Threat Intelligence Aggregation:

- **Overview**: ML algorithms can aggregate and analyze threat intelligence from various sources, such as security feeds, threat reports, and social media. This helps in identifying trends, new threats, and vulnerabilities.
- **Techniques**: Data mining, NLP, and clustering methods to extract and categorize threat information.
- **Applications**: Enhancing threat intelligence platforms, providing actionable insights for threat analysts.

2.2. Vulnerability Management:

- **Overview**: ML can assist in identifying and prioritizing vulnerabilities based on their potential impact and exploitation likelihood. By analyzing historical data and threat trends, ML models can recommend remediation actions.
- **Techniques**: Predictive modeling and risk scoring algorithms to assess vulnerabilities and their impact.
- **Applications**: Prioritizing patch management and vulnerability remediation efforts.

3. Incident Response and Automation

3.1. Automated Incident Response:

- **Overview**: ML can automate incident response actions by analyzing alerts, identifying the nature of the attack, and taking predefined actions. This reduces response time and improves the efficiency of handling incidents.
- **Techniques**: Rule-based systems combined with ML algorithms to automate response workflows and decision-making processes.
- **Applications**: Automating responses to security incidents, reducing manual intervention, and mitigating threats in real-time.

3.2. Security Operations Center (SOC) Enhancement:

- **Overview**: ML enhances SOC operations by providing advanced analytics and insights into security events. It helps SOC analysts by prioritizing alerts, reducing false positives, and providing contextual information.
- **Techniques**: Anomaly detection, alert correlation, and predictive analytics to improve the efficiency of SOC operations.

- **Applications**: Improving threat detection capabilities, reducing alert fatigue, and streamlining security operations.

4. User and Entity Behavior Analytics (UEBA)

4.1. Anomaly Detection in User Behavior:

- **Overview**: ML analyzes user behavior patterns to detect anomalies that may indicate insider threats or compromised accounts. By learning normal behavior patterns, ML models can identify deviations that suggest malicious activity.
- **Techniques**: Unsupervised learning algorithms, such as clustering and Principal Component Analysis (PCA), to model and detect unusual behavior.
- **Applications**: Detecting insider threats, compromised user accounts, and unauthorized access.

4.2. Risk Assessment and Scoring:

- **Overview**: ML can assess the risk level of users and entities based on their behavior, access patterns, and historical data. Risk scores help prioritize security measures and responses.
- **Techniques**: Risk scoring algorithms, including supervised learning models, to assess and categorize risk levels.
- **Applications**: Enhancing access control policies, identifying high-risk users, and tailoring security measures.

5. Security Policy Enforcement

5.1. Policy Violation Detection:

- **Overview**: ML can monitor and analyze system configurations and user actions to detect violations of security policies. It ensures that security policies are adhered to and identifies deviations that could lead to security breaches.
- **Techniques**: Rule-based systems enhanced with ML for pattern recognition and anomaly detection.
- **Applications**: Monitoring compliance with security policies, detecting unauthorized changes, and enforcing security controls.

5.2. Adaptive Security Policies:

- **Overview**: ML enables adaptive security policies that dynamically adjust based on real-time data and threat intelligence. This helps in responding to emerging threats and changing attack vectors.
- **Techniques**: Reinforcement Learning and dynamic policy adjustment algorithms to adapt security measures based on current threats.
- **Applications**: Implementing adaptive access controls, adjusting security configurations, and responding to evolving threats.

6. Fraud Detection

6.1. Financial Fraud Detection:

- **Overview**: ML algorithms analyze financial transactions to detect fraudulent activities, such as credit card fraud and money laundering. By learning from historical fraud patterns, ML models can identify suspicious transactions in real-time.
- **Techniques**: Supervised learning algorithms like Random Forests and Deep Learning for detecting anomalies in transaction patterns.
- **Applications**: Preventing financial fraud, protecting customer accounts, and enhancing transaction security.

6.2. Identity Theft Prevention:

- **Overview**: ML helps in identifying and preventing identity theft by analyzing patterns in user behavior and detecting anomalies that suggest compromised identities.
- **Techniques**: Behavioral analysis, anomaly detection, and pattern recognition algorithms to identify potential identity theft.
- **Applications**: Enhancing identity verification processes, detecting stolen credentials, and protecting user identities.

7. Network Security

7.1. Network Traffic Analysis:

- **Overview**: ML can analyze network traffic to detect anomalies, identify potential threats, and prevent attacks. By learning normal network patterns, ML models can flag unusual activities that may indicate malicious behavior.
- **Techniques**: Supervised and unsupervised learning methods for traffic analysis, including clustering and anomaly detection algorithms.

- **Applications**: Monitoring network traffic, detecting DDoS attacks, and identifying network-based threats.

7.2. Network Anomaly Detection:

- **Overview**: ML algorithms detect deviations from normal network behavior, such as unusual traffic patterns or unauthorized access attempts. This helps in identifying potential security incidents and mitigating threats.
- **Techniques**: Anomaly detection methods, including statistical models and machine learning algorithms for network monitoring.
- **Applications**: Detecting network intrusions, monitoring traffic anomalies, and improving network security.

Machine Learning has become an integral part of modern cybersecurity strategies, providing advanced capabilities for threat detection, prevention, and response. By leveraging ML techniques such as anomaly detection, predictive analytics, and automated incident response, organizations can enhance their ability to defend against evolving cyber threats. As cybersecurity challenges continue to grow in complexity, the application of ML will play a crucial role in improving security measures, protecting assets, and maintaining the integrity of digital systems. Understanding and implementing these ML applications can significantly enhance an organization's cybersecurity posture and resilience.

Chapter 4: AI in Threat Detection

Chapter 4 explores the pivotal role of artificial intelligence (AI) in enhancing threat detection capabilities. As cyber threats become more sophisticated and frequent, traditional methods of threat detection often struggle to keep up. AI offers a powerful solution, providing advanced tools and techniques to identify and respond to threats with unprecedented speed and accuracy.

We start by examining the integration of AI into Intrusion Detection Systems (IDS) and Intrusion Prevention Systems (IPS), showcasing how AI algorithms can analyze vast amounts of data to detect and block suspicious activities. AI's ability to learn from historical data and adapt to new patterns makes these systems more effective at identifying and mitigating threats.

Next, we delve into behavioral analysis and anomaly detection, two key areas where AI excels. By analyzing normal behavior patterns and flagging deviations, AI can identify potential threats that might otherwise go unnoticed. This proactive approach helps in detecting zero-day exploits and other advanced attack methods.

The chapter also includes real-world case studies, illustrating how organizations have successfully implemented AI-powered threat detection systems. These examples highlight the practical benefits and challenges of using AI in threat detection and provide valuable insights into best practices.

By the end of this chapter, you'll have a clear understanding of how AI transforms threat detection, enhancing the ability to protect against emerging cyber threats. AI's role in threat detection is a cornerstone of modern cybersecurity, offering advanced capabilities that are crucial for staying ahead in the digital arms race.

4.1 Intrusion Detection Systems (IDS)

Intrusion Detection Systems (IDS) are critical components of modern cybersecurity infrastructures, designed to monitor and analyze network traffic and system activities to detect and respond to potential security threats. IDS play a crucial role in identifying unauthorized access, malicious activities, and policy violations within a network or system. This section explores the fundamentals of IDS, their types, and the application of Machine Learning (ML) in enhancing their effectiveness.

1. Overview of Intrusion Detection Systems

1.1. Definition:

Intrusion Detection Systems (IDS): IDS are security solutions that continuously monitor network or system activities to detect suspicious or anomalous behavior that may indicate a security threat or breach. They alert administrators to potential intrusions, enabling timely responses to mitigate risks.

1.2. Objectives:

- **Threat Detection**: Identifying malicious activities such as unauthorized access, data breaches, and attacks.
- **Alerting**: Providing real-time alerts to administrators about potential security incidents.
- **Analysis**: Offering insights and context for detected anomalies to assist in incident investigation and response.
- **Forensics**: Collecting and storing data for post-incident analysis and understanding attack vectors.

2. Types of Intrusion Detection Systems

2.1. Network-Based IDS (NIDS):

Definition: NIDS monitor and analyze network traffic to detect suspicious patterns and activities. They are typically deployed at strategic points within the network to capture and analyze traffic data.

Features:

- **Traffic Analysis**: Examines packet headers and payloads to identify unusual patterns or anomalies.
- **Signature-Based Detection**: Compares network traffic against known attack signatures or patterns.
- **Anomaly Detection**: Identifies deviations from established network baselines or normal behavior.
- **Applications**: Effective for detecting network-level attacks such as Distributed Denial of Service (DDoS) and unauthorized access attempts.

2.2. Host-Based IDS (HIDS):

Definition: HIDS monitor and analyze activities on individual hosts or devices, such as servers and workstations. They focus on system-level events and file integrity.

Features:

- **System Monitoring**: Tracks changes in system files, configurations, and processes.
- **Log Analysis**: Reviews system logs and audit trails for signs of suspicious behavior.
- **File Integrity** Checking: Monitors changes to critical system files and directories.
- **Applications**: Useful for detecting attacks that target specific hosts, such as malware infections and unauthorized changes.

2.3. Hybrid IDS:

Definition: Hybrid IDS combine elements of both NIDS and HIDS to provide comprehensive monitoring and detection capabilities. They leverage the strengths of both network and host-based approaches.

Features:

- **Integrated Analysis**: Correlates data from both network and host sources to provide a unified view of security events.
- **Cross-Referencing**: Enhances detection accuracy by combining network traffic analysis with host-level data.
- **Applications**: Suitable for environments requiring detailed visibility across both network and host levels.

3. Machine Learning in IDS

3.1. Overview:

Machine Learning (ML): ML algorithms enhance IDS by enabling automated, data-driven detection of threats. ML models can analyze large volumes of data, identify complex patterns, and adapt to evolving attack methods.

3.2. Applications of ML in IDS:

3.2.1. Anomaly Detection:

- **Technique**: ML algorithms analyze network and system behavior to detect deviations from normal patterns. Anomalies may indicate potential threats or malicious activities.
- **Algorithms**: Unsupervised learning methods, such as clustering and Principal Component Analysis (PCA), are commonly used for anomaly detection.
- **Benefits**: ML models can identify previously unknown threats and adapt to changing attack patterns.

3.2.2. Signature-Based Detection:

- **Technique**: ML enhances signature-based detection by automating the generation and updating of attack signatures. It can identify subtle variations of known threats.
- **Algorithms**: Supervised learning methods, such as Decision Trees and Neural Networks, are used to classify and detect known attack patterns.
- **Benefits**: Improves detection accuracy and reduces the time required to update signatures.

3.2.3. Behavioral Analysis:

- **Technique**: ML models analyze user and system behavior to identify deviations that may indicate malicious activities. Behavioral analysis can detect insider threats and compromised accounts.
- **Algorithms**: Techniques such as Random Forests and Support Vector Machines (SVM) are used to classify behavior as normal or suspicious.
- **Benefits**: Provides contextual insights and improves the detection of advanced threats.

3.2.4. Correlation Analysis:

- **Technique**: ML correlates data from multiple sources, such as network traffic and system logs, to identify patterns and relationships indicative of attacks.
- **Algorithms**: Ensemble methods and deep learning models are used to combine and analyze data from various sources.
- **Benefits**: Enhances the ability to detect multi-stage and sophisticated attacks.

3.2.5. Automated Response:

- **Technique**: ML models can automate response actions based on detected threats, such as blocking malicious traffic or isolating compromised hosts.
- **Algorithms**: Reinforcement Learning and decision-making algorithms are used to determine the appropriate response actions.
- **Benefits**: Reduces response time and improves the efficiency of incident handling.

4. Challenges and Considerations

4.1. False Positives and False Negatives:

- **Challenge**: Balancing the detection of real threats with the avoidance of false positives (incorrectly identifying benign activities as threats) and false negatives (failing to detect actual threats).
- **Solution**: Fine-tuning ML models, incorporating feedback loops, and combining multiple detection techniques.

4.2. Data Quality and Volume:

- **Challenge**: ML models require large amounts of high-quality data for training. Ensuring data accuracy and completeness is essential for effective detection.
- **Solution**: Implementing data preprocessing and normalization techniques to improve data quality.

4.3. Evolving Threat Landscape:

- **Challenge**: Attack techniques and strategies continuously evolve, requiring IDS to adapt and update their detection methods.
- **Solution**: Using adaptive ML algorithms that can learn from new data and emerging threats.

4.4. Resource Consumption:

- **Challenge**: ML algorithms can be computationally intensive, requiring significant processing power and memory.
- **Solution**: Optimizing algorithms and leveraging cloud-based solutions to manage resource demands.

4.5. Privacy and Compliance:

- **Challenge**: Ensuring that IDS implementations comply with privacy regulations and data protection requirements.
- **Solution**: Implementing data anonymization and encryption techniques, and adhering to relevant regulatory standards.

Intrusion Detection Systems (IDS) are essential for safeguarding networks and systems against security threats. By leveraging Machine Learning (ML), IDS can enhance their detection capabilities, adapt to evolving threats, and automate responses to incidents. However, challenges such as managing false positives, handling large volumes of data, and adapting to new attack techniques must be addressed to maximize the effectiveness of IDS. As the cybersecurity landscape continues to evolve, the integration of ML with IDS will play a pivotal role in enhancing threat detection and response capabilities.

4.2 Intrusion Prevention Systems (IPS)

Intrusion Prevention Systems (IPS) are advanced security solutions designed to actively detect and prevent malicious activities within a network or system. Unlike Intrusion Detection Systems (IDS), which primarily focus on monitoring and alerting, IPS take proactive measures to block or mitigate threats in real-time. This section explores the fundamentals of IPS, their types, and the role of Machine Learning (ML) in enhancing their effectiveness.

1. Overview of Intrusion Prevention Systems

1.1. Definition:

Intrusion Prevention Systems (IPS): IPS are security mechanisms that monitor network traffic or system activities and automatically take action to block or mitigate detected threats. They operate in-line with network traffic or system processes, providing real-time protection against attacks.

1.2. Objectives:

- **Threat Prevention**: Actively blocking malicious activities and attacks before they can cause harm.
- **Real-Time Response**: Providing immediate responses to detected threats, reducing the risk of damage or data loss.

- **Policy Enforcement**: Ensuring compliance with security policies by enforcing access controls and other security measures.

2. Types of Intrusion Prevention Systems

2.1. Network-Based IPS (NIPS):

Definition: NIPS are deployed at strategic points within a network to monitor and analyze network traffic. They are designed to detect and prevent attacks targeting network infrastructure and communication channels.

Features:

- **Traffic Inspection**: Analyzes incoming and outgoing network traffic for signs of malicious activity.
- **Signature-Based Prevention**: Uses predefined signatures of known attacks to identify and block malicious traffic.
- **Anomaly Detection**: Detects deviations from normal traffic patterns that may indicate an attack.
- **Applications**: Effective for preventing network-based attacks such as DDoS, port scanning, and exploitation of vulnerabilities.

2.2. Host-Based IPS (HIPS):

Definition: HIPS are installed on individual hosts or devices to monitor and protect system-level activities. They focus on detecting and preventing attacks that target specific systems or applications.

Features:

- **System Monitoring**: Tracks changes to system files, configurations, and processes to detect malicious activities.
- **Application Control**: Monitors and controls the execution of applications to prevent unauthorized actions.
- **File Integrity Checking**: Ensures the integrity of critical system files and detects unauthorized modifications.
- **Applications**: Useful for preventing host-specific attacks such as malware infections, unauthorized access, and privilege escalation.

2.3. Hybrid IPS:

Definition: Hybrid IPS combine elements of both network-based and host-based approaches to provide comprehensive protection. They leverage the strengths of both types to offer a unified security solution.

Features:

- **Integrated Monitoring**: Combines network traffic analysis with system-level monitoring for a holistic view of security.
- **Cross-Referencing**: Correlates data from network and host sources to identify complex attacks and anomalies.
- **Applications**: Suitable for environments requiring detailed visibility and protection across both network and host levels.

3. Machine Learning in IPS

3.1. Overview:

Machine Learning (ML): ML algorithms enhance IPS by enabling automated, data-driven detection and prevention of threats. ML models can analyze vast amounts of data, identify complex patterns, and adapt to evolving attack techniques.

3.2. Applications of ML in IPS:

3.2.1. Real-Time Threat Detection:

- **Technique**: ML algorithms analyze network traffic and system behavior in real-time to detect and prevent threats. By learning from historical data, ML models can identify patterns indicative of malicious activities.
- **Algorithms**: Unsupervised learning methods, such as clustering and anomaly detection, and supervised methods, like Neural Networks and Decision Trees.
- **Benefits**: Enables rapid detection and prevention of new and emerging threats.

3.2.2. Signature Generation and Updating:

- **Technique**: ML automates the generation and updating of attack signatures, improving the accuracy and efficiency of signature-based detection. It can identify subtle variations of known threats and generate new signatures.
- **Algorithms**: Supervised learning algorithms and Natural Language Processing (NLP) for analyzing attack patterns and creating signatures.

- **Benefits**: Reduces the time required to update signatures and enhances the detection of variant attacks.

3.2.3. Behavioral Analysis:

- **Technique**: ML models analyze user and system behavior to identify anomalies that may indicate malicious activities. Behavioral analysis helps in detecting insider threats and compromised accounts.
- **Algorithms**: Algorithms such as Random Forests, Support Vector Machines (SVM), and Deep Learning for classifying normal and suspicious behavior.
- **Benefits**: Provides contextual insights and improves the detection of sophisticated attacks.

3.2.4. Automated Response Actions:

- **Technique**: ML can automate response actions based on detected threats, such as blocking malicious traffic, isolating compromised hosts, or terminating malicious processes.
- **Algorithms**: Reinforcement Learning and decision-making algorithms for determining appropriate response actions.
- **Benefits**: Reduces response time and improves the efficiency of threat mitigation.

3.2.5. Risk Assessment and Prioritization:

- **Technique**: ML models assess the risk level of detected threats based on their potential impact and likelihood of exploitation. This helps in prioritizing response actions and resource allocation.
- **Algorithms**: Predictive modeling and risk scoring algorithms to evaluate and rank threats.
- **Benefits**: Enhances the ability to focus on high-priority threats and allocate resources effectively.

4. Challenges and Considerations

4.1. False Positives and False Negatives:

- **Challenge** Balancing the prevention of real threats with the avoidance of false positives (incorrectly blocking benign activities) and false negatives (failing to block actual threats).

- **Solution**: Fine-tuning ML models, incorporating feedback loops, and combining multiple detection techniques.

4.2. Data Quality and Volume:

- **Challenge**: ML models require high-quality data for training and accurate detection. Ensuring data accuracy and completeness is essential for effective prevention.
- **Solution**: Implementing data preprocessing, normalization techniques, and continuous data monitoring.

4.3. Evolving Threat Landscape:

- **Challenge**: Attack techniques and strategies continuously evolve, requiring IPS to adapt and update their prevention methods.
- **Solution**: Using adaptive ML algorithms that can learn from new data and emerging threats.

4.4. Resource Consumption:

- **Challenge**: ML algorithms can be computationally intensive, requiring significant processing power and memory.
- **Solution**: Optimizing algorithms, leveraging cloud-based solutions, and implementing efficient processing techniques.

4.5. Privacy and Compliance:

- **Challenge**: Ensuring that IPS implementations comply with privacy regulations and data protection requirements.
- **Solution**: Implementing data anonymization, encryption techniques, and adhering to relevant regulatory standards.

Intrusion Prevention Systems (IPS) are essential for actively protecting networks and systems against security threats. By leveraging Machine Learning (ML), IPS can enhance their detection and prevention capabilities, providing real-time protection and automated response to attacks. However, challenges such as managing false positives, handling large volumes of data, and adapting to evolving threats must be addressed to maximize the effectiveness of IPS. As the cybersecurity landscape continues to evolve, the integration of ML with IPS will play a pivotal role in enhancing threat prevention and safeguarding critical assets.

4.3 Behavioral Analysis

Behavioral Analysis in cybersecurity refers to the technique of examining and interpreting patterns of behavior within a network or system to identify potential security threats. This approach focuses on detecting anomalies and deviations from established norms that may indicate malicious activities or security breaches. By understanding and analyzing normal behavior patterns, security systems can more effectively spot and respond to irregularities that suggest potential threats. This section explores the principles, methodologies, applications, and challenges of behavioral analysis in cybersecurity.

1. Overview of Behavioral Analysis

1.1. Definition:

Behavioral Analysis: A security technique that involves monitoring and analyzing user and system behavior to identify deviations from established norms. The goal is to detect abnormal activities that could indicate security incidents such as insider threats, compromised accounts, or malware infections.

1.2. Objectives:

- **Anomaly Detection**: Identifying unusual behavior that deviates from the norm, which may suggest malicious activity or system compromise.
- **Threat Detection**: Detecting potential security threats based on behavioral deviations rather than known attack signatures.
- **Contextual Insight**: Providing context and understanding of user and system behaviors to improve incident response and investigation.

2. Methodologies in Behavioral Analysis

2.1. Baseline Behavior Modeling:

- **Definition**: Establishing a baseline of normal behavior by analyzing historical data to understand typical patterns of user and system activities.

Techniques:

- **Statistical Analysis**: Using statistical methods to define normal behavior patterns and detect deviations.
- **Machine Learning Models**: Employing unsupervised learning techniques to model and understand normal behavior.
- **Applications**: Creating baseline profiles for users, devices, and applications to identify deviations.

2.2. Anomaly Detection:

Definition: Identifying deviations from normal behavior that may indicate security threats. Anomalies are flagged based on their deviation from established baselines.

Techniques:

- **Unsupervised Learning**: Techniques such as clustering and Principal Component Analysis (PCA) to detect anomalies without predefined labels.
- **Statistical Methods**: Statistical tests and algorithms to identify outliers and deviations.
- **Applications**: Detecting unusual login patterns, unexpected data access, or abnormal network traffic.

2.3. Behavioral Profiling:

Definition: Creating detailed profiles of user and system behaviors to understand and monitor normal activities. Profiles are used to compare with real-time data to identify anomalies.

Techniques:

- **Feature Extraction**: Identifying key features of user and system behavior to build comprehensive profiles.
- **Pattern Recognition**: Using pattern recognition algorithms to match behaviors with established profiles.
- **Applications**: Monitoring user activity, detecting insider threats, and identifying behavioral changes that may indicate compromised accounts.

2.4. Contextual Analysis:

Definition: Analyzing the context in which behavioral anomalies occur to understand their significance and potential impact. Contextual analysis provides additional insights into detected anomalies.

Techniques:

- **Correlation Analysis**: Correlating behavioral anomalies with other security events, such as network activity or system changes.
- **Risk Assessment**: Evaluating the risk level of detected anomalies based on contextual information.
- **Applications**: Enhancing incident investigation, prioritizing threats, and improving response strategies.

3. Applications of Behavioral Analysis

3.1. Insider Threat Detection:

- **Overview**: Behavioral analysis helps identify potential insider threats by monitoring for unusual or unauthorized activities performed by legitimate users.
- **Techniques**: Analyzing deviations in user behavior, such as accessing sensitive data or performing unusual operations.
- **Applications**: Detecting disgruntled employees, compromised accounts, or unauthorized data access.

3.2. Compromised Account Detection:

- **Overview**: Identifying compromised accounts by analyzing behavior patterns that deviate from normal usage, which may indicate that an account has been hijacked.
- **Techniques**: Monitoring login patterns, access behaviors, and data usage for anomalies.
- **Applications**: Detecting credential theft, unauthorized access, and account abuse.

3.3. Malware Detection:

- **Overview**: Behavioral analysis helps in detecting malware by monitoring for unusual system activities and behaviors that are indicative of malicious software.
- **Techniques**: Analyzing file and process behaviors, network communications, and system changes.

- **Applications**: Identifying and mitigating malware infections, preventing lateral movement, and detecting ransomware activities.

3.4. Network Security Monitoring:

- **Overview**: Monitoring network traffic and behaviors to detect anomalies and potential threats that could impact network security.
- **Techniques**: Analyzing traffic patterns, communication behaviors, and network anomalies.
- **Applications**: Detecting network intrusions, preventing data exfiltration, and identifying unauthorized access.

3.5. Fraud Detection:

- **Overview**: Behavioral analysis can identify fraudulent activities by analyzing transaction patterns and user behaviors for deviations.
- **Techniques**: Monitoring transaction behaviors, access patterns, and user interactions for anomalies.
- **Applications**: Detecting financial fraud, preventing unauthorized transactions, and identifying account takeovers.

4. Challenges and Considerations

4.1. False Positives and False Negatives:

- **Challenge**: Balancing the detection of genuine threats with the avoidance of false positives (incorrectly identifying benign activities as threats) and false negatives (failing to detect actual threats).
- **Solution**: Fine-tuning behavioral models, incorporating feedback loops, and combining behavioral analysis with other detection methods.

4.2. Data Volume and Complexity:

- **Challenge**: Managing and analyzing large volumes of behavioral data can be complex and resource-intensive.
- **Solution**: Implementing efficient data processing techniques, using scalable storage solutions, and leveraging cloud-based analytics.

4.3. Evolving Threat Landscape:

- **Challenge**: Adapting to new and evolving threats that may not conform to established behavioral patterns.
- **Solution**: Using adaptive ML algorithms that continuously learn from new data and emerging threats.

4.4. Privacy Concerns:

- **Challenge**: Ensuring that behavioral analysis respects user privacy and complies with data protection regulations.
- **Solution**: Implementing data anonymization techniques, ensuring compliance with regulations, and transparently communicating data usage policies.

4.5. Integration with Other Security Measures:

- **Challenge**: Integrating behavioral analysis with other security solutions, such as firewalls, IDS, and IPS, to provide comprehensive protection.
- **Solution**: Ensuring interoperability between security tools and implementing coordinated response strategies.

Behavioral Analysis is a powerful technique for enhancing cybersecurity by monitoring and interpreting user and system behavior to detect potential threats. By establishing baseline behaviors, detecting anomalies, and analyzing contextual information, organizations can improve their ability to identify and respond to security incidents. Despite challenges such as managing false positives, handling large data volumes, and ensuring privacy, behavioral analysis offers valuable insights and enhances overall security posture. As the threat landscape continues to evolve, incorporating behavioral analysis into cybersecurity strategies will be crucial for detecting and mitigating sophisticated and emerging threats.

4.4 Anomaly Detection Algorithms

Anomaly detection algorithms are crucial tools in cybersecurity for identifying unusual or unexpected patterns within data that may indicate potential threats or security breaches. These algorithms are designed to recognize deviations from normal behavior, making them effective in detecting a wide range of security issues, including unauthorized access, data breaches, and system intrusions. This section explores various anomaly detection algorithms, their methodologies, applications, and challenges.

1. Overview of Anomaly Detection Algorithms

1.1. Definition:

Anomaly Detection Algorithms: These are algorithms used to identify data points or patterns that significantly deviate from the norm. In cybersecurity, they help detect unusual activities that could suggest security threats or system anomalies.

1.2. Objectives:

- **Threat Identification**: Detecting deviations from normal behavior that may indicate malicious activities or system compromise.
- **Early Warning**: Providing early alerts to potential security incidents based on observed anomalies.
- **System Integrity**: Ensuring the integrity of systems by identifying and addressing unusual activities that could impact security.

2. Types of Anomaly Detection Algorithms

2.1. Statistical Methods:

Overview: Statistical methods involve analyzing data distributions and identifying outliers based on statistical properties such as mean, variance, and standard deviation.

Techniques:

- **Z-Score**: Measures how many standard deviations a data point is from the mean. Data points with high z-scores are considered anomalies.
- **Grubbs' Test**: Detects outliers in univariate data by evaluating the maximum deviation from the mean.
- **Chi-Square Test**: Used for categorical data to identify deviations from expected frequencies.
- **Applications**: Effective for detecting deviations in structured data and identifying outliers in simpler datasets.

2.2. Machine Learning-Based Methods:

Overview: Machine learning methods use algorithms that learn from historical data to identify patterns and detect anomalies. They can adapt to changing data patterns and complex scenarios.

Techniques:

Unsupervised Learning:

- **Clustering Algorithms**: Techniques like K-Means and DBSCAN group similar data points and identify outliers as those not fitting into any cluster.
- **Principal Component Analysis (PCA):** Reduces data dimensionality and identifies anomalies based on reconstruction errors.

Supervised Learning:

- **Support Vector Machines (SVM):** Classifies data points as normal or anomalous by finding a hyperplane that maximizes the margin between classes.
- **Decision Trees**: Classifies data based on feature values and identifies anomalies as data points with unusual feature combinations.
- **Applications**: Suitable for complex datasets and scenarios where patterns and relationships are not easily discernible.

2.3. Ensemble Methods:

Overview: Ensemble methods combine multiple anomaly detection techniques to improve accuracy and robustness. They leverage the strengths of different algorithms to enhance detection performance.

Techniques:

- **Isolation Forest**: Isolates anomalies by randomly selecting features and splitting data points. Anomalies are identified as points requiring fewer splits to be isolated.
- **Random Cut Forest**: Uses a collection of trees to detect anomalies based on the frequency of data point isolation across trees.
- **Hybrid Models**: Combine statistical, machine learning, and domain-specific methods to improve detection capabilities.
- **Applications**: Effective for handling diverse and heterogeneous datasets, providing improved accuracy and reduced false positives.

2.4. Deep Learning Methods:

Overview: Deep learning methods leverage neural networks with multiple layers to model complex patterns and detect anomalies. They are particularly useful for large-scale and high-dimensional data.

Techniques:

- **Autoencoders**: Neural networks that learn to compress and reconstruct data. Anomalies are identified based on high reconstruction errors.
- **Recurrent Neural Networks (RNN):** Used for sequential data to detect anomalies based on temporal patterns and deviations.
- **Generative Adversarial Networks (GANs):** Consist of two networks, a generator and a discriminator, to learn data distributions and detect anomalies based on discrepancies.
- **Applications**: Suitable for complex data types such as images, time-series data, and unstructured data.

3. Applications of Anomaly Detection Algorithms

3.1. Network Security:

- **Overview**: Detecting unusual network traffic patterns, unauthorized access attempts, and data exfiltration activities.
- **Techniques**: Using clustering algorithms and machine learning models to identify deviations from normal network behavior.

3.2. System Monitoring:

- **Overview**: Monitoring system processes, file modifications, and application behaviors to detect anomalies.
- **Techniques**: Applying statistical methods and deep learning models to identify unusual system activities.

3.3. Fraud Detection:

- **Overview**: Identifying fraudulent transactions and activities by analyzing deviations from typical transaction patterns.
- **Techniques**: Utilizing supervised learning algorithms and ensemble methods to detect anomalies in financial transactions.

3.4. Insider Threat Detection:

- **Overview**: Detecting unusual user behavior that may indicate insider threats or compromised accounts.
- **Techniques**: Leveraging behavioral analysis and machine learning models to identify deviations in user activities.

3.5. Cloud Security:

- **Overview**: Monitoring cloud environments for unusual activities, unauthorized access, and data breaches.
- **Techniques**: Using deep learning methods and ensemble models to analyze cloud data and detect anomalies.

4. Challenges and Considerations

4.1. False Positives and False Negatives:

- **Challenge**: Balancing the detection of genuine anomalies with the avoidance of false positives (incorrectly identifying normal activities as anomalies) and false negatives (failing to detect actual anomalies).
- **Solution**: Fine-tuning algorithms, incorporating feedback loops, and combining multiple detection methods.

4.2. Data Quality and Volume:

- **Challenge**: Handling large volumes of data and ensuring data quality for accurate anomaly detection.
- **Solution**: Implementing data preprocessing techniques, using scalable storage solutions, and applying efficient data management practices.

4.3. Evolving Threat Landscape:

- **Challenge**: Adapting to new and evolving threats that may not conform to established patterns or anomalies.
- **Solution**: Using adaptive algorithms that continuously learn from new data and emerging threats.

4.4. Computational Resources:

- **Challenge**: Anomaly detection algorithms, especially deep learning methods, can be computationally intensive.
- **Solution**: Optimizing algorithms, leveraging cloud-based solutions, and implementing efficient processing techniques.

4.5. Privacy and Compliance:

- **Challenge**: Ensuring that anomaly detection practices comply with privacy regulations and data protection requirements.
- **Solution**: Implementing data anonymization techniques, ensuring regulatory compliance, and transparently communicating data usage policies.

Anomaly detection algorithms play a critical role in cybersecurity by identifying deviations from normal behavior that may indicate potential threats. From statistical methods and machine learning to deep learning techniques, a variety of approaches are available to address different types of data and scenarios. Despite challenges such as managing false positives, handling large data volumes, and ensuring privacy, effective anomaly detection is essential for enhancing security posture and protecting against evolving threats. Integrating these algorithms into a comprehensive security strategy can significantly improve threat detection and response capabilities.

4.5 Real-World Case Studies

Real-world case studies provide valuable insights into how anomaly detection algorithms are applied in practical scenarios and the impact they have on enhancing cybersecurity. By examining actual incidents where these algorithms were used, organizations can learn from both successes and challenges. This section presents several case studies that illustrate the effectiveness of anomaly detection in various contexts.

1. Case Study: Detection of Insider Threats at a Financial Institution

1.1. Background:

- **Organization**: A large financial institution with extensive internal and external networks.
- **Challenge**: The organization faced difficulties in detecting insider threats due to the complexity of user behaviors and the vast amount of data generated.

1.2. Solution:

Approach: The organization implemented a behavioral analysis system that utilized anomaly detection algorithms to monitor user activities and identify unusual patterns.

Techniques:

- **Baseline Behavior Modeling**: Created baseline profiles for user activities based on historical data.
- **Unsupervised Learning**: Used clustering algorithms to detect deviations from normal behavior.
- **Behavioral Profiling**: Monitored specific actions like large data transfers and access to sensitive files.

1.3. Results:

Successes:

- **Early Detection**: Identified an insider threat that involved an employee accessing and downloading large volumes of sensitive data.
- **Preventive Measures**: Allowed for timely intervention and prevention of potential data leakage.

Challenges:

- **False Positives**: Initial implementation generated some false positives, requiring fine-tuning of algorithms.
- **Adaptation**: Adjusted behavioral profiles to reduce false positives and improve detection accuracy.

1.4. Lessons Learned:

- **Importance of Baselines**: Establishing accurate baselines for normal behavior is crucial for effective anomaly detection.
- **Continuous Monitoring**: Ongoing adjustments and monitoring are needed to adapt to changing user behaviors and minimize false positives.

2. Case Study: Ransomware Attack Detection in a Healthcare Network

2.1. Background:

- **Organization**: A healthcare network with critical systems handling patient data and medical records.
- **Challenge**: The network experienced a ransomware attack that encrypted essential files and disrupted operations.

2.2. Solution:

Approach: Deployed an anomaly detection system to monitor network traffic and identify unusual patterns indicative of ransomware activity.

Techniques:

- **Network Anomaly Detection**: Used statistical and machine learning algorithms to analyze network traffic for signs of encryption activities and unauthorized file access.
- **Behavioral Analysis**: Monitored patterns of file modifications and data transfers.

2.3. Results:

Successes:

- **Early Warning**: Detected unusual encryption patterns before the ransomware fully propagated, enabling containment measures.
- **Incident Response**: Provided actionable insights that helped IT staff isolate affected systems and prevent further damage.

Challenges:

- **Complexity of Ransomware**: The sophistication of the ransomware required continuous adaptation of detection methods.
- **Impact on Operations**: Some legitimate network activities were flagged as anomalies, causing temporary disruptions.

2.4. Lessons Learned:

- **Real-Time Monitoring**: Real-time anomaly detection is essential for timely identification and response to ransomware attacks.
- **Adaptive Techniques**: Regular updates and adaptations to detection algorithms are necessary to handle evolving threats.

3. Case Study: Fraud Detection in an E-Commerce Platform

3.1. Background:

- **Organization**: A major e-commerce platform processing a high volume of transactions daily.
- **Challenge**: The platform struggled with fraudulent transactions, including payment fraud and account takeovers.

3.2. Solution:

Approach: Implemented an anomaly detection system focused on transaction patterns and user behaviors.

Techniques:

- **Supervised Learning**: Applied decision tree and SVM algorithms to classify transactions as legitimate or fraudulent.
- **Unsupervised Learning**: Utilized clustering techniques to detect unusual transaction patterns.
- **Behavioral Profiling**: Monitored user behaviors such as purchase frequency, shipping addresses, and login patterns.

3.3. Results:

Successes:

- **Fraud Reduction**: Significantly reduced the number of fraudulent transactions by identifying and blocking suspicious activities.
- **Enhanced Detection**: Improved the platform's ability to detect account takeovers and payment fraud.

Challenges:

- **Data Volume**: Handling the large volume of transactions posed challenges in terms of processing speed and accuracy.
- **False Positives**: Balancing fraud detection with the need to avoid flagging legitimate transactions.

2.4. Lessons Learned:

- **Scalability**: Implementing scalable solutions to manage high data volumes is critical for effective fraud detection.
- **Balance of Sensitivity**: Finding the right balance between sensitivity and specificity is essential to minimize false positives while maintaining effective fraud detection.

4. Case Study: Network Intrusion Detection in a Government Agency

4.1. Background:

- **Organization**: A government agency responsible for handling sensitive and classified information.
- **Challenge**: The agency faced threats from sophisticated network intrusions and cyber espionage attempts.

4.2. Solution:

Approach: Deployed a network intrusion detection system (NIDS) incorporating anomaly detection algorithms to identify and prevent unauthorized access.

Techniques:

- **Anomaly Detection**: Applied machine learning algorithms to detect deviations in network traffic patterns and unauthorized access attempts.
- **Hybrid Models**: Combined statistical methods with machine learning to improve detection accuracy.

4.3. Results:

Successes:

- **Effective Detection**: Identified and blocked several sophisticated intrusion attempts, preventing unauthorized access to sensitive data.
- **Improved Security Posture**: Enhanced the overall security posture of the agency by integrating anomaly detection with other security measures.

Challenges:

- **Complex Threats**: The complexity of advanced persistent threats required continuous updates and refinements to detection algorithms.
- **Resource Intensive**: The system's resource requirements impacted network performance and required optimization.

4.4. Lessons Learned:

- **Integration**: Integrating anomaly detection with other security solutions can provide a more comprehensive defense against complex threats.
- **Continuous Improvement**: Ongoing refinement and adaptation of detection algorithms are necessary to stay ahead of evolving threats.

These real-world case studies demonstrate the effectiveness and challenges of implementing anomaly detection algorithms across various domains. From detecting insider threats and ransomware attacks to preventing fraud and network intrusions, anomaly detection plays a crucial role in enhancing cybersecurity. Key lessons include the importance of establishing accurate baselines, continuous adaptation of detection methods, and balancing sensitivity with operational impact. By learning from these case studies, organizations can improve their anomaly detection strategies and better protect their assets against emerging threats.

Chapter 5: AI in Incident Response

Chapter 5 delves into how artificial intelligence (AI) is revolutionizing incident response in cybersecurity. In the face of increasingly complex and rapid cyber threats, the ability to respond swiftly and effectively is critical. AI offers powerful solutions that enhance the efficiency and effectiveness of incident response processes.

We begin by exploring automated incident response systems powered by AI. These systems can analyze security events in real-time, categorize incidents, and initiate appropriate responses without human intervention. This automation not only speeds up reaction times but also reduces the potential for human error.

Next, we examine AI-driven forensic analysis. AI tools can sift through large volumes of data to uncover critical evidence, identify attack vectors, and understand the full scope of a breach. This capability is essential for accurately diagnosing incidents and determining appropriate remediation steps.

The chapter also covers how AI can integrate with Security Operations Centers (SOCs) to streamline incident management. By enhancing situational awareness and providing actionable insights, AI supports SOC teams in managing and responding to threats more effectively.

Additionally, we present case studies showcasing successful implementations of AI in incident response. These real-world examples illustrate the tangible benefits and challenges of leveraging AI in managing and mitigating cybersecurity incidents.

By the end of this chapter, you will gain a comprehensive understanding of how AI transforms incident response, making it faster, more accurate, and less reliant on manual processes. AI's role in incident response represents a critical advancement in modern cybersecurity, enabling organizations to better protect themselves against evolving threats.

5.1 Automated Incident Response Systems

Automated Incident Response Systems (AIRS) are designed to streamline and accelerate the process of responding to security incidents. These systems leverage automation and artificial intelligence to detect, analyze, and respond to threats with minimal human intervention. By automating repetitive tasks and orchestrating response actions, AIRS help organizations manage and mitigate security incidents more efficiently. This section explores the key components, functionalities, benefits, and challenges of automated incident response systems.

1. Overview of Automated Incident Response Systems

1.1. Definition:

Automated Incident Response Systems (AIRS): Platforms and tools that use automation and artificial intelligence to manage and respond to security incidents. They aim to reduce the time and effort required to detect, analyze, and address threats, enhancing the overall efficiency of incident response.

1.2. Objectives:

- **Efficiency:** Streamline incident response processes to reduce response times and minimize manual effort.
- **Consistency:** Ensure standardized and repeatable response actions to common threats.
- **Scalability:** Handle a high volume of incidents and threats without requiring proportional increases in human resources.

2. Key Components of Automated Incident Response Systems

2.1. Threat Detection:

Overview: Automated systems use various techniques to detect potential security incidents. This includes monitoring network traffic, system logs, and user behavior for signs of anomalies or known threats.

Techniques:

- **Anomaly Detection:** Identifies deviations from normal behavior that may indicate potential threats.
- **Signature-Based Detection:** Uses predefined signatures of known threats to identify malicious activities.
- **Behavioral Analysis:** Monitors and analyzes patterns of behavior to detect suspicious activities.

2.2. Incident Analysis:

Overview: Once a potential incident is detected, automated systems analyze the threat to determine its nature, scope, and potential impact.

Techniques:

- **Contextual Analysis**: Provides context around the detected threat, including affected systems, potential impact, and associated risks.
- **Correlation**: Correlates information from multiple sources to build a comprehensive picture of the incident.
- **Threat Intelligence Integration**: Incorporates threat intelligence feeds to enrich incident analysis with external threat data.

2.3. Response Orchestration:

Overview: Automated systems orchestrate response actions based on predefined playbooks and workflows. This ensures a consistent and timely response to incidents.

Techniques:

- **Playbooks**: Predefined workflows that outline the steps to be taken in response to specific types of incidents.
- **Automated Actions**: Executes response actions such as isolating affected systems, blocking IP addresses, or applying patches.
- **Escalation Procedures**: Defines how and when to escalate incidents to human analysts for further investigation.

2.4. Reporting and Documentation:

Overview: Automated systems generate reports and documentation related to security incidents, providing valuable insights and records for post-incident analysis and compliance.

Techniques:

- **Incident Reports**: Detailed reports on the nature, scope, and resolution of incidents.
- **Audit Trails**: Records of all actions taken during the incident response process.
- **Compliance Reporting**: Generates reports to meet regulatory and compliance requirements.

3. Benefits of Automated Incident Response Systems

3.1. Faster Response Times:

- **Overview**: Automated systems reduce the time required to detect and respond to security incidents by eliminating manual tasks and accelerating response actions.
- **Impact**: Minimizes the window of opportunity for attackers and reduces potential damage.

3.2. Increased Efficiency:

- **Overview**: Automation streamlines incident response processes, allowing security teams to handle more incidents with fewer resources.
- **Impact**: Frees up security personnel to focus on more complex tasks and strategic initiatives.

3.3. Consistency and Standardization:

- **Overview**: Automated systems ensure that response actions are consistent and adhere to predefined playbooks and workflows.
- **Impact**: Reduces variability in incident handling and ensures adherence to best practices.

3.4. Scalability:

- **Overview**: Automated systems can scale to handle a high volume of incidents without requiring proportional increases in human resources.
- **Impact**: Enables organizations to manage growing threats and larger attack surfaces effectively.

3.5. Improved Accuracy:

- **Overview**: Automation reduces the likelihood of human error in incident response actions and analysis.
- **Impact**: Enhances the accuracy and effectiveness of response efforts.

4. Challenges of Automated Incident Response Systems

4.1. Complexity of Implementation:

- **Challenge**: Deploying and configuring automated incident response systems can be complex and require significant initial setup and integration efforts.
- **Solution**: Careful planning, testing, and phased implementation can help address these complexities.

4.2. False Positives and Negatives:

- **Challenge**: Automated systems may generate false positives (incorrectly identifying benign activities as threats) or false negatives (failing to detect actual threats).
- **Solution**: Fine-tuning algorithms, integrating contextual information, and using hybrid approaches can help improve accuracy.

4.3. Integration with Existing Systems:

- **Challenge**: Integrating automated incident response systems with existing security tools and infrastructure can be challenging.
- **Solution**: Ensure compatibility with existing systems and establish clear integration processes and standards.

4.4. Dependence on Predefined Playbooks:

- **Challenge**: Automated systems rely on predefined playbooks and workflows, which may not account for all possible scenarios or evolving threats.
- **Solution**: Regularly update and review playbooks, and incorporate flexibility to adapt to new threats and situations.

4.5. Security and Privacy Concerns:

- **Challenge**: Automated systems may introduce additional security and privacy concerns, such as the risk of automation being exploited or mishandling sensitive data.
- **Solution**: Implement strong security measures, access controls, and data protection practices to mitigate risks.

5. Examples of Automated Incident Response Systems

5.1. SIEM Integration:

- **Example**: Integration of Security Information and Event Management (SIEM) systems with automated response tools to enhance threat detection and response capabilities.
- **Impact**: Enables real-time correlation of security events and automated response actions.

5.2. SOAR Platforms:

- **Example**: Security Orchestration, Automation, and Response (SOAR) platforms that provide comprehensive automation and orchestration capabilities for incident response.
- **Impact**: Streamlines and coordinates response actions across multiple security tools and systems.

5.3. Automated Phishing Response:

- **Example**: Automated systems that detect and respond to phishing attacks by blocking malicious emails and alerting users.
- **Impact**: Reduces the risk of successful phishing attacks and enhances user awareness.

5.4. Endpoint Detection and Response (EDR):

- **Example**: EDR solutions that automate the detection and response to threats on endpoints, including isolating affected systems and applying remediation actions.
- **Impact**: Enhances endpoint security and minimizes the impact of attacks.

Automated Incident Response Systems play a crucial role in modern cybersecurity by enhancing the speed, efficiency, and accuracy of incident response. By leveraging automation and artificial intelligence, these systems streamline detection, analysis, and response processes, allowing organizations to manage and mitigate threats more effectively. Despite challenges such as complexity, false positives, and integration issues, the benefits of automated incident response—faster response times, increased efficiency, consistency, and scalability—make it an essential component of a robust security strategy. As threats continue to evolve, automated incident response systems will play an increasingly vital role in protecting organizations against emerging cyber threats.

5.2 AI-Powered Forensic Analysis

AI-Powered Forensic Analysis refers to the use of artificial intelligence (AI) and machine learning (ML) technologies to enhance the processes involved in digital forensics. This involves applying AI techniques to analyze digital evidence, uncover hidden patterns, and accelerate investigations. AI-powered tools can handle large volumes of data, identify complex correlations, and provide actionable insights that may not be immediately apparent through traditional forensic methods. This section explores the key aspects of AI-powered forensic analysis, its applications, benefits, and challenges.

1. Overview of AI-Powered Forensic Analysis

1.1. Definition:

AI-Powered Forensic Analysis: The application of artificial intelligence and machine learning techniques to digital forensic investigations to improve the detection, analysis, and interpretation of digital evidence.

1.2. Objectives:

- **Enhanced Data Analysis**: Improve the ability to process and analyze large volumes of digital evidence.
- **Pattern Recognition**: Identify hidden patterns and correlations in data that may be relevant to investigations.
- **Efficiency**: Accelerate forensic analysis and reduce the time required to uncover critical evidence.

2. Key Components of AI-Powered Forensic Analysis

2.1. Data Collection and Processing:

Overview: AI-powered forensic analysis begins with the collection and preprocessing of digital evidence from various sources, including computers, mobile devices, and cloud services.

Techniques:

- **Data Acquisition**: Using automated tools to collect data from digital devices while preserving its integrity.

- **Data Cleansing**: Removing noise and irrelevant information to focus on critical data points.
- **Data Integration**: Combining data from multiple sources to provide a comprehensive view of the evidence.

2.2. AI-Driven Analysis:

Overview: AI-driven analysis involves applying machine learning and AI algorithms to examine digital evidence and uncover relevant information.

Techniques:

- **Pattern Recognition**: Identifying recurring patterns, anomalies, and correlations in data that may indicate suspicious or criminal activity.
- **Natural Language Processing (NLP):** Analyzing text-based data to extract meaningful information, such as identifying keywords, sentiments, or entities.
- **Image and Video Analysis**: Using computer vision techniques to analyze images and videos, detecting objects, faces, and activities.

2.3. Correlation and Interpretation:

Overview: Correlation and interpretation involve linking disparate pieces of evidence and providing context to understand their significance.

Techniques:

- **Link Analysis**: Mapping relationships between entities (e.g., people, devices, transactions) to uncover connections and networks.
- **Timeline Reconstruction**: Creating chronological sequences of events based on analyzed data to reconstruct the sequence of activities.
- **Contextual Analysis**: Providing context to the evidence by integrating external information, such as threat intelligence and historical data.

2.4. Reporting and Visualization:

Overview: AI-powered forensic analysis includes generating reports and visualizations to present findings in a clear and actionable manner.

Techniques:

- **Automated Reporting**: Creating detailed forensic reports that summarize key findings, methodologies, and conclusions.
- **Data Visualization**: Using charts, graphs, and interactive dashboards to visualize data and highlight critical insights.
- **Presentation**: Preparing visual and textual presentations for stakeholders, including law enforcement and legal teams.

3. Benefits of AI-Powered Forensic Analysis

3.1. Speed and Efficiency:

- **Overview**: AI-powered tools can process and analyze large volumes of data more quickly than manual methods, significantly reducing the time required for forensic investigations.
- **Impact**: Accelerates the investigation process and allows for timely responses to incidents.

3.2. Enhanced Accuracy:

- **Overview**: AI algorithms can reduce human error and improve the accuracy of data analysis by identifying patterns and correlations that may be missed manually.
- **Impact**: Provides more reliable and precise evidence for investigations and legal proceedings.

3.3. Scalability:

- **Overview**: AI-powered forensic tools can handle vast amounts of data from diverse sources, making them suitable for large-scale investigations.
- **Impact**: Enables investigations involving extensive digital footprints and multiple devices.

3.4. Improved Pattern Recognition:

- **Overview**: AI techniques excel at detecting complex patterns and anomalies in data that may be indicative of criminal activities or security incidents.
- **Impact**: Enhances the ability to uncover hidden or subtle evidence.

3.5. Cost-Effectiveness:

- **Overview**: Automating forensic analysis can reduce the need for extensive manual labor, lowering overall investigation costs.
- **Impact**: Provides cost savings while maintaining high-quality forensic analysis.

4. Challenges of AI-Powered Forensic Analysis

4.1. Data Privacy and Security:

- **Challenge**: Handling sensitive or personal data during forensic analysis raises privacy and security concerns.
- **Solution**: Implement robust data protection measures, encryption, and access controls to safeguard data integrity and privacy.

4.2. Complexity of AI Algorithms:

- **Challenge**: The complexity of AI algorithms can make it difficult to understand how decisions are made, potentially impacting the credibility of findings.
- **Solution**: Ensure transparency and explainability of AI models, and provide clear documentation of the analysis process.

4.3. Integration with Existing Tools:

- **Challenge**: Integrating AI-powered forensic tools with existing forensic workflows and tools can be challenging.
- **Solution**: Develop interoperable solutions and ensure compatibility with existing forensic infrastructure.

4.4. Quality of Training Data:

- **Challenge**: The effectiveness of AI algorithms depends on the quality and quantity of training data used to develop them.
- **Solution**: Use high-quality, diverse training datasets and continuously update models to improve accuracy and relevance.

4.5. Ethical and Legal Considerations:

- **Challenge**: AI-powered forensic analysis must adhere to legal and ethical standards, particularly concerning data collection and evidence handling.
- **Solution**: Ensure compliance with legal and regulatory requirements and follow best practices for ethical forensic analysis.

5. Examples of AI-Powered Forensic Analysis

5.1. Email Analysis:

- **Example**: Using AI to analyze email communications for patterns of phishing, spear-phishing, or insider threats.
- **Impact**: Identifies malicious or suspicious emails and tracks communication patterns.

5.2. Social Media Investigations:

- **Example**: Leveraging AI to analyze social media posts, interactions, and networks for evidence related to criminal activities or threats.
- **Impact**: Uncovers connections and behaviors related to investigations.

5.3. Cybercrime Investigations:

- **Example**: Applying AI to analyze malware samples, identify their behavior, and track their distribution.
- **Impact**: Enhances the understanding of malware operations and helps in developing countermeasures.

5.4. Digital Evidence Recovery:

- **Example**: Using AI to recover and reconstruct deleted or corrupted digital evidence from storage devices.
- **Impact**: Retrieves critical evidence that might otherwise be lost.

5.5. Video Surveillance Analysis:

- **Example**: Implementing AI for video surveillance systems to detect unusual activities, recognize faces, and track movements.
- **Impact**: Enhances security and provides actionable insights from surveillance footage.

AI-Powered Forensic Analysis represents a significant advancement in the field of digital forensics. By leveraging artificial intelligence and machine learning, forensic investigators can process and analyze vast amounts of data more efficiently and accurately. The benefits of AI-powered forensic analysis, including speed, accuracy, scalability, and improved pattern recognition, make it a valuable tool in modern investigations. However, challenges such as data privacy, algorithm complexity, and integration with existing tools must be addressed to fully realize the potential of AI in forensic analysis. As technology continues to evolve, AI-powered forensic tools will play an increasingly important role in uncovering evidence, solving crimes, and ensuring justice.

5.3 Reducing Response Time with AI

Reducing response time is crucial in cybersecurity to mitigate the impact of threats and minimize damage. AI plays a significant role in accelerating response times by automating detection, analysis, and response processes. This section explores how AI can be leveraged to reduce response time, the key techniques involved, and the impact on overall incident management.

1. Overview of Reducing Response Time with AI

1.1. Definition:

Reducing Response Time with AI: Utilizing artificial intelligence technologies to accelerate the detection, analysis, and response to cybersecurity incidents, thereby minimizing the time between threat identification and effective mitigation.

1.2. Objectives:

- **Speed**: Enhance the speed of detecting and responding to security incidents.
- **Efficiency**: Automate repetitive tasks to free up human resources for more complex tasks.
- **Impact Mitigation**: Reduce the potential damage and impact of security incidents by responding more quickly.

2. Key Techniques for Reducing Response Time with AI

2.1. Automated Threat Detection:

Overview: AI-driven tools can continuously monitor network traffic, system logs, and user behavior to detect potential threats in real-time.

Techniques:

- **Anomaly Detection**: Identifies deviations from normal behavior that may indicate a threat, such as unusual network traffic or system activities.
- **Signature-Based Detection**: Uses predefined signatures of known threats to quickly identify malicious activities.
- **Behavioral Analysis**: Analyzes patterns of behavior to detect suspicious or abnormal activities.

2.2. Rapid Incident Analysis:

Overview: AI accelerates the process of analyzing detected threats by correlating data, assessing the scope, and determining the nature of the incident.

Techniques:

- **Contextual Analysis**: Provides context around detected threats, including affected systems, potential impact, and associated risks.
- **Machine Learning Models**: Employs advanced models to assess and categorize threats based on historical data and learned patterns.
- **Threat Intelligence Integration**: Incorporates external threat intelligence to enrich the analysis and provide additional context.

2.3. Automated Response Actions:

Overview: AI systems can execute predefined response actions automatically based on the nature and severity of the threat.

Techniques:

- **Playbook Automation**: Executes predefined response playbooks for common threats, such as isolating affected systems or blocking malicious IP addresses.
- **Real-Time Response**: Implements immediate actions, such as quarantining suspicious files or cutting off network access, to contain the threat.
- **Orchestration**: Coordinates response actions across multiple security tools and systems to ensure a unified and timely response.

2.4. Adaptive Learning and Improvement:

Overview: AI systems continuously learn from new threats and incidents to improve detection and response capabilities over time.

Techniques:

- **Feedback Loops**: Incorporates feedback from previous incidents to refine detection algorithms and response strategies.
- **Self-Tuning Models**: Adjusts models and algorithms based on evolving threat landscapes and emerging attack patterns.
- **Continuous Monitoring**: Continuously monitors system performance and adjusts response mechanisms as needed.

3. Benefits of Reducing Response Time with AI

3.1. Faster Incident Detection:

- **Overview**: AI-driven detection systems can identify threats more quickly than manual methods, reducing the time it takes to become aware of an incident.
- **Impact**: Minimizes the time attackers have to exploit vulnerabilities and reduces the potential impact of the attack.

3.2. Accelerated Incident Response:

- **Overview**: Automated response actions ensure that threats are addressed promptly, without waiting for human intervention.
- **Impact**: Limits the spread of the threat and reduces the overall damage caused by the incident.

3.3. Improved Efficiency:

- **Overview**: Automating repetitive tasks and response actions frees up human resources to focus on more complex and strategic aspects of incident management.
- **Impact**: Enhances the overall efficiency of the security team and optimizes resource allocation.

3.4. Reduced Human Error:

- **Overview**: AI systems minimize the risk of human error in threat detection and response by executing predefined actions accurately.
- **Impact**: Improves the reliability and effectiveness of incident response efforts.

3.5. Enhanced Threat Mitigation:

- **Overview**: Rapid detection and response capabilities enable organizations to mitigate the impact of threats more effectively.
- **Impact**: Reduces the overall impact of security incidents on operations and business continuity.

4. Challenges of Reducing Response Time with AI

4.1. False Positives and Negatives:

- **Challenge**: AI systems may generate false positives (incorrectly identifying benign activities as threats) or false negatives (failing to detect actual threats).
- **Solution**: Fine-tune algorithms and use hybrid approaches to improve accuracy and reduce false alerts.

4.2. Complexity of Integration:

- **Challenge**: Integrating AI-driven detection and response systems with existing security infrastructure can be complex and require significant effort.
- **Solution**: Develop interoperable solutions and establish clear integration processes and standards.

4.3. Dependency on Training Data:

- **Challenge**: The effectiveness of AI models depends on the quality and diversity of training data used to develop them.
- **Solution**: Use comprehensive and representative training datasets and regularly update models to ensure relevance.

4.4. Security and Privacy Concerns:

- **Challenge**: Implementing AI systems involves handling sensitive data, raising privacy and security concerns.
- **Solution**: Implement strong data protection measures, encryption, and access controls to safeguard data integrity and privacy.

4.5. Maintenance and Adaptation:

- **Challenge**: AI systems require ongoing maintenance and adaptation to stay effective against evolving threats.
- **Solution**: Establish regular update cycles and continuous monitoring to ensure systems remain current and effective.

5. Examples of Reducing Response Time with AI

5.1. Automated Firewall Management:

- **Example**: AI-driven firewall systems that automatically block suspicious IP addresses and traffic patterns based on real-time analysis.
- **Impact**: Reduces the time required to respond to network-based threats and prevent unauthorized access.

5.2. AI-Enhanced Endpoint Protection:

- **Example**: Endpoint security solutions that use AI to detect and respond to malware and other threats on individual devices.
- **Impact**: Provides immediate protection and remediation for compromised endpoints.

5.3. Security Incident and Event Management (SIEM) Integration:

- **Example**: SIEM systems integrated with AI to automatically correlate security events and trigger response actions.
- **Impact**: Enhances the speed and accuracy of incident detection and response.

5.4. Automated Phishing Defense:

- **Example**: AI-powered email security solutions that automatically detect and block phishing emails before they reach users.
- **Impact**: Reduces the time it takes to prevent phishing attacks and protect users from malicious emails.

5.5. Real-Time Threat Intelligence:

- **Example**: AI systems that analyze and disseminate threat intelligence in real-time to inform and guide response efforts.
- **Impact**: Provides timely and actionable information to enhance threat response strategies.

Reducing response time with AI is a critical component of modern cybersecurity strategies. By leveraging artificial intelligence to automate detection, analysis, and response processes, organizations can significantly enhance their ability to address security incidents promptly and effectively. The benefits of AI-driven response, including faster detection, accelerated response actions, and improved efficiency, contribute to a more robust and resilient security posture. Despite challenges such as false positives, integration complexity, and data dependency, the potential for AI to transform incident response and mitigate the impact of threats makes it an invaluable tool in the cybersecurity arsenal. As AI technologies continue to evolve, their role in reducing response times and improving security outcomes will only become more significant.

5.4 Integration with Security Operations Centers (SOCs)

Integrating AI with Security Operations Centers (SOCs) represents a significant advancement in enhancing the capabilities and efficiency of cybersecurity operations. SOCs are central hubs responsible for monitoring, detecting, and responding to security threats within an organization. By incorporating AI technologies, SOCs can improve their effectiveness in threat detection, incident response, and overall security management. This section explores how AI integration enhances SOC operations, the key components involved, and the associated benefits and challenges.

1. Overview of AI Integration with SOCs

1.1. Definition:

AI Integration with SOCs: The incorporation of artificial intelligence and machine learning technologies into the workflows and processes of Security Operations Centers to enhance their ability to detect, analyze, and respond to security incidents.

1.2. Objectives:

- **Enhanced Detection**: Improve the accuracy and speed of threat detection through AI-powered analysis.
- **Efficient Response**: Streamline incident response processes with automated actions and decision support.
- **Operational Excellence**: Optimize SOC operations by automating routine tasks and providing advanced analytical capabilities.

2. Key Components of AI Integration with SOCs

2.1. Threat Intelligence Integration:

Overview: AI enhances SOCs by integrating threat intelligence data to provide context and improve threat detection and response.

Techniques:

- **Automated Threat Feeds**: Incorporates real-time threat intelligence feeds to enrich SOC operations with up-to-date information on emerging threats.
- **Contextual Analysis**: Uses AI to correlate threat intelligence with internal data to identify relevant threats and vulnerabilities.
- **Predictive Analytics**: Applies AI models to forecast potential threats and prepare proactive response strategies.

2.2. AI-Driven Incident Detection:

Overview: AI technologies enhance SOC capabilities by improving the detection of security incidents through advanced analytics.

Techniques:

- **Anomaly Detection**: AI algorithms detect deviations from normal behavior that may indicate potential security incidents.
- **Behavioral Analysis**: Analyzes patterns and trends in user and network behavior to identify suspicious activities.
- **Correlation Engines**: Uses AI to correlate data from multiple sources to identify complex attack patterns and indicators of compromise (IoCs).

2.3. Automated Incident Response:

Overview: AI facilitates faster and more efficient incident response by automating routine actions and decision-making processes.

Techniques:

- **Playbook Automation**: Executes predefined response actions based on detected threats, such as isolating affected systems or blocking malicious IP addresses.

- **Decision Support Systems**: Provides recommendations and decision-making support for SOC analysts based on AI analysis of the incident.
- **Orchestration**: Coordinates response actions across various security tools and platforms to ensure a cohesive and timely response.

2.4. AI-Powered Analytics and Reporting:

Overview: AI enhances the analytical capabilities of SOCs by providing advanced analytics and reporting features.

Techniques:

- **Automated Reporting**: Generates detailed reports on security incidents, including analysis, impact assessment, and response actions taken.
- **Data Visualization**: Uses AI to create interactive dashboards and visualizations that highlight key metrics and trends.
- **Post-Incident Analysis**: Provides insights and recommendations based on the analysis of past incidents to improve future response strategies.

2.5. Continuous Learning and Adaptation:

Overview: AI systems continuously learn from new data and incidents to improve their performance and adapt to evolving threats.

Techniques:

- **Feedback Loops**: Incorporates feedback from SOC analysts and past incidents to refine AI models and algorithms.
- **Adaptive Learning**: Uses machine learning to adapt to new threat patterns and behaviors, enhancing detection and response capabilities.
- **Model Updates**: Regularly updates AI models to reflect the latest threat intelligence and emerging attack techniques.

3. Benefits of AI Integration with SOCs

3.1. Improved Threat Detection:

- **Overview**: AI enhances SOC capabilities by improving the accuracy and speed of threat detection, reducing the likelihood of missed or delayed incidents.

- **Impact**: Enables SOCs to identify and respond to threats more effectively, reducing the risk of successful attacks.

3.2. Accelerated Incident Response:

- **Overview**: Automated response actions and decision support systems enable SOCs to address security incidents more quickly and efficiently.
- **Impact**: Minimizes the impact of security incidents and reduces the time to recover from attacks.

3.3. Enhanced Operational Efficiency:

- **Overview**: AI automates routine tasks and provides advanced analytical capabilities, allowing SOC analysts to focus on more complex and strategic activities.
- **Impact**: Optimizes resource allocation and improves overall SOC performance.

3.4. Advanced Analytics and Insights:

- **Overview**: AI provides SOCs with advanced analytics and reporting capabilities, offering deeper insights into security incidents and trends.
- **Impact**: Enhances the ability to make informed decisions and develop proactive security strategies.

3.5. Scalability:

- **Overview**: AI technologies can handle large volumes of data and scale with the increasing complexity of security threats.
- **Impact**: Allows SOCs to manage growing threats and larger attack surfaces effectively.

4. Challenges of AI Integration with SOCs

4.1. Integration Complexity:

- **Challenge**: Integrating AI technologies with existing SOC infrastructure and workflows can be complex and require significant effort.
- **Solution**: Develop interoperable solutions and establish clear integration processes to facilitate smooth implementation.

4.2. Data Privacy and Security:

- **Challenge**: Handling sensitive data and integrating various data sources raises privacy and security concerns.
- **Solution**: Implement robust data protection measures, encryption, and access controls to safeguard data integrity and privacy.

4.3. False Positives and Negatives:

- **Challenge**: AI systems may generate false positives (incorrectly identifying benign activities as threats) or false negatives (failing to detect actual threats).
- **Solution**: Fine-tune AI algorithms and use hybrid approaches to improve detection accuracy and reduce false alerts.

4.4. Model Maintenance and Updates:

- **Challenge**: AI models require ongoing maintenance and updates to remain effective against evolving threats.
- **Solution**: Establish regular update cycles and continuous monitoring to ensure models stay current and relevant.

4.5. Skill and Training Requirements:

- **Challenge**: Integrating AI with SOCs may require new skills and training for SOC analysts to effectively utilize AI tools and technologies.
- **Solution**: Provide training and resources to ensure SOC staff are equipped to work with AI-driven systems and tools.

5. Examples of AI Integration with SOCs

5.1. AI-Enhanced SIEM Systems:

- **Example**: SIEM systems integrated with AI for advanced threat detection and response, providing real-time analysis and automated actions.
- **Impact**: Enhances the effectiveness of SIEM systems in identifying and addressing security incidents.

5.2. Automated Incident Management:

- **Example**: AI-powered incident management platforms that automatically classify, prioritize, and assign incidents to SOC analysts.
- **Impact**: Streamlines incident handling and ensures timely and appropriate response actions.

5.3. AI-Driven Threat Hunting:

- **Example**: AI tools that assist SOC teams in proactive threat hunting by analyzing data and identifying potential indicators of compromise.
- **Impact**: Improves the ability to uncover and address hidden threats before they escalate.

5.4. Contextual Threat Intelligence:

- **Example**: AI systems that provide contextual threat intelligence by correlating internal and external data to inform SOC operations.
- **Impact**: Enhances the relevance and accuracy of threat intelligence for better decision-making.

5.5. Real-Time Threat Visualization:

- **Example**: AI-powered visualization tools that present real-time data and threat metrics through interactive dashboards and visualizations.
- **Impact**: Provides SOC teams with clear and actionable insights into security events and trends.

Integrating AI with Security Operations Centers (SOCs) represents a transformative approach to enhancing cybersecurity operations. By leveraging AI technologies, SOCs can improve threat detection, accelerate incident response, and optimize overall operational efficiency. The benefits of AI integration, including advanced analytics, automated actions, and enhanced scalability, contribute to a more robust and effective security posture. However, challenges such as integration complexity, data privacy, and model maintenance must be addressed to fully realize the potential of AI in SOC operations. As AI technologies continue to advance, their role in supporting and enhancing SOC functions will become increasingly vital to safeguarding organizational assets and managing security threats.

5.5 Case Studies of Successful Implementations

Integrating AI into Security Operations Centers (SOCs) can significantly enhance their ability to detect, analyze, and respond to security incidents. Real-world case studies offer valuable insights into the practical benefits, challenges, and outcomes of AI implementations in SOCs. This section explores several case studies that demonstrate successful use of AI technologies in improving SOC operations and cybersecurity outcomes.

1. Case Study: Large Financial Institution

1.1. Background:

- **Organization**: A major global financial institution with a complex IT infrastructure and extensive data assets.
- **Challenge**: The institution faced challenges with detecting sophisticated cyber threats and managing a high volume of security alerts.

1.2. AI Implementation:

Solution: The organization integrated an AI-powered Security Information and Event Management (SIEM) system with advanced threat detection and response capabilities.

Features:

- **Anomaly Detection**: AI algorithms analyzed network traffic and user behavior to identify unusual patterns indicative of potential threats.
- **Automated Response**: The SIEM system automated response actions such as isolating affected systems and blocking suspicious IP addresses.
- **Threat Intelligence Integration**: Real-time threat intelligence feeds were integrated to enhance detection accuracy and provide contextual information.

1.3. Outcomes:

- **Improved Detection**: The AI-powered SIEM significantly reduced false positives and improved the accuracy of threat detection.
- **Faster Response**: Automated response actions reduced the time required to address security incidents, minimizing potential damage.
- **Enhanced Efficiency**: SOC analysts were able to focus on complex threats and strategic tasks, thanks to automation of routine tasks.

1.4. Impact:

- **Reduced Threat Impact**: The improved detection and response capabilities led to a noticeable reduction in the impact of security incidents.
- **Increased Confidence**: The organization gained greater confidence in its ability to manage and mitigate cyber threats effectively.

2. Case Study: Healthcare Provider

2.1. Background:

- **Organization**: A large healthcare provider with sensitive patient data and critical healthcare systems.
- **Challenge**: The organization struggled with managing and responding to a high volume of security alerts and protecting patient information.

2.2. AI Implementation:

Solution: The healthcare provider deployed an AI-driven threat detection and incident response platform.

Features:

- **Behavioral Analysis**: AI analyzed user and network behavior to detect anomalies and potential threats.
- **Automated Incident Management**: The platform automated incident classification, prioritization, and response actions.
- **Integration with Existing Tools**: The AI system was integrated with existing security tools and systems for seamless operation.

2.3. Outcomes:

- **Efficient Alert Management**: AI reduced alert fatigue by filtering out false positives and prioritizing high-risk incidents.
- **Faster Incident Response**: Automated response actions improved response times and reduced the risk of data breaches.
- **Enhanced Data Protection**: The system enhanced the protection of sensitive patient data by identifying and addressing threats more effectively.

2.4. Impact:

- **Improved Security Posture**: The healthcare provider experienced a strengthened security posture and improved incident management capabilities.
- **Reduced Operational Overhead**: Automation reduced the operational overhead of managing security alerts and incidents.

3. Case Study: E-Commerce Company

3.1. Background:

- **Organization**: A major e-commerce company with a large online presence and significant customer data.
- **Challenge**: The company faced challenges with detecting and mitigating fraud and cyber attacks targeting customer accounts.

3.2. AI Implementation:

Solution: The e-commerce company implemented an AI-powered fraud detection and response system.

Features:

- **Real-Time Fraud Detection**: AI algorithms monitored transactions and user behavior to detect fraudulent activities in real-time.
- **Automated Fraud Prevention**: The system automated actions such as flagging suspicious transactions and blocking compromised accounts.
- **Adaptive Learning**: The AI system continuously learned from new fraud patterns and adjusted its detection algorithms accordingly.

3.3. Outcomes:

- **Reduced Fraud Incidents**: The AI system effectively identified and mitigated fraudulent activities, reducing the number of successful fraud attempts.
- **Improved Customer Trust**: Enhanced fraud detection and prevention improved customer trust and satisfaction.
- **Operational Efficiency**: Automation of fraud detection and prevention reduced the manual workload for security teams.

3.4. Impact:

- **Enhanced Security**: The company achieved a more secure online environment for customers, protecting sensitive financial information.
- **Increased Revenue Protection**: Effective fraud prevention contributed to protecting revenue and minimizing financial losses.

4. Case Study: Government Agency

4.1. Background:

- **Organization**: A government agency responsible for national security and critical infrastructure protection.
- **Challenge**: The agency needed to improve its ability to detect and respond to advanced persistent threats (APTs) and cyber espionage activities.

4.2. AI Implementation:

Solution: The agency adopted an AI-based advanced threat detection and response system.

Features:

- **Advanced Threat Detection**: AI models analyzed network traffic and endpoint data to identify indicators of APTs and cyber espionage.
- **Automated Threat Hunting**: The system automated threat hunting tasks and provided SOC analysts with actionable intelligence.
- **Enhanced Forensics**: AI-powered forensic analysis tools provided deeper insights into the nature and impact of detected threats.

4.3. Outcomes:

- **Improved Threat Visibility**: The AI system provided enhanced visibility into advanced threats and malicious activities.
- **Faster Threat Detection**: The system reduced the time required to detect and investigate sophisticated attacks.
- **Strengthened Security Measures**: The agency improved its overall security measures and response strategies.

4.4. Impact:

- **Enhanced National Security**: The AI-driven system contributed to strengthening national security and protecting critical infrastructure.
- **Effective Threat Mitigation**: The agency achieved more effective threat mitigation and incident management capabilities.

The case studies presented illustrate the transformative impact of AI integration in Security Operations Centers (SOCs). From financial institutions and healthcare providers to e-commerce companies and government agencies, AI technologies have demonstrated their ability to enhance threat detection, automate response actions, and improve overall security operations. The successful implementations highlight the benefits of AI in reducing false positives, accelerating response times, and optimizing SOC efficiency. Despite challenges such as integration complexity and model maintenance, the positive outcomes achieved through AI integration underscore its value in modern cybersecurity strategies. As AI technologies continue to evolve, their role in enhancing SOC capabilities and addressing emerging threats will become increasingly crucial.

Chapter 6: AI for Network Security

Chapter 6 focuses on the transformative impact of artificial intelligence (AI) on network security. As networks become more complex and diverse, protecting them from a wide array of threats requires advanced solutions. AI offers powerful tools to enhance network security, ensuring robust protection against evolving cyber threats.

We start by exploring AI's role in network traffic analysis. AI algorithms can analyze vast amounts of network data in real-time, identifying unusual patterns and potential threats. This capability is crucial for detecting network anomalies that may indicate malicious activity, such as DDoS attacks or unauthorized access.

Next, we delve into AI applications for securing Internet of Things (IoT) devices. With the proliferation of IoT devices, securing these often vulnerable endpoints is essential. AI helps in monitoring and managing IoT networks, detecting threats specific to IoT environments, and enforcing security policies.

The chapter also covers AI in cloud security, highlighting how AI can protect cloud infrastructures from various threats. We explore AI-driven solutions for monitoring cloud environments, detecting vulnerabilities, and managing security configurations to safeguard sensitive data and applications.

Furthermore, we examine the role of AI in Software-Defined Networking (SDN) and Network Function Virtualization (NFV). AI enhances these modern network architectures by optimizing traffic flows, managing resources, and providing adaptive security measures.

Real-world case studies illustrate how organizations have successfully integrated AI into their network security strategies. These examples provide insights into the practical benefits and challenges of deploying AI in network security.

By the end of this chapter, you will have a clear understanding of how AI enhances network security, providing advanced tools and techniques to protect against a wide range of cyber threats. AI's integration into network security is a crucial advancement, offering enhanced capabilities to defend against complex and evolving threats.

6.1 Network Traffic Analysis

Network traffic analysis is a fundamental aspect of network security, providing critical insights into the flow of data across a network. AI technologies have greatly enhanced this process, enabling more sophisticated detection and response to potential threats. This section explores the principles of network traffic analysis, the role of AI in enhancing this analysis, and the practical applications and benefits of integrating AI into network traffic monitoring.

1. Overview of Network Traffic Analysis

1.1. Definition:

Network Traffic Analysis: The process of monitoring, inspecting, and analyzing data packets transmitted across a network to detect anomalies, security threats, and performance issues.

1.2. Objectives:

- **Threat Detection**: Identify malicious activities, such as intrusions, data exfiltration, and denial-of-service attacks.
- **Performance Monitoring**: Assess network performance, detect bottlenecks, and optimize bandwidth usage.
- **Compliance**: Ensure adherence to regulatory and organizational security policies by monitoring network traffic patterns.

2. Key Components of Network Traffic Analysis

2.1. Data Collection:

Overview: Collecting network traffic data involves capturing packets transmitted across the network using various tools and techniques.

Techniques:

- **Packet Capture**: Tools such as Wireshark or tcpdump capture raw packet data for analysis.
- **NetFlow/SFlow**: Protocols that provide aggregated traffic data and statistics, such as flow records.
- **Network Sensors**: Devices or software that monitor network traffic in real-time and generate logs.

2.2. Data Inspection:

Overview: Inspecting network traffic involves analyzing captured data to identify patterns, anomalies, and potential threats.

Techniques:

- **Deep Packet Inspection (DPI):** Examines the content of network packets to identify protocols, applications, and potential threats.
- **Traffic Analysis**: Analyzes traffic patterns, such as volume and flow direction, to detect unusual behavior or anomalies.
- **Log Analysis**: Reviews logs generated by network devices to identify and investigate suspicious activities.

2.3. Anomaly Detection:

Overview: Anomaly detection involves identifying deviations from normal network behavior that may indicate potential security threats or performance issues.

Techniques:

- **Statistical Analysis**: Uses statistical methods to establish baseline traffic patterns and detect deviations.
- **Behavioral Analysis**: Monitors network behavior to identify unusual activities, such as unexpected data transfers or abnormal traffic spikes.
- **Machine Learning Models**: Employs machine learning algorithms to learn normal traffic patterns and detect anomalies based on learned behavior.

2.4. Threat Identification:

Overview: Threat identification involves correlating network traffic data with known threat signatures or indicators to detect malicious activities.

Techniques:

- **Signature-Based Detection**: Compares network traffic against known threat signatures to identify potential attacks.
- **Heuristic Analysis**: Uses heuristic methods to identify suspicious activities based on known attack patterns and behaviors.

- **Threat Intelligence Integration**: Incorporates external threat intelligence to enhance detection capabilities and provide context.

3. Role of AI in Enhancing Network Traffic Analysis

3.1. Advanced Anomaly Detection:

Overview: AI enhances anomaly detection by leveraging advanced algorithms to identify subtle deviations from normal traffic patterns.

Techniques:

- **Anomaly Detection Models**: Machine learning models that learn from historical data to detect unusual patterns and behaviors.
- **Real-Time Analysis**: AI algorithms that analyze network traffic in real-time to quickly identify and respond to anomalies.
- **Contextual Analysis**: AI integrates context from various data sources to improve the accuracy of anomaly detection.

3.2. Improved Threat Detection:

Overview: AI enhances threat detection by analyzing large volumes of network traffic data and identifying complex attack patterns.

Techniques:

- **Behavioral Analytics**: AI analyzes patterns of network behavior to detect sophisticated threats and zero-day attacks.
- **Correlation Engines**: AI correlates data from multiple sources to identify potential threats that may not be detected by traditional methods.
- **Adaptive Learning**: AI systems continuously learn and adapt to new threats, improving detection capabilities over time.

3.3. Automation of Network Monitoring:

Overview: AI automates network monitoring tasks, reducing the need for manual intervention and enabling more efficient analysis.

Techniques:

- **Automated Alerts:** AI generates automated alerts for detected anomalies or potential threats, reducing response times.
- **Incident Response Automation**: AI systems automate response actions, such as isolating affected systems or blocking suspicious traffic.
- **Dashboard Visualization**: AI provides interactive dashboards and visualizations to simplify network traffic analysis and monitoring.

3.4. Enhanced Performance Analysis:

Overview: AI improves performance analysis by providing advanced analytics and insights into network performance and optimization.

Techniques:

- **Traffic Flow Analysis**: AI analyzes traffic flow patterns to identify bottlenecks and optimize network performance.
- **Predictive Analytics**: AI uses historical data to predict future traffic patterns and potential performance issues.
- **Resource Allocation**: AI assists in optimizing resource allocation and bandwidth usage based on traffic analysis.

4. Benefits of AI in Network Traffic Analysis

4.1. Faster Detection of Threats:

- **Overview**: AI enables faster detection of security threats by analyzing network traffic in real-time and identifying anomalies more quickly.
- **Impact**: Reduces the time required to identify and address potential security incidents, minimizing potential damage.

4.2. Reduced False Positives:

- **Overview**: AI enhances the accuracy of anomaly detection and threat identification, reducing the number of false positives.
- **Impact**: Improves the efficiency of network monitoring and reduces alert fatigue for security teams.

4.3. Improved Accuracy and Precision:

- **Overview**: AI algorithms provide more accurate and precise analysis of network traffic, leading to better threat detection and performance monitoring.
- **Impact**: Enhances the overall effectiveness of network security measures and performance optimization efforts.

4.4. Scalability:

- **Overview**: AI systems can handle large volumes of network traffic data and scale with growing network complexity.
- **Impact**: Enables organizations to manage increasing amounts of data and more complex network environments effectively.

4.5. Enhanced Insight and Reporting:

- **Overview**: AI provides advanced analytics and reporting capabilities, offering deeper insights into network performance and security.
- **Impact**: Facilitates better decision-making and strategic planning for network management and security.

5. Challenges of AI in Network Traffic Analysis

5.1. Data Privacy and Security:

- **Challenge**: Analyzing network traffic involves handling sensitive data, raising privacy and security concerns.
- **Solution**: Implement strong data protection measures, encryption, and access controls to safeguard data integrity and privacy.

5.2. Integration Complexity:

- **Challenge**: Integrating AI technologies with existing network monitoring tools and systems can be complex.
- **Solution**: Develop interoperable solutions and establish clear integration processes to facilitate smooth implementation.

5.3. Model Accuracy and Maintenance:

- **Challenge**: AI models require ongoing maintenance and updates to remain effective against evolving threats and traffic patterns.

- **Solution**: Regularly update models and algorithms based on new data and threat intelligence.

5.4. Skill and Training Requirements:

- **Challenge**: Implementing AI in network traffic analysis may require new skills and training for network security professionals.
- **Solution**: Provide training and resources to ensure staff are equipped to work with AI-driven tools and technologies.

5.5. Cost of Implementation:

- **Challenge**: AI technologies can be costly to implement and maintain.
- **Solution**: Assess the cost-benefit ratio and consider long-term savings and efficiencies gained through AI integration.

6. Examples of AI in Network Traffic Analysis

6.1. Real-Time Intrusion Detection:

- **Example**: An AI-based intrusion detection system (IDS) that monitors network traffic for signs of unauthorized access and intrusions in real-time.
- **Impact**: Provides early detection of potential threats and enables timely response to mitigate risks.

6.2. Automated Traffic Monitoring:

- **Example**: AI-powered network monitoring tools that automatically analyze traffic patterns, detect anomalies, and generate alerts.
- **Impact**: Enhances the efficiency of network monitoring and reduces the manual workload for security teams.

6.3. Performance Optimization:

- **Example**: AI-driven analytics platforms that analyze network traffic to identify performance bottlenecks and optimize bandwidth usage.
- **Impact**: Improves network performance and ensures efficient use of resources.

6.4. Threat Intelligence Integration:

- **Example**: AI systems that integrate threat intelligence feeds with network traffic analysis to provide context and enhance threat detection capabilities.
- **Impact**: Provides a more comprehensive view of potential threats and improves the accuracy of detection.

6.5. Predictive Analytics for Traffic Management:

- **Example**: AI tools that use predictive analytics to forecast future traffic patterns and potential performance issues.
- **Impact**: Enables proactive management of network resources and performance optimization.

AI-driven network traffic analysis represents a significant advancement in network security and performance management. By leveraging advanced algorithms and machine learning models, AI enhances the ability to detect and respond to threats, optimize network performance, and provide deeper insights into network behavior. The integration of AI into network traffic analysis offers numerous benefits, including faster threat detection, reduced false positives, and improved accuracy. However, challenges such as data privacy, integration complexity, and cost must be addressed to fully realize the potential of AI in this domain. As AI technologies continue to evolve, their role in enhancing network traffic analysis and overall network security will become increasingly important.

6.2 AI for Securing Internet of Things (IoT)

The Internet of Things (IoT) has rapidly expanded, connecting a vast array of devices and systems across various sectors. While this connectivity brings numerous benefits, it also introduces significant security challenges. AI has emerged as a powerful tool for enhancing the security of IoT environments. This section explores how AI can be leveraged to secure IoT networks, addresses the unique security challenges associated with IoT, and examines the benefits and applications of AI in this domain.

1. Understanding IoT Security Challenges

1.1. Vast Attack Surface:

- **Overview**: The proliferation of IoT devices creates a broad attack surface that can be exploited by cybercriminals.

- **Challenge**: Each connected device represents a potential entry point for attackers, increasing the risk of unauthorized access and data breaches.

1.2. Limited Device Resources:

- **Overview**: Many IoT devices have limited processing power, memory, and storage.
- **Challenge**: These limitations make it difficult to deploy traditional security measures, such as antivirus software or firewalls, on IoT devices.

1.3. Lack of Standardization:

- **Overview**: The IoT ecosystem lacks uniform security standards and protocols.
- **Challenge**: Inconsistent security practices and protocols across devices and manufacturers can lead to vulnerabilities and compatibility issues.

1.4. Data Privacy Concerns:

- **Overview**: IoT devices often collect and transmit sensitive data, such as personal information and operational data.
- **Challenge**: Ensuring the privacy and protection of this data is critical, especially in sectors such as healthcare, finance, and smart homes.

1.5. Complexity of IoT Networks:

- **Overview**: IoT networks can be highly complex, with numerous interconnected devices and systems.
- **Challenge**: Managing and securing such complex networks requires sophisticated and scalable security solutions.

2. Role of AI in IoT Security

2.1. Anomaly Detection:

Overview: AI can enhance anomaly detection by analyzing patterns of behavior and identifying deviations that may indicate security threats.

Techniques:

- **Behavioral Analysis**: AI models analyze normal behavior patterns of IoT devices and detect unusual activities that may signal a compromise.
- **Statistical Methods**: Statistical models establish baseline metrics and identify deviations from expected behavior.

2.2. Threat Detection and Response:

Overview: AI improves threat detection by analyzing large volumes of data from IoT devices to identify potential security threats.

Techniques:

- **Signature-Based Detection**: AI systems can recognize known attack signatures and patterns within IoT traffic.
- **Heuristic Analysis**: AI uses heuristic techniques to identify previously unknown threats based on behavior and traffic patterns.

2.3. Automated Incident Response:

Overview: AI can automate responses to detected threats, reducing the need for manual intervention and improving response times.

Techniques:

- **Automated Actions**: AI systems can trigger predefined actions, such as isolating compromised devices or blocking malicious traffic.
- **Adaptive Response**: AI algorithms can adapt and refine response actions based on ongoing analysis and evolving threats.

2.4. Network Traffic Analysis:

Overview: AI enhances network traffic analysis by providing deeper insights into IoT traffic patterns and identifying potential security issues.

Techniques:

- **Traffic Monitoring**: AI tools analyze traffic flow, volume, and patterns to detect anomalies or signs of attacks.
- **Correlation Analysis**: AI correlates data from various IoT devices and network sources to provide a comprehensive view of potential threats.

2.5. Device Authentication and Access Control:

Overview: AI can improve device authentication and access control mechanisms, ensuring that only authorized devices and users can access IoT networks.

Techniques:

- **Behavioral Biometrics**: AI analyzes behavioral patterns, such as device usage or interaction patterns, to authenticate users and devices.
- **Dynamic Access Control**: AI systems adjust access controls dynamically based on real-time analysis of device and user behavior.

3. Practical Applications of AI in IoT Security

3.1. Smart Home Security:

Overview: AI enhances security in smart home environments by monitoring connected devices and detecting potential threats.

Applications:

- **Intrusion Detection**: AI detects unusual activities or unauthorized access attempts within a smart home network.
- **Privacy Protection**: AI ensures that personal data collected by smart home devices is securely managed and protected.

3.2. Industrial IoT (IIoT) Security:

Overview: AI improves security in industrial IoT environments by monitoring and protecting critical infrastructure and operational technology.

Applications:

- **Operational Monitoring**: AI analyzes data from industrial sensors and equipment to detect anomalies and prevent potential failures or attacks.
- **Predictive Maintenance**: AI uses predictive analytics to foresee potential issues and optimize maintenance schedules, enhancing operational security.

3.3. Healthcare IoT Security:

Overview: AI enhances security in healthcare IoT environments by protecting sensitive patient data and medical devices.

Applications:

- **Device Integrity**: AI monitors medical devices for signs of tampering or unauthorized access, ensuring patient safety.
- **Data Security**: AI ensures the confidentiality and integrity of patient data collected by IoT devices, preventing data breaches.

3.4. Smart Cities:

Overview: AI enhances the security of smart city infrastructures by monitoring various IoT devices and systems, such as traffic lights, surveillance cameras, and environmental sensors.

Applications:

- **Surveillance and Monitoring**: AI analyzes data from smart city sensors and cameras to detect and respond to security threats or anomalies.
- **Infrastructure Protection**: AI protects critical infrastructure, such as power grids and water supply systems, from cyber threats and attacks.

4. Benefits of AI in IoT Security

4.1. Enhanced Threat Detection:

- **Overview**: AI provides advanced threat detection capabilities by analyzing vast amounts of data and identifying subtle patterns indicative of security threats.
- **Impact**: Improves the ability to detect and respond to emerging threats and attacks in IoT environments.

4.2. Reduced Response Times:

- **Overview**: AI automates incident response actions, reducing the time required to address security incidents and mitigate potential damage.
- **Impact**: Enhances overall security posture and reduces the impact of security breaches.

4.3. Improved Scalability:

- **Overview**: AI systems can scale with the growing number of IoT devices and the increasing volume of data generated.
- **Impact**: Provides effective security solutions for large and complex IoT networks.

4.4. Enhanced Data Privacy:

- **Overview**: AI helps protect sensitive data collected by IoT devices by ensuring secure data transmission and storage.
- **Impact**: Ensures compliance with data privacy regulations and protects user information.

4.5. Cost Efficiency:

- **Overview**: AI can reduce the cost of security management by automating routine tasks and improving the efficiency of security operations.
- **Impact**: Provides cost-effective solutions for managing and securing IoT environments.

5. Challenges and Considerations

5.1. Data Privacy and Compliance:

- **Challenge**: Ensuring that AI systems handle sensitive data in compliance with privacy regulations and standards.
- **Solution**: Implement strong data protection measures, encryption, and adherence to regulatory requirements.

5.2. Integration with Existing Systems:

- **Challenge**: Integrating AI-based security solutions with existing IoT infrastructure and security systems.
- **Solution**: Develop interoperable solutions and establish clear integration processes to facilitate seamless implementation.

5.3. Model Accuracy and Maintenance:

- **Challenge**: AI models require ongoing maintenance and updates to remain effective against evolving threats and IoT environments.

- **Solution**: Regularly update models based on new data and threat intelligence to ensure continued effectiveness.

5.4. Complexity of AI Systems:

- **Challenge**: Managing the complexity of AI systems and ensuring they are properly configured and optimized for IoT security.
- **Solution**: Provide adequate training and resources to security teams and continuously monitor and adjust AI systems.

5.5. Cost of Implementation:

- **Challenge**: The initial cost of implementing AI-based security solutions for IoT environments can be high.
- **Solution**: Assess the cost-benefit ratio and consider long-term savings and efficiencies gained through AI integration.

AI plays a crucial role in enhancing the security of IoT environments by addressing unique challenges such as the vast attack surface, limited device resources, and lack of standardization. By leveraging advanced techniques in anomaly detection, threat identification, and automated response, AI provides significant benefits including improved threat detection, reduced response times, and enhanced data privacy. Despite challenges related to data privacy, integration, and cost, AI offers a powerful and scalable solution for securing IoT networks and ensuring the safe and efficient operation of connected devices. As IoT continues to expand, the role of AI in securing these networks will become increasingly important, driving the need for continued innovation and adaptation in security strategies.

6.3 Cloud Security Solutions

The widespread adoption of cloud computing has transformed how organizations store, process, and manage data. While the cloud offers numerous benefits, including scalability, flexibility, and cost-efficiency, it also introduces unique security challenges. This section explores the role of AI in cloud security solutions, the key challenges associated with cloud security, and how AI technologies can address these challenges to protect cloud environments effectively.

1. Understanding Cloud Security Challenges

1.1. Data Breaches:

- **Overview**: Cloud environments are attractive targets for cybercriminals seeking to access sensitive data.
- **Challenge**: Ensuring the protection of data stored and processed in the cloud is critical to preventing breaches and unauthorized access.

1.2. Insufficient Access Controls:

- **Overview**: Managing access to cloud resources and data can be complex, particularly in environments with multiple users and roles.
- **Challenge**: Implementing effective access controls and ensuring only authorized users have appropriate permissions is essential for cloud security.

1.3. Shared Responsibility Model:

- **Overview**: In cloud environments, security responsibilities are shared between the cloud service provider (CSP) and the customer.
- **Challenge**: Clearly defining and managing security responsibilities to ensure comprehensive protection is crucial.

1.4. Data Loss and Recovery:

- **Overview**: Data loss can occur due to various reasons, including accidental deletion, corruption, or malicious attacks.
- **Challenge**: Implementing robust data backup and recovery solutions is necessary to ensure data integrity and availability.

1.5. Compliance and Regulatory Issues:

- **Overview**: Organizations must adhere to various regulatory requirements and industry standards related to data security and privacy.
- **Challenge**: Ensuring compliance with regulations, such as GDPR, HIPAA, and PCI-DSS, while leveraging cloud services is essential for avoiding legal and financial penalties.

2. Role of AI in Cloud Security

2.1. Threat Detection and Prevention:

Overview: AI enhances threat detection and prevention by analyzing cloud traffic and identifying potential security threats.

Techniques:

- **Behavioral Analysis**: AI models analyze normal cloud usage patterns and detect deviations that may indicate security threats.
- **Signature-Based Detection**: AI systems recognize known attack signatures and patterns in cloud traffic and data.
- **Anomaly Detection**: AI identifies unusual activities or patterns that could signify potential threats or breaches.

2.2. Automated Security Operations:

Overview: AI can automate various security operations, reducing the need for manual intervention and improving efficiency.

Techniques:

- **Automated Alerts**: AI generates real-time alerts for detected threats or anomalies, enabling timely response.
- **Incident Response Automation**: AI systems can trigger predefined actions, such as isolating affected resources or blocking malicious traffic, based on detected threats.

2.3. Access Control and Identity Management:

Overview: AI enhances access control and identity management by analyzing user behavior and ensuring proper authorization.

Techniques:

- **Behavioral Biometrics**: AI analyzes user behavior patterns to detect anomalies and verify identities.
- **Adaptive Access Control**: AI adjusts access controls dynamically based on real-time analysis of user activities and risk levels.

2.4. Data Encryption and Privacy Protection:

Overview: AI can improve data encryption and privacy protection by automating encryption processes and monitoring data access.

Techniques:

- **Automated Encryption**: AI systems can automatically encrypt sensitive data based on predefined policies and access controls.
- **Privacy Monitoring**: AI analyzes data access patterns to detect unauthorized access and protect user privacy.

2.5. Compliance Monitoring:

Overview: AI aids in compliance monitoring by continuously analyzing cloud environments to ensure adherence to regulatory requirements and standards.

Techniques:

- **Automated Audits**: AI performs automated audits of cloud resources and configurations to identify compliance gaps and potential issues.
- **Regulatory Reporting**: AI generates reports and documentation to support compliance efforts and demonstrate adherence to regulations.

3. Practical Applications of AI in Cloud Security

3.1. Cloud Security Incident Detection:

Overview: AI enhances the detection of security incidents in cloud environments by analyzing vast amounts of data and identifying potential threats.

Applications:

- **Intrusion Detection**: AI monitors cloud traffic and resources for signs of unauthorized access or malicious activities.
- **Malware Detection**: AI identifies and responds to malware threats in cloud environments by analyzing file behavior and network traffic.

3.2. Cloud Security Automation:

Overview: AI automates security tasks in cloud environments, improving efficiency and reducing the risk of human error.

Applications:

- **Automated Response**: AI systems automate response actions, such as quarantining compromised resources or blocking suspicious activities.
- **Security Policy Enforcement**: AI enforces security policies and configurations across cloud environments to ensure consistent protection.

3.3. Data Loss Prevention (DLP):

Overview: AI improves data loss prevention by monitoring cloud storage and preventing unauthorized access or data leaks.

Applications:

- **Data Monitoring**: AI analyzes data access patterns and detects potential data leakage or unauthorized transfers.
- **Policy Enforcement**: AI enforces data protection policies and ensures that sensitive information is securely managed.

3.4. Threat Intelligence Integration:

Overview: AI integrates threat intelligence feeds with cloud security solutions to enhance threat detection and response.

Applications:

- **Contextual Analysis**: AI correlates threat intelligence with cloud activity to provide context and improve detection accuracy.
- **Predictive Analytics**: AI uses threat intelligence to predict and prepare for potential future attacks based on emerging threat trends.

3.5. Cloud Security Posture Management:

Overview: AI enhances cloud security posture management by continuously analyzing cloud configurations and identifying vulnerabilities.

Applications:

- **Configuration Analysis**: AI analyzes cloud configurations to identify misconfigurations and potential security weaknesses.
- **Risk Assessment**: AI assesses the risk associated with cloud resources and provides recommendations for improving security posture.

4. Benefits of AI in Cloud Security

4.1. Enhanced Threat Detection and Prevention:

- **Overview**: AI improves threat detection and prevention capabilities by analyzing large volumes of data and identifying subtle threats.
- **Impact**: Provides better protection against evolving threats and reduces the risk of security breaches.

4.2. Improved Operational Efficiency:

- **Overview**: AI automates various security tasks, reducing the need for manual intervention and improving operational efficiency.
- **Impact**: Enhances the overall effectiveness of cloud security operations and reduces the workload on security teams.

4.3. Real-Time Monitoring and Response:

- **Overview**: AI enables real-time monitoring and response to security incidents, allowing for swift action and mitigation.
- **Impact**: Reduces the time required to detect and respond to threats, minimizing potential damage.

4.4. Cost Savings:

- **Overview**: AI-driven security solutions can reduce the cost of managing and maintaining cloud security by automating tasks and improving efficiency.
- **Impact**: Provides cost-effective security solutions and reduces the financial burden of managing cloud environments.

4.5. Enhanced Compliance and Reporting:

- **Overview**: AI assists with compliance monitoring and reporting by automating audits and generating documentation.

- **Impact**: Ensures adherence to regulatory requirements and simplifies compliance efforts.

5. Challenges and Considerations

5.1. Data Privacy and Compliance:

- **Challenge**: Ensuring that AI systems handle sensitive data in compliance with privacy regulations and standards.
- **Solution**: Implement strong data protection measures, encryption, and adherence to regulatory requirements.

5.2. Integration with Existing Systems:

- **Challenge**: Integrating AI-based security solutions with existing cloud infrastructure and security systems.
- **Solution**: Develop interoperable solutions and establish clear integration processes to facilitate seamless implementation.

5.3. Model Accuracy and Maintenance:

- **Challenge**: AI models require ongoing maintenance and updates to remain effective against evolving threats and cloud environments.
- **Solution**: Regularly update models based on new data and threat intelligence to ensure continued effectiveness.

5.4. Complexity of AI Systems:

- **Challenge**: Managing the complexity of AI systems and ensuring they are properly configured and optimized for cloud security.
- **Solution**: Provide adequate training and resources to security teams and continuously monitor and adjust AI systems.

5.5. Cost of Implementation:

- **Challenge**: The initial cost of implementing AI-based security solutions for cloud environments can be high.
- **Solution**: Assess the cost-benefit ratio and consider long-term savings and efficiencies gained through AI integration.

AI plays a critical role in enhancing cloud security by addressing unique challenges such as data breaches, insufficient access controls, and compliance issues. By leveraging advanced techniques in threat detection, automated security operations, and access control, AI provides significant benefits including improved threat detection, operational efficiency, and compliance monitoring. Despite challenges related to data privacy, integration, and cost, AI offers a powerful and scalable solution for securing cloud environments and ensuring the protection of data and resources. As cloud computing continues to evolve, the role of AI in cloud security will become increasingly important, driving the need for continued innovation and adaptation in security strategies.

6.4 AI in Software-Defined Networking (SDN)

Software-Defined Networking (SDN) represents a transformative approach to network management that decouples the control plane from the data plane, allowing for centralized control and increased flexibility. This paradigm shift offers numerous advantages, including improved network agility, simplified management, and cost savings. However, it also introduces unique security challenges that can be addressed effectively with the help of Artificial Intelligence (AI). This section explores how AI can enhance the security and functionality of SDN environments, the challenges associated with integrating AI into SDN, and practical applications of AI in this domain.

1. Understanding SDN Security Challenges

1.1. Centralized Control Vulnerabilities:

- **Overview**: In SDN, a centralized controller manages the entire network, making it a single point of control.
- **Challenge**: A compromised controller can lead to widespread network disruptions, data breaches, or unauthorized access.

1.2. Dynamic and Scalable Network Architectures:

- **Overview**: SDN enables dynamic and scalable network architectures, which can be challenging to monitor and secure.
- **Challenge**: Ensuring security in a constantly evolving network requires adaptive and real-time security measures.

1.3. API Security:

- **Overview**: SDN relies heavily on APIs for communication between the controller and network devices.
- **Challenge**: Securing APIs from vulnerabilities and unauthorized access is crucial to maintaining network integrity.

1.4. Network Traffic Analysis:

- **Overview**: SDN introduces new traffic patterns and flows that need to be monitored and analyzed for security purposes.
- **Challenge**: Identifying and responding to suspicious or malicious traffic in SDN environments requires advanced analytical tools.

1.5. Configuration and Policy Management:

- **Overview**: Managing network configurations and security policies in SDN can be complex due to the dynamic nature of the network.
- **Challenge**: Ensuring consistent and secure configuration management across the network is essential.

2. Role of AI in Enhancing SDN Security

2.1. Advanced Threat Detection:

Overview: AI enhances threat detection in SDN by analyzing network traffic and identifying anomalies that may indicate security threats.

Techniques:

- **Behavioral Analysis**: AI models analyze normal network behavior and detect deviations that could signify potential attacks.
- **Anomaly Detection**: AI identifies unusual traffic patterns or network behaviors that may indicate security issues.

2.2. Automated Network Management:

Overview: AI automates network management tasks, improving efficiency and reducing the risk of human error.

Techniques:

- **Automated Configuration**: AI systems automatically configure network settings based on predefined policies and real-time analysis.
- **Policy Enforcement**: AI enforces network security policies and adjusts configurations dynamically in response to changing conditions.

2.3. Real-Time Traffic Analysis:

Overview: AI provides real-time traffic analysis to monitor network performance and security.

Techniques:

- **Traffic Monitoring**: AI analyzes network traffic in real-time to detect and respond to potential threats or anomalies.
- **Pattern Recognition**: AI identifies patterns in network traffic that may indicate malicious activities or vulnerabilities.

2.4. Intrusion Detection and Prevention:

Overview: AI enhances intrusion detection and prevention in SDN environments by analyzing network traffic and identifying potential intrusions.

Techniques:

- **Signature-Based Detection**: AI recognizes known attack signatures and patterns within network traffic.
- **Heuristic Analysis**: AI uses heuristic techniques to detect unknown threats based on behavior and traffic patterns.

2.5. Dynamic Threat Response:

Overview: AI enables dynamic threat response by automating actions based on real-time threat analysis.

Techniques:

- **Automated Mitigation**: AI systems can automatically isolate affected network segments or block malicious traffic based on detected threats.

- **Adaptive Response**: AI adapts response actions based on ongoing analysis and evolving threat landscapes.

3. Practical Applications of AI in SDN

3.1. Network Traffic Optimization:

Overview: AI optimizes network traffic by analyzing patterns and adjusting network configurations to improve performance and security.

Applications:

- **Traffic Routing**: AI optimizes traffic routing to minimize congestion and enhance network efficiency.
- **Load Balancing**: AI distributes network load effectively to prevent overloads and maintain performance.

3.2. Policy-Based Security Management:

Overview: AI assists in managing security policies based on network conditions and traffic patterns.

Applications:

- **Policy Adaptation**: AI adjusts security policies dynamically in response to real-time network conditions and threats.
- **Policy Enforcement**: AI ensures consistent application of security policies across the network.

3.3. Threat Intelligence Integration:

Overview: AI integrates threat intelligence with SDN to enhance threat detection and response capabilities.

Applications:

- **Contextual Analysis**: AI correlates threat intelligence with network data to provide context and improve detection accuracy.
- **Predictive Analytics**: AI uses threat intelligence to anticipate and prepare for emerging threats.

3.4. Network Anomaly Detection:

Overview: AI enhances anomaly detection in SDN by identifying deviations from normal network behavior.

Applications:

- **Behavioral Anomalies**: AI detects unusual network behaviors or traffic patterns that may indicate security threats.
- **Traffic Analysis**: AI analyzes traffic flows to identify anomalies and potential security issues.

3.5. Security Automation and Orchestration:

Overview: AI automates security tasks and orchestrates responses to improve efficiency and effectiveness.

Applications:

- **Automated Incident Response**: AI automates responses to detected threats, such as isolating affected segments or blocking malicious activities.
- **Security Orchestration**: AI coordinates security efforts across multiple network components to ensure a unified defense strategy.

4. Benefits of AI in SDN Security

4.1. Enhanced Threat Detection and Prevention:

- **Overview**: AI improves threat detection and prevention capabilities by analyzing network traffic and identifying subtle threats.
- **Impact**: Provides better protection against sophisticated attacks and reduces the risk of network breaches.

4.2. Increased Operational Efficiency:

- **Overview**: AI automates network management and security tasks, reducing the need for manual intervention and improving efficiency.
- **Impact**: Enhances the overall effectiveness of network operations and reduces the workload on network administrators.

4.3. Real-Time Monitoring and Response:

- **Overview**: AI enables real-time monitoring and response to network threats and anomalies.
- **Impact**: Reduces the time required to detect and address security issues, minimizing potential damage.

4.4. Improved Network Performance:

- **Overview**: AI optimizes network traffic and configurations to enhance performance and reliability.
- **Impact**: Ensures efficient network operation and reduces the risk of performance-related issues.

4.5. Scalability and Flexibility:

- **Overview**: AI provides scalable and flexible security solutions that adapt to dynamic SDN environments.
- **Impact**: Supports the growth and evolution of network infrastructures while maintaining security and performance.

5. Challenges and Considerations

5.1. Integration with Existing SDN Systems:

- **Challenge**: Integrating AI-based security solutions with existing SDN infrastructure and components.
- **Solution**: Develop interoperable solutions and establish clear integration processes to facilitate seamless implementation.

5.2. Model Accuracy and Maintenance:

- **Challenge**: AI models require ongoing maintenance and updates to remain effective in dynamic SDN environments.
- **Solution**: Regularly update models based on new data and evolving threat landscapes to ensure continued effectiveness.

5.3. Complexity of AI Systems:

- **Challenge**: Managing the complexity of AI systems and ensuring they are properly configured for SDN environments.
- **Solution**: Provide adequate training and resources to network teams and continuously monitor and adjust AI systems.

5.4. Data Privacy and Compliance:

- **Challenge**: Ensuring that AI systems handle network data in compliance with privacy regulations and standards.
- **Solution**: Implement strong data protection measures and adhere to regulatory requirements.

5.5. Cost of Implementation:

- **Challenge**: The initial cost of implementing AI-based security solutions for SDN environments can be high.
- **Solution**: Assess the cost-benefit ratio and consider long-term savings and efficiencies gained through AI integration.

AI plays a crucial role in enhancing the security and functionality of Software-Defined Networking (SDN) by addressing challenges such as centralized control vulnerabilities, dynamic network architectures, and API security. By leveraging advanced techniques in threat detection, automated network management, and real-time traffic analysis, AI provides significant benefits including improved threat prevention, increased operational efficiency, and enhanced network performance. Despite challenges related to integration, model accuracy, and cost, AI offers a powerful and scalable solution for securing SDN environments and ensuring the reliability and security of modern network infrastructures. As SDN continues to evolve, the role of AI in network security will become increasingly important, driving the need for continued innovation and adaptation in security strategies.

6.5 Practical Applications and Tools

Artificial Intelligence (AI) has revolutionized how network security is managed in Software-Defined Networking (SDN) environments. By applying AI to various aspects of SDN, organizations can enhance security, improve efficiency, and address complex challenges more effectively. This section delves into practical applications of AI in SDN, highlighting specific tools and technologies that leverage AI to secure and optimize network environments.

1. Practical Applications of AI in SDN

1.1. Automated Network Configuration and Management:

Overview: AI can automate the configuration and management of SDN networks, ensuring optimal performance and security.

Applications:

- **Dynamic Configuration**: AI systems automatically adjust network configurations based on real-time analysis of traffic and network conditions.
- **Policy Management**: AI enforces security policies and updates configurations to respond to evolving threats and network demands.

1.2. Intelligent Traffic Routing:

Overview: AI enhances traffic routing in SDN by analyzing traffic patterns and optimizing routes for efficiency and security.

Applications:

- **Load Balancing**: AI algorithms distribute network traffic across multiple paths to prevent congestion and ensure balanced load.
- **Path Optimization**: AI selects the most efficient paths for data transmission, improving network performance and reducing latency.

1.3. Real-Time Anomaly Detection:

Overview: AI enables real-time detection of anomalies in network traffic, helping to identify and respond to potential security threats.

Applications:

- **Behavioral Analysis**: AI analyzes normal network behavior and detects deviations that may indicate malicious activities or intrusions.
- **Anomaly Detection Systems**: AI systems continuously monitor network traffic and alert administrators to unusual patterns or behaviors.

1.4. Enhanced Intrusion Detection and Prevention:

Overview: AI improves intrusion detection and prevention in SDN environments by analyzing network data and identifying potential threats.

Applications:

- **Intrusion Detection Systems (IDS):** AI-powered IDS can detect and respond to known and unknown threats based on traffic analysis and behavior.
- **Intrusion Prevention Systems (IPS):** AI-driven IPS can automatically block or mitigate threats in real-time, enhancing network security.

1.5. Adaptive Security Policy Enforcement:

Overview: AI helps enforce security policies dynamically, adapting to changing network conditions and threat landscapes.

Applications:

- **Policy Adaptation**: AI adjusts security policies based on real-time analysis of network conditions and detected threats.
- **Automated Enforcement**: AI systems ensure consistent application of security policies across the network, reducing the risk of misconfigurations.

2. AI Tools and Technologies for SDN

2.1. AI-Based Network Traffic Analysis Tools:

Overview: These tools use AI to analyze and monitor network traffic, providing insights into performance and security.

Examples:

- **Darktrace**: Utilizes machine learning to detect and respond to anomalies and threats in network traffic.
- **Cisco Stealthwatch**: Employs AI to monitor network behavior and detect potential threats through advanced traffic analysis.

2.2. AI-Enhanced Intrusion Detection and Prevention Systems (IDPS):

Overview: AI-powered IDPS solutions enhance threat detection and prevention capabilities in SDN environments.

Examples:

- **Vectra AI**: Uses AI and machine learning to detect and respond to advanced threats and anomalies in network traffic.
- **Splunk**: Integrates AI and machine learning to provide comprehensive intrusion detection and prevention across network environments.

2.3. AI-Driven Security Information and Event Management (SIEM) Systems:

Overview: SIEM systems leverage AI to collect, analyze, and correlate security events and data from various sources.

Examples:

- **IBM QRadar**: Utilizes AI and machine learning to analyze security data and provide actionable insights for threat detection and response.
- **Elastic Security**: Employs AI to correlate security events and provide real-time visibility into network security.

2.4. AI-Based Network Optimization and Management Tools:

Overview: These tools use AI to optimize network performance and manage configurations efficiently.

Examples:

- **Arista Networks**: Integrates AI for network management and optimization, providing insights into traffic patterns and network performance.
- **Juniper Networks**: Uses AI and machine learning to automate network operations and improve overall network efficiency.

2.5. AI-Powered Threat Intelligence Platforms:

Overview: Threat intelligence platforms leverage AI to analyze and integrate threat data, enhancing security posture.

Examples:

- **Recorded Future**: Utilizes AI to aggregate and analyze threat intelligence from various sources, providing actionable insights for threat management.
- **ThreatConnect**: Employs AI to enhance threat intelligence and enable proactive threat detection and response.

3. Benefits of AI Tools in SDN Security

3.1. Improved Threat Detection and Response:

- **Overview**: AI tools enhance the ability to detect and respond to threats by analyzing large volumes of network data and identifying subtle patterns.
- **Impact**: Provides timely detection of advanced threats and reduces the risk of security breaches.

3.2. Increased Efficiency and Automation:

- **Overview**: AI tools automate various network management tasks, reducing manual intervention and improving operational efficiency.
- **Impact**: Streamlines network operations and reduces the workload on network administrators.

3.3. Enhanced Visibility and Insights:

- **Overview**: AI tools provide comprehensive visibility into network traffic and performance, offering valuable insights for security and optimization.
- **Impact**: Improves decision-making and enables proactive management of network security and performance.

3.4. Adaptive and Dynamic Security:

- **Overview**: AI tools enable adaptive and dynamic security measures, responding to changing network conditions and emerging threats.
- **Impact**: Ensures continuous protection and adjustment of security measures based on real-time analysis.

3.5. Scalability and Flexibility:

- **Overview**: AI tools provide scalable and flexible solutions that adapt to evolving network environments and demands.

- **Impact**: Supports growth and changes in network infrastructure while maintaining security and performance.

4. Challenges and Considerations

4.1. Integration with Existing Systems:

- **Challenge**: Integrating AI tools with existing SDN infrastructure and systems may be complex.
- **Solution**: Develop interoperable solutions and establish clear integration processes to facilitate seamless implementation.

4.2. Accuracy and Reliability of AI Models:

- **Challenge**: AI models require ongoing maintenance and updates to remain effective in dynamic SDN environments.
- **Solution**: Regularly update models based on new data and evolving network conditions to ensure continued effectiveness.

4.3. Complexity of AI Tools:

- **Challenge**: Managing the complexity of AI tools and ensuring they are properly configured and optimized for SDN environments.
- **Solution**: Provide adequate training and resources to network teams and continuously monitor and adjust AI systems.

4.4. Data Privacy and Compliance:

- **Challenge**: Ensuring that AI tools handle network data in compliance with privacy regulations and standards.
- **Solution**: Implement strong data protection measures and adhere to regulatory requirements.

4.5. Cost of Implementation:

- **Challenge**: The initial cost of implementing AI-based tools for SDN security can be high.
- **Solution**: Assess the cost-benefit ratio and consider long-term savings and efficiencies gained through AI integration.

AI offers significant advantages for enhancing security and optimizing performance in Software-Defined Networking (SDN) environments. By leveraging AI for automated network management, intelligent traffic routing, real-time anomaly detection, and adaptive security policy enforcement, organizations can address complex challenges and improve overall network security. AI tools, such as network traffic analyzers, intrusion detection systems, and threat intelligence platforms, provide valuable capabilities for securing and managing SDN environments. Despite challenges related to integration, model accuracy, and cost, AI offers a powerful and scalable solution for modern network security, driving the need for continued innovation and adaptation in security strategies.

Chapter 7: AI in Endpoint Security

Chapter 7 delves into the critical role of artificial intelligence (AI) in enhancing endpoint security. As endpoints such as computers, mobile devices, and other connected devices become primary targets for cyber attacks, AI provides advanced solutions to protect these crucial elements of the IT infrastructure.

We start by examining AI-based antivirus and anti-malware solutions. Traditional antivirus tools rely on signature-based detection methods, which can be ineffective against new and evolving threats. AI-powered solutions, however, leverage machine learning to detect malicious behavior and anomalies, offering superior protection against both known and unknown threats.

Next, we explore the concept of Endpoint Detection and Response (EDR) systems. AI enhances EDR by providing real-time analysis of endpoint activities, identifying suspicious behavior, and automating response actions. This proactive approach helps in mitigating threats before they can cause significant damage.

The chapter also addresses the challenges of securing mobile and remote devices. With the rise of remote work and mobile computing, securing these endpoints is more important than ever. AI helps by monitoring mobile traffic, detecting vulnerabilities, and enforcing security policies across diverse and distributed environments.

Additionally, we include case studies of organizations that have successfully implemented AI-driven endpoint security solutions. These real-world examples illustrate the effectiveness of AI in protecting endpoints and provide valuable insights into best practices and potential pitfalls.

By the end of this chapter, you will have a comprehensive understanding of how AI enhances endpoint security. From advanced malware detection to proactive threat mitigation, AI plays a pivotal role in safeguarding endpoints against an increasingly sophisticated threat landscape.

7.1 AI-Based Antivirus Solutions

Artificial Intelligence (AI) has fundamentally transformed the landscape of antivirus solutions, enhancing their ability to detect, prevent, and respond to a broad spectrum of malware threats. Traditional antivirus solutions primarily relied on signature-based detection, which required a database of known malware signatures to identify threats. In contrast, AI-based antivirus solutions leverage advanced techniques in machine learning and data analysis to provide more proactive and adaptive protection. This section explores how AI improves antivirus solutions, the key technologies involved, and practical applications of AI in combating malware.

1. Overview of Traditional Antivirus Solutions

1.1. Signature-Based Detection:

Overview: Traditional antivirus solutions rely on a database of known malware signatures to identify and block threats.

Limitations:

- **Known Threats Only**: Signature-based detection is effective only against known malware and cannot identify new or modified threats.
- **Database Updates**: Frequent updates are required to maintain an up-to-date signature database, which can be time-consuming and resource-intensive.

1.2. Heuristic Analysis:

Overview: Heuristic analysis involves examining the behavior and characteristics of files to identify potentially malicious activities.

Limitations:

- **False Positives**: Heuristic analysis can generate false positives, flagging benign files as threats.
- **Limited Scope**: Heuristic analysis is not as effective at detecting sophisticated or zero-day threats.

2. How AI Enhances Antivirus Solutions

2.1. Machine Learning for Threat Detection:

Overview: AI-based antivirus solutions use machine learning algorithms to detect and identify malware based on patterns and behaviors rather than signatures.

Techniques:

- **Supervised Learning**: Trains models on labeled datasets of known malware and benign files to classify new files.
- **Unsupervised Learning**: Identifies new and unknown malware by analyzing patterns and anomalies in data without predefined labels.

2.2. Behavioral Analysis:

Overview: AI-based antivirus solutions monitor the behavior of programs and files to detect malicious activities in real-time.

Techniques:

- **Dynamic Analysis**: Executes files in a controlled environment (sandbox) to observe their behavior and identify potential threats.
- **Behavioral Modeling**: Uses AI to create models of normal and malicious behaviors, detecting deviations from established patterns.

2.3. Advanced Threat Intelligence:

Overview: AI integrates threat intelligence from various sources to enhance detection and response capabilities.

Techniques:

- **Threat Correlation**: AI correlates data from multiple threat intelligence feeds to identify emerging threats and attack patterns.
- **Predictive Analytics**: Uses historical data and trends to predict and prepare for potential future threats.

2.4. Real-Time and Continuous Monitoring:

Overview: AI-based antivirus solutions provide real-time monitoring and continuous analysis of system activities and network traffic.

Techniques:

- **Continuous Scanning**: AI continuously scans files and processes for signs of malicious activities.

- **Real-Time Alerts**: Provides instant alerts and responses to detected threats, minimizing potential damage.

3. Key Technologies in AI-Based Antivirus Solutions

3.1. Machine Learning Algorithms:

Overview: Various machine learning algorithms are used to enhance antivirus capabilities.

Examples:

- **Neural Networks**: Deep learning algorithms that analyze complex patterns and relationships in data.
- **Support Vector Machines (SVM):** Classifies files based on learned patterns and decision boundaries.
- **Random Forests**: Uses ensembles of decision trees to make predictions and classify files.

3.2. Natural Language Processing (NLP):

Overview: NLP techniques are used to analyze and interpret textual data related to malware threats.

Applications:

- **Threat Analysis**: NLP processes threat reports, malware descriptions, and other textual data to enhance threat intelligence.
- **Communication Analysis**: Analyzes communication patterns and messages within malware to detect suspicious activities.

3.3. Sandbox Environments:

Overview: Sandbox environments isolate and execute suspicious files to observe their behavior without affecting the actual system.

Applications:

- **Behavioral Analysis**: AI analyzes the behavior of files in the sandbox to identify potential threats.

- **Dynamic Analysis**: Provides insights into the actions and impact of malware in a controlled environment.

3.4. Threat Intelligence Feeds:

Overview: AI-based antivirus solutions integrate threat intelligence feeds to stay updated on the latest threats and attack vectors.

Applications:

- **Threat Updates**: AI receives and processes real-time updates on new malware strains and attack techniques.
- **Intelligence Correlation**: Correlates threat intelligence with observed behaviors to enhance detection accuracy.

4. Practical Applications of AI-Based Antivirus Solutions

4.1. Endpoint Protection:

Overview: AI-based antivirus solutions provide comprehensive protection for individual devices and endpoints.

Applications:

- **Endpoint Detection and Response (EDR)**: Monitors and responds to threats on endpoints in real-time.
- **Malware Removal**: Identifies and removes malicious files and processes from infected endpoints.

4.2. Network Security:

Overview: AI enhances network security by analyzing traffic and detecting malicious activities across the network.

Applications:

- **Network Threat Detection**: AI monitors network traffic for signs of malware and attacks.
- **Intrusion Prevention**: Provides real-time responses to detected threats, preventing network breaches.

4.3. Cloud Security:

Overview: AI-based antivirus solutions protect cloud environments from malware and other security threats.

Applications:

- **Cloud Workload Protection**: Monitors and secures virtual machines and containers in cloud environments.
- **Cloud Access Security**: Analyzes user behavior and access patterns to detect potential threats.

4.4. Email Security:

Overview: AI enhances email security by detecting and blocking malicious attachments and links.

Applications:

- **Phishing Detection**: AI analyzes email content and patterns to identify and block phishing attempts.
- **Attachment Scanning**: Scans email attachments for signs of malware and potential threats.

5. Benefits of AI-Based Antivirus Solutions

5.1. Enhanced Detection Accuracy:

- **Overview**: AI improves detection accuracy by analyzing complex patterns and behaviors rather than relying on signatures.
- **Impact**: Reduces false positives and improves the identification of new and unknown threats.

5.2. Proactive Threat Prevention:

- **Overview**: AI-based antivirus solutions provide proactive protection by predicting and preventing potential threats before they can cause harm.
- **Impact**: Minimizes the risk of malware infections and reduces the impact of security breaches.

5.3. Real-Time Response:

- **Overview**: AI enables real-time monitoring and response to threats, reducing the time between detection and remediation.
- **Impact**: Limits the potential damage caused by malware and enhances overall security posture.

5.4. Reduced Resource Requirements:

- **Overview**: AI automates many security tasks, reducing the need for manual intervention and lowering resource requirements.
- **Impact**: Improves efficiency and allows security teams to focus on more complex and strategic tasks.

5.5. Adaptive and Scalable Protection:

- **Overview**: AI-based solutions adapt to changing threat landscapes and scale with growing network and endpoint environments.
- **Impact**: Provides continuous protection as new threats emerge and network environments evolve.

6. Challenges and Considerations

6.1. Model Accuracy and Reliability:

- **Challenge**: Ensuring the accuracy and reliability of AI models in detecting and classifying threats.
- **Solution**: Continuously update and refine models based on new data and evolving threat landscapes.

6.2. Integration with Existing Systems:

- **Challenge**: Integrating AI-based antivirus solutions with existing security infrastructure and systems.
- **Solution**: Develop interoperable solutions and establish clear integration processes to ensure seamless operation.

6.3. Resource and Computational Demands:

- **Challenge**: AI-based solutions can be resource-intensive and require significant computational power.
- **Solution**: Optimize algorithms and leverage cloud-based resources to manage computational demands.

6.4. Privacy and Data Protection:

- **Challenge**: Ensuring that AI-based solutions handle sensitive data in compliance with privacy regulations and standards.
- **Solution**: Implement strong data protection measures and adhere to regulatory requirements.

6.5. Cost of Implementation:

- **Challenge**: The initial cost of implementing AI-based antivirus solutions can be high.
- **Solution**: Assess the cost-benefit ratio and consider long-term savings and efficiencies gained through AI integration.

AI-based antivirus solutions represent a significant advancement in malware protection, offering enhanced detection capabilities, proactive threat prevention, and real-time response. By leveraging machine learning, behavioral analysis, and advanced threat intelligence, AI improves the accuracy and effectiveness of antivirus solutions beyond traditional signature-based methods. Despite challenges related to model accuracy, integration, and resource demands, AI-based antivirus solutions provide valuable benefits for endpoint protection, network security, cloud environments, and email security. As the threat landscape continues to evolve, AI-based solutions will play an increasingly crucial role in safeguarding digital assets and ensuring robust security defenses.

7.2 AI-Based Anti-Malware Solutions

AI-based anti-malware solutions represent a significant leap forward in the fight against malicious software. Unlike traditional anti-malware tools that rely heavily on signature-based detection, AI-driven solutions harness the power of advanced machine learning and data analysis techniques to offer dynamic, proactive, and adaptive protection. This section explores how AI enhances anti-malware capabilities, the key technologies involved, and practical applications of AI in combating a variety of malware threats.

1. Overview of Traditional Anti-Malware Solutions

1.1. Signature-Based Detection:

Overview: Traditional anti-malware solutions use a database of known malware signatures to identify and block malicious software.

Limitations:

- **Known Threats Only**: Effective only against previously identified malware. New or modified threats are not detected.
- **Database Maintenance**: Requires constant updates to the malware signature database to remain effective, which can be resource-intensive.

1.2. Behavioral Analysis:

Overview: Behavioral analysis focuses on the behavior of software to detect potential threats.

Limitations:

- **False Positives**: Can generate false positives by flagging benign software exhibiting suspicious behavior.
- **Limited Efficacy**: May not be effective against sophisticated malware that mimics legitimate behavior.

2. How AI Enhances Anti-Malware Solutions

2.1. Machine Learning for Threat Detection:

Overview: AI-based anti-malware solutions use machine learning to analyze and classify software based on patterns and behaviors rather than signatures.

Techniques:

- **Supervised Learning**: Trains models on labeled datasets of known malware and clean software to recognize new threats.
- **Unsupervised Learning**: Identifies anomalies and unknown malware by analyzing patterns and deviations in data without predefined labels.

2.2. Dynamic Behavior Analysis:

Overview: AI enhances behavior-based analysis by examining the real-time behavior of software in a controlled environment.

Techniques:

- **Sandboxing**: Executes suspicious software in a virtual environment to monitor its behavior and detect malicious actions.
- **Behavioral Profiling**: AI creates profiles of normal software behavior and detects deviations that may indicate malicious activity.

2.3. Advanced Threat Intelligence Integration:

Overview: AI integrates threat intelligence from various sources to improve detection and response capabilities.

Techniques:

- **Threat Correlation**: AI correlates threat data from multiple sources to identify emerging threats and attack vectors.
- **Predictive Analytics**: Uses historical data to forecast potential malware threats and proactively adjust defenses.

2.4. Real-Time Monitoring and Response:

Overview: AI-based anti-malware solutions provide continuous monitoring and immediate response to threats.

Techniques:

- **Continuous Scanning**: AI continuously scans files and processes for malicious activities, providing up-to-date protection.
- **Instant Alerts**: Generates real-time alerts and automated responses to detected threats, minimizing potential damage.

3. Key Technologies in AI-Based Anti-Malware Solutions

3.1. Machine Learning Algorithms:

Overview: Various machine learning algorithms are employed to enhance anti-malware detection and analysis.

Examples:

- **Deep Learning**: Utilizes neural networks to analyze complex patterns and classify software as malicious or benign.
- **Clustering**: Groups similar data points to identify unusual patterns and potential malware.
- **Decision Trees**: Builds decision models based on features and characteristics of software to classify threats.

3.2. Natural Language Processing (NLP):

Overview: NLP techniques analyze textual data related to malware, such as descriptions and documentation.

Applications:

- **Threat Analysis**: Processes and interprets threat reports and malware descriptions to enhance detection and response.
- **Communication Analysis**: Examines communication patterns within malware to identify malicious intents.

3.3. Sandbox Environments:

Overview: AI-based anti-malware solutions use sandboxing to execute and analyze suspicious software in isolation.

Applications:

- **Behavioral Observation**: Monitors software actions in a controlled environment to identify malicious behavior.
- **Dynamic Analysis**: Provides insights into the potential impact and actions of malware without risking the actual system.

3.4. Threat Intelligence Feeds:

Overview: AI integrates threat intelligence feeds to stay updated on the latest malware threats and attack trends.

Applications:

- **Real-Time Updates**: Receives and processes updates on new malware strains and attack methods.
- **Correlation and Analysis**: Correlates threat data with observed behaviors to enhance detection capabilities.

4. Practical Applications of AI-Based Anti-Malware Solutions

4.1. Endpoint Protection:

Overview: AI-based anti-malware solutions protect individual devices and endpoints from malicious software.

Applications:

- **Endpoint Detection and Response (EDR):** Provides real-time monitoring and response to malware threats on endpoints.
- **Malware Removal**: Detects and removes malicious software from infected devices.

4.2. Network Security:

Overview: AI enhances network security by analyzing traffic and identifying malware within network communications.

Applications:

- **Network Threat Detection**: Monitors network traffic for signs of malware and other malicious activities.
- **Intrusion Prevention**: Implements real-time responses to block or mitigate detected malware threats.

4.3. Cloud Security:

Overview: AI-based anti-malware solutions extend protection to cloud environments, safeguarding virtualized resources.

Applications:

- **Cloud Workload Protection**: Monitors and secures virtual machines and containers in cloud environments.
- **Cloud Storage Security**: Analyzes cloud storage for signs of malicious activity and data breaches.

4.4. Email Security:

Overview: AI enhances email security by detecting and blocking malicious attachments and phishing attempts.

Applications:

- **Phishing Detection**: Analyzes email content and links to identify and block phishing attempts.
- **Attachment Scanning**: Scans email attachments for malware and potential threats.

5. Benefits of AI-Based Anti-Malware Solutions

5.1. Enhanced Detection Capabilities:

- **Overview**: AI improves detection accuracy by analyzing complex patterns and behaviors rather than relying solely on signatures.
- **Impact**: Reduces false positives and enhances the identification of new and evolving threats.

5.2. Proactive Threat Prevention:

- **Overview**: AI-based solutions provide proactive protection by anticipating and mitigating potential threats before they cause harm.
- **Impact**: Minimizes the risk of malware infections and reduces the impact of security breaches.

5.3. Real-Time and Continuous Protection:

- **Overview**: AI enables real-time monitoring and continuous analysis of software and network activities.
- **Impact**: Provides immediate responses to detected threats, limiting potential damage and enhancing overall security.

5.4. Adaptive and Scalable Security:

- **Overview**: AI-based anti-malware solutions adapt to changing threat landscapes and scale with growing environments.
- **Impact**: Ensures ongoing protection as new threats emerge and network environments expand.

5.5. Reduced Operational Overhead:

- **Overview**: AI automates many aspects of malware detection and response, reducing the need for manual intervention.
- **Impact**: Lowers the workload on IT and security teams, allowing them to focus on more strategic tasks.

6. Challenges and Considerations

6.1. Accuracy of AI Models:

- **Challenge**: Ensuring the accuracy and reliability of AI models in detecting and classifying malware.
- **Solution**: Continuously update and refine models based on new data and emerging threat patterns.

6.2. Integration with Existing Systems:

- **Challenge**: Integrating AI-based anti-malware solutions with existing security infrastructure and tools.
- **Solution**: Develop interoperable solutions and establish clear integration processes to ensure smooth operation.

6.3. Resource and Computational Demands:

- **Challenge**: AI-based solutions can be resource-intensive and require significant computational power.
- **Solution**: Optimize algorithms and utilize cloud-based resources to manage computational demands effectively.

6.4. Privacy and Data Protection:

- **Challenge**: Ensuring that AI-based solutions handle sensitive data in compliance with privacy regulations.
- **Solution**: Implement robust data protection measures and adhere to relevant privacy standards.

6.5. Cost of Implementation:

- **Challenge**: The initial cost of implementing AI-based anti-malware solutions can be high.
- **Solution**: Evaluate the cost-benefit ratio and consider long-term savings and efficiencies gained through AI integration.

AI-based anti-malware solutions represent a significant advancement in malware protection, offering enhanced detection capabilities, proactive threat prevention, and real-time response. By leveraging machine learning, behavioral analysis, and advanced threat intelligence, AI improves upon traditional methods and provides robust defense against evolving malware threats. Despite challenges related to model accuracy, integration, and resource demands, AI-based solutions offer valuable benefits for endpoint protection, network security, cloud environments, and email security. As malware continues to evolve, AI will play an increasingly crucial role in maintaining effective and adaptive security defenses.

7.3 Endpoint Detection and Response (EDR)

Endpoint Detection and Response (EDR) is a critical component of modern cybersecurity strategies, designed to provide comprehensive visibility into endpoint activities and enable rapid response to threats. EDR solutions leverage advanced technologies, including artificial intelligence (AI), to enhance the detection, investigation, and remediation of security incidents. This section delves into the role of AI in EDR, the technologies and techniques employed, and the practical applications of EDR solutions in defending against cyber threats.

1. Overview of Endpoint Detection and Response (EDR)

1.1. Definition and Purpose:

Overview: EDR refers to a category of security solutions that focus on detecting, investigating, and responding to threats on endpoint devices such as computers, servers, and mobile devices.

Purpose:

- **Detection**: Identifies suspicious activities and potential threats on endpoints.
- **Response**: Provides tools and capabilities for investigating and mitigating detected threats.
- **Visibility**: Offers comprehensive visibility into endpoint activities to aid in threat analysis and response.

1.2. Traditional EDR Capabilities:

Overview: Traditional EDR solutions often include features such as signature-based detection, behavioral analysis, and log management.

Capabilities:

- **Threat Detection**: Monitors endpoint activities for known and unknown threats.
- **Incident Response**: Provides tools for investigating and responding to security incidents.
- **Data Collection**: Gathers and analyzes endpoint data to support threat analysis and forensic investigations.

2. How AI Enhances EDR Solutions

2.1. Advanced Threat Detection:

Overview: AI enhances EDR solutions by using machine learning algorithms to detect sophisticated and emerging threats that may evade traditional detection methods.

Techniques:

- **Anomaly Detection**: AI analyzes endpoint behavior to identify deviations from normal patterns, which may indicate malicious activity.
- **Pattern Recognition**: Utilizes machine learning to recognize patterns associated with known threats and emerging attack techniques.

2.2. Automated Response and Remediation:

Overview: AI-driven EDR solutions automate response actions to detected threats, reducing the time required to mitigate potential damage.

Techniques:

- **Automated Containment**: AI can automatically isolate compromised endpoints to prevent the spread of malware.
- **Automated Remediation**: AI provides automated tools for cleaning and restoring affected endpoints, minimizing manual intervention.

2.3. Behavioral Analysis and Profiling:

Overview: AI enhances behavioral analysis by creating detailed profiles of normal endpoint behavior and identifying deviations that may signal malicious activity.

Techniques:

- **Behavioral Baselines**: AI establishes baselines of normal endpoint behavior to detect anomalies indicative of threats.
- **Contextual Analysis**: Analyzes context and intent behind endpoint activities to differentiate between benign and malicious actions.

2.4. Threat Intelligence Integration:

Overview: AI-driven EDR solutions integrate threat intelligence feeds to provide real-time updates on emerging threats and attack vectors.

Techniques:

- **Threat Correlation**: AI correlates endpoint activities with threat intelligence to identify potential threats and attack patterns.
- **Predictive Analytics**: Uses historical threat data to predict future threats and enhance detection capabilities.

3. Key Technologies in AI-Based EDR Solutions

3.1. Machine Learning Algorithms:

Overview: Machine learning algorithms play a crucial role in enhancing the capabilities of EDR solutions.

Examples:

- **Deep Learning**: Utilizes neural networks to analyze complex patterns and behaviors on endpoints.
- **Clustering Algorithms**: Groups similar activities to identify unusual patterns that may indicate threats.
- **Decision Trees**: Builds decision models based on features and characteristics of endpoint activities.

3.2. Behavioral Analytics:

Overview: Behavioral analytics focuses on understanding and analyzing endpoint behavior to detect and respond to threats.

Applications:

- **Activity Monitoring**: Monitors and analyzes endpoint activities in real-time to identify suspicious behavior.
- **Anomaly Detection**: Detects deviations from established behavioral baselines that may indicate malicious activities.

3.3. Threat Intelligence Feeds:

Overview: Integration of threat intelligence feeds provides real-time updates and context for EDR solutions.

Applications:

- **Real-Time Threat Updates**: Receives and processes updates on new malware strains, attack techniques, and threat actors.
- **Contextual Analysis**: Enhances threat detection and response by correlating endpoint activities with threat intelligence.

3.4. Automated Response Mechanisms:

Overview: AI-driven EDR solutions provide automated mechanisms for responding to and mitigating detected threats.

Applications:

- **Incident Containment**: Automatically isolates compromised endpoints to prevent further spread of malware.
- **Threat Remediation**: Provides automated tools for cleaning and restoring affected systems.

4. Practical Applications of AI-Based EDR Solutions

4.1. Enhanced Threat Detection:

Overview: AI-based EDR solutions improve the detection of sophisticated threats by analyzing complex patterns and behaviors.

Applications:

- **Zero-Day Threats**: Identifies and responds to new and unknown threats that do not have existing signatures.
- **Advanced Persistent Threats (APTs):** Detects subtle and sophisticated attacks that may evade traditional detection methods.

4.2. Real-Time Incident Response:

Overview: AI-driven EDR solutions enable real-time monitoring and response to security incidents on endpoints.

Applications:

- **Immediate Containment**: Quickly isolates compromised endpoints to prevent further damage.
- **Rapid Remediation**: Automates the process of cleaning and restoring affected systems.

4.3. Forensic Analysis and Investigation:

Overview: AI-based EDR solutions provide tools for conducting thorough forensic investigations following a security incident.

Applications:

- **Data Analysis**: Analyzes endpoint data to identify the scope and impact of a security breach.

- **Incident Reconstruction**: Reconstructs the sequence of events leading to an incident to understand the attack method and origin.

4.4. Proactive Threat Hunting:

Overview: AI-driven EDR solutions support proactive threat hunting by analyzing endpoint data for indicators of compromise.

Applications:

- **Suspicious Activity Detection**: Identifies and investigates unusual activities that may indicate potential threats.
- **Threat Intelligence Correlation**: Correlates endpoint data with threat intelligence to uncover hidden threats.

5. Benefits of AI-Based EDR Solutions

5.1. Improved Detection Accuracy:

- **Overview**: AI enhances detection accuracy by analyzing complex patterns and behaviors, reducing false positives and false negatives.
- **Impact**: Increases the effectiveness of threat detection and minimizes the risk of undetected threats.

5.2. Faster Incident Response:

- **Overview**: AI-driven EDR solutions automate and accelerate incident response, reducing the time to contain and remediate threats.
- **Impact**: Limits the potential damage caused by security incidents and enhances overall security posture.

5.3. Comprehensive Visibility:

- **Overview**: AI provides comprehensive visibility into endpoint activities, enabling detailed analysis and investigation of threats.
- **Impact**: Supports effective threat analysis and response by providing a complete view of endpoint activities.

5.4. Reduced Operational Overhead:

- **Overview**: AI automates many aspects of endpoint monitoring and response, reducing the need for manual intervention.
- **Impact**: Lowers the operational burden on IT and security teams, allowing them to focus on more strategic tasks.

5.5. Scalability and Adaptability:

- **Overview**: AI-based EDR solutions scale with growing environments and adapt to changing threat landscapes.
- **Impact**: Provides continuous protection as endpoints and threat vectors evolve.

6. Challenges and Considerations

6.1. Model Accuracy and Reliability:

- **Challenge**: Ensuring the accuracy and reliability of AI models in detecting and classifying threats.
- **Solution**: Continuously update and refine models based on new data and emerging threats.

6.2. Integration with Existing Security Infrastructure:

- **Challenge**: Integrating AI-based EDR solutions with existing security tools and infrastructure.
- **Solution**: Develop interoperable solutions and establish clear integration processes to ensure smooth operation.

6.3. Resource and Computational Demands:

- **Challenge**: AI-based EDR solutions can be resource-intensive and require significant computational power.
- **Solution**: Optimize algorithms and utilize cloud-based resources to manage computational demands effectively.

6.4. Privacy and Data Protection:

- **Challenge**: Ensuring that AI-based EDR solutions handle sensitive endpoint data in compliance with privacy regulations.
- **Solution**: Implement robust data protection measures and adhere to relevant privacy standards.

6.5. Cost of Implementation:

- **Challenge**: The initial cost of implementing AI-based EDR solutions can be high.
- **Solution**: Evaluate the cost-benefit ratio and consider long-term savings and efficiencies gained through AI integration.

AI-based Endpoint Detection and Response (EDR) solutions offer a transformative approach to endpoint security, enhancing detection capabilities, accelerating response times, and providing comprehensive visibility into endpoint activities. By leveraging advanced machine learning, behavioral analysis, and threat intelligence, AI-driven EDR solutions address the limitations of traditional methods and provide robust defense against evolving cyber threats. Despite challenges related to model accuracy, integration, and resource demands, AI-based EDR solutions deliver significant benefits for detecting, investigating, and mitigating endpoint threats. As the cybersecurity landscape continues to evolve, AI will play an increasingly vital role in maintaining effective and adaptive endpoint protection.

7.4 Protecting Mobile and Remote Devices

In the modern digital landscape, mobile and remote devices are integral to both personal and professional life. With the rise of remote work, BYOD (Bring Your Own Device) policies, and the proliferation of mobile applications, securing these devices has become crucial. This section explores how AI enhances the protection of mobile and remote devices, focusing on the technologies and strategies employed to safeguard these endpoints against a variety of threats.

1. Overview of Mobile and Remote Device Security

1.1. Mobile Device Security:

Overview: Mobile devices, including smartphones and tablets, are increasingly targeted by cyber threats due to their widespread use and the sensitive data they often store.

Challenges:

- **Varied Operating Systems**: Different mobile operating systems (iOS, Android) present unique security challenges and vulnerabilities.

- **App Ecosystem**: Mobile applications can be a source of malware and privacy breaches.
- **Loss and Theft**: Mobile devices are prone to loss or theft, increasing the risk of unauthorized access to sensitive data.

1.2. Remote Device Security:

Overview: Remote devices, such as laptops and desktops used outside the corporate network, face security challenges due to their connection over potentially insecure networks.

Challenges:

- **Unsecured Networks**: Remote devices often connect to public or unsecured networks, exposing them to potential attacks.
- **Data Leakage**: Sensitive data accessed or stored on remote devices may be vulnerable to theft or leakage.
- **Inconsistent Security Policies**: Ensuring consistent security policies and updates on remote devices can be challenging.

2. How AI Enhances Mobile and Remote Device Security

2.1. AI-Powered Threat Detection:

Overview: AI enhances the detection of threats on mobile and remote devices by analyzing patterns and behaviors that may indicate malicious activities.

Techniques:

- **Behavioral Analysis**: AI monitors device behavior to detect anomalies and potential threats.
- **Anomaly Detection**: Identifies deviations from normal activity patterns that may signal malware or unauthorized access.

2.2. Automated Incident Response:

Overview: AI-driven solutions provide automated response mechanisms to quickly address security incidents on mobile and remote devices.

Techniques:

- **Automated Containment**: AI can automatically isolate compromised devices to prevent further spread of malware or unauthorized access.
- **Real-Time Alerts**: Generates instant alerts for detected threats, enabling rapid response and mitigation.

2.3. Mobile Threat Defense:

Overview: AI enhances mobile threat defense by analyzing mobile apps and network traffic for potential security risks.

Techniques:

- **App Analysis**: AI scans and evaluates mobile applications for security vulnerabilities and malicious behavior.
- **Network Traffic Analysis**: Monitors network traffic for suspicious activities and potential threats.

2.4. Remote Device Management:

Overview: AI supports the management and security of remote devices by providing tools for monitoring and enforcing security policies.

Techniques:

- **Policy Enforcement**: AI ensures that remote devices adhere to corporate security policies and configurations.
- **Remote Monitoring**: Provides continuous monitoring of remote devices for compliance and security threats.

3. Key Technologies in AI-Based Mobile and Remote Device Security

3.1. Machine Learning Algorithms:

Overview: Machine learning algorithms are used to enhance the security of mobile and remote devices by analyzing data and detecting threats.

Examples:

- **Deep Learning:** Utilizes neural networks to analyze complex patterns and detect advanced threats.
- **Clustering Algorithms**: Groups similar activities to identify unusual patterns that may indicate malicious behavior.
- **Decision Trees**: Builds decision models based on features and characteristics of device activities.

3.2. Behavioral Analytics:

Overview: Behavioral analytics focuses on understanding and analyzing device behavior to detect potential threats.

Applications:

- **Mobile App Behavior**: Analyzes the behavior of mobile applications to identify suspicious activities and potential risks.
- **Remote Device Activity**: Monitors and analyzes remote device activities for signs of unauthorized access or malicious actions.

3.3. Threat Intelligence Integration:

Overview: Integration of threat intelligence feeds provides real-time updates and context for mobile and remote device security.

Applications:

- **Real-Time Updates**: Receives and processes updates on new threats and attack methods targeting mobile and remote devices.
- **Contextual Analysis**: Enhances threat detection by correlating device activities with threat intelligence.

3.4. Automated Response Mechanisms:

Overview: AI-driven solutions provide automated mechanisms for responding to threats on mobile and remote devices.

Applications:

- **Incident Containment**: Automatically isolates compromised devices to prevent further damage.

- **Threat Remediation**: Provides automated tools for cleaning and restoring affected devices.

4. Practical Applications of AI-Based Mobile and Remote Device Security

4.1. Enhanced Mobile Threat Detection:

Overview: AI-based solutions improve the detection of threats on mobile devices by analyzing app behavior, network traffic, and user activities.

Applications:

- **Malware Detection**: Identifies and mitigates malware on mobile devices.
- **Phishing Protection**: Detects and blocks phishing attempts targeting mobile users.

4.2. Secure Remote Access:

Overview: AI enhances the security of remote access solutions by monitoring and securing connections to corporate resources.

Applications:

- **Secure VPNs**: Analyzes VPN connections for potential security risks and unauthorized access.
- **Access Control**: Ensures that remote access adheres to corporate security policies and permissions.

4.3. Mobile Device Management (MDM):

Overview: AI-based MDM solutions provide comprehensive management and security for mobile devices.

Applications:

- **Policy Enforcement**: Enforces security policies on mobile devices to ensure compliance and protection.
- **Remote Wiping**: Enables remote wiping of lost or stolen devices to protect sensitive data.

4.4. Remote Device Monitoring and Management:

Overview: AI supports the monitoring and management of remote devices to ensure security and compliance.

Applications:

- **Real-Time Monitoring**: Continuously monitors remote devices for security threats and policy compliance.
- **Automated Updates**: Ensures that remote devices receive timely security updates and patches.

5. Benefits of AI-Based Mobile and Remote Device Security

5.1. Improved Threat Detection:

- **Overview**: AI enhances the detection of sophisticated threats on mobile and remote devices by analyzing complex patterns and behaviors.
- **Impact**: Reduces the risk of undetected threats and improves overall device security.

5.2. Faster Incident Response:

- **Overview**: AI-driven solutions automate and accelerate incident response, minimizing the time required to address security incidents.
- **Impact**: Limits the potential damage caused by security breaches and enhances overall security posture.

5.3. Enhanced Visibility and Control:

- **Overview**: AI provides comprehensive visibility into mobile and remote device activities, enabling better control and management.
- **Impact**: Supports effective threat analysis and response by offering a complete view of device activities.

5.4. Reduced Operational Overhead:

- **Overview**: AI automates many aspects of device security, reducing the need for manual intervention and management.

- **Impact**: Lowers the operational burden on IT and security teams, allowing them to focus on more strategic tasks.

5.5. Scalability and Adaptability:

- **Overview**: AI-based solutions scale with growing environments and adapt to evolving threat landscapes.
- **Impact**: Provides continuous protection as the number of devices and threat vectors increases.

6. Challenges and Considerations

6.1. Diverse Device Ecosystems:

- **Challenge**: Securing a wide range of mobile and remote devices with varying operating systems and configurations.
- **Solution**: Develop comprehensive security solutions that accommodate diverse device ecosystems and provide consistent protection.

6.2. Privacy and Data Protection:

- **Challenge**: Ensuring that AI-based solutions handle sensitive data in compliance with privacy regulations.
- **Solution**: Implement robust data protection measures and adhere to relevant privacy standards.

6.3. Integration with Existing Security Infrastructure:

- **Challenge**: Integrating AI-based solutions with existing security tools and infrastructure.
- **Solution**: Develop interoperable solutions and establish clear integration processes to ensure smooth operation.

6.4. Resource and Computational Demands:

- **Challenge**: AI-based solutions can be resource-intensive and require significant computational power.
- **Solution**: Optimize algorithms and utilize cloud-based resources to manage computational demands effectively.

6.5. Cost of Implementation:

- **Challenge**: The initial cost of implementing AI-based device security solutions can be high.
- **Solution**: Evaluate the cost-benefit ratio and consider long-term savings and efficiencies gained through AI integration.

AI-based protection for mobile and remote devices offers a robust and adaptive approach to securing endpoints in a rapidly evolving digital landscape. By leveraging advanced machine learning, behavioral analysis, and threat intelligence, AI-driven solutions enhance threat detection, automate response, and provide comprehensive visibility into device activities. Despite challenges related to device diversity, privacy, and integration, AI-based solutions deliver significant benefits for securing mobile and remote devices, ensuring consistent protection as threats and technologies continue to evolve.

7.5 Case Studies and Best Practices

The protection of mobile and remote devices is a critical aspect of cybersecurity, particularly in the modern landscape where these devices are increasingly targeted by sophisticated threats. This section explores real-world case studies and best practices for implementing AI-driven security solutions for mobile and remote devices. By examining successful implementations and lessons learned, we can gain insights into effective strategies for enhancing device security.

1. Case Studies

1.1. Case Study: Financial Institution's Mobile Security Enhancement

Overview: A leading financial institution faced challenges in securing a large fleet of mobile devices used by employees for financial transactions and sensitive communications.

Challenge:

- **Risk of Data Breach**: The institution was concerned about potential data breaches and unauthorized access to financial data.
- **Complex Device Ecosystem**: The organization had to manage a diverse range of mobile devices with different operating systems and configurations.

Solution:

- **AI-Based Threat Detection**: Implemented an AI-powered mobile threat defense solution that analyzed app behavior and network traffic for anomalies.
- **Automated Response**: Integrated automated incident response capabilities to quickly contain and remediate threats on mobile devices.
- **Mobile Device Management (MDM):** Deployed an AI-driven MDM solution to enforce security policies and ensure compliance.

Results:

- **Enhanced Security**: Improved detection and mitigation of mobile threats, reducing the risk of data breaches.
- **Efficient Management**: Streamlined device management and policy enforcement, increasing operational efficiency.

1.2. Case Study: Tech Company's Remote Device Protection Strategy

Overview: A technology company with a large remote workforce needed to secure remote devices accessing corporate resources.

Challenge:

- **Unsecured Networks**: Remote devices frequently connected to public and unsecured networks, increasing the risk of cyberattacks.
- **Inconsistent Security Policies**: Ensuring consistent application of security policies across remote devices was a challenge.

Solution:

- **AI-Powered Endpoint Security**: Deployed an AI-based endpoint detection and response (EDR) solution to monitor and secure remote devices.
- **Threat Intelligence Integration**: Utilized threat intelligence feeds to provide real-time updates and context for detecting and responding to threats.
- **Secure Remote Access**: Implemented AI-driven secure VPN solutions to protect remote connections to corporate resources.

Results:

- **Improved Threat Detection**: Enhanced visibility into remote device activities and quicker identification of security threats.
- **Faster Incident Response**: Automated response mechanisms reduced response times and minimized the impact of security incidents.

1.3. Case Study: Healthcare Provider's Mobile Device Protection

Overview: A healthcare provider needed to secure mobile devices used by medical staff for accessing patient records and sensitive health information.

Challenge:

- **Compliance Requirements**: Required compliance with stringent regulations for protecting patient data.
- **Risk of Mobile Threats**: Faced threats from malicious apps and potential data breaches due to lost or stolen devices.

Solution:

- **AI-Based Mobile Threat Defense**: Implemented an AI-powered solution for real-time app analysis and network traffic monitoring.
- **Data Encryption**: Enforced data encryption on mobile devices to protect sensitive health information.
- **Remote Wiping**: Deployed remote wiping capabilities to protect data in case of lost or stolen devices.

Results:

- **Regulatory Compliance**: Achieved compliance with healthcare data protection regulations.
- **Enhanced Security**: Reduced the risk of data breaches and improved overall mobile device security.

2. Best Practices

2.1. Implement Comprehensive Mobile and Remote Device Security Policies

Overview: Develop and enforce comprehensive security policies for mobile and remote devices to ensure consistent protection.

Best Practices:

- **Policy Development**: Create detailed policies for device usage, data access, and security practices.
- **Regular Updates**: Regularly review and update policies to address new threats and technological advancements.
- **User Education**: Educate employees on security best practices and the importance of adhering to security policies.

2.2. Leverage AI for Threat Detection and Response

Overview: Utilize AI-driven solutions to enhance threat detection, analysis, and response on mobile and remote devices.

Best Practices:

- **Behavioral Analytics**: Implement AI-based behavioral analytics to monitor and analyze device activities for suspicious behavior.
- **Anomaly Detection**: Use AI to detect deviations from normal behavior patterns and identify potential threats.
- **Automated Response**: Deploy automated response mechanisms to quickly contain and remediate detected threats.

2.3. Integrate Threat Intelligence for Real-Time Updates

Overview: Integrate threat intelligence feeds to provide real-time updates and context for detecting and responding to threats.

Best Practices:

- **Threat Feed Integration**: Incorporate threat intelligence feeds into security solutions to stay informed about emerging threats and attack methods.
- **Contextual Analysis**: Use threat intelligence to enhance the contextual analysis of device activities and improve threat detection accuracy.

2.4. Ensure Consistent Security Policies Across Devices

Overview: Implement and enforce consistent security policies across all mobile and remote devices to ensure comprehensive protection.

Best Practices:

- **Unified Policy Management**: Use centralized management tools to enforce security policies across diverse device ecosystems.
- **Regular Audits**: Conduct regular audits to ensure compliance with security policies and identify areas for improvement.

2.5. Invest in Scalable and Adaptable Security Solutions

Overview: Choose security solutions that are scalable and adaptable to accommodate growing environments and evolving threats.

Best Practices:

- **Scalability**: Select AI-driven solutions that can scale with the number of devices and users in the organization.
- **Adaptability**: Ensure solutions can adapt to changing threat landscapes and technological advancements.

2.6. Address Privacy and Data Protection Concerns

Overview: Ensure that security solutions handle sensitive data in compliance with privacy regulations and best practices.

Best Practices:

- **Data Encryption**: Implement data encryption to protect sensitive information stored on mobile and remote devices.
- **Privacy Compliance**: Adhere to relevant privacy regulations and standards to protect user data and maintain trust.

The case studies and best practices outlined in this section provide valuable insights into effective strategies for securing mobile and remote devices using AI-driven solutions. By leveraging advanced threat detection, automated response mechanisms, and comprehensive security policies, organizations can enhance their protection against evolving threats. Real-world examples highlight the success of AI-based solutions in addressing security challenges, improving incident response, and ensuring regulatory compliance. Adopting these best practices will help organizations safeguard their mobile and remote devices, maintain robust security postures, and adapt to the dynamic cybersecurity landscape.

Chapter 8: AI in Threat Intelligence

Chapter 8 explores how artificial intelligence (AI) is transforming threat intelligence, a crucial component of modern cybersecurity strategies. Threat intelligence involves collecting, analyzing, and using information about current and emerging threats to improve security posture and proactively defend against cyber attacks. AI enhances this process by providing advanced tools for analyzing and interpreting vast amounts of data.

We start by discussing AI-driven threat intelligence platforms. These platforms leverage machine learning algorithms to analyze large volumes of data from various sources, such as threat feeds, logs, and social media. By automating data collection and analysis, AI can identify patterns, correlations, and emerging threats more effectively than traditional methods.

Next, we delve into data collection and analysis techniques. AI enables the aggregation and normalization of threat data from diverse sources, including dark web forums, security blogs, and industry reports. This comprehensive approach allows for more accurate and timely threat assessments.

We then explore predictive analytics and its application in threat intelligence. AI models can forecast potential threats based on historical data and current trends, helping organizations anticipate and prepare for future attacks. This proactive approach enhances the ability to respond to emerging threats before they can cause significant damage.

The chapter also covers the integration of AI with existing threat intelligence feeds. By enriching these feeds with AI-driven insights, organizations can gain a deeper understanding of threats and improve their overall security posture. We highlight how AI can automate the correlation of threat data with organizational assets and vulnerabilities.

Real-world case studies demonstrate the successful implementation of AI in threat intelligence. These examples provide practical insights into how AI can enhance threat detection, response, and overall security strategy.

By the end of this chapter, you will have a thorough understanding of how AI is revolutionizing threat intelligence. AI's ability to analyze and interpret vast amounts of data enhances threat detection, predictive capabilities, and overall cybersecurity strategy, making it an indispensable tool in the modern security landscape.

8.1 AI-Driven Threat Intelligence Platforms

Threat intelligence platforms (TIPs) are essential tools for organizations seeking to stay ahead of cyber threats by aggregating, analyzing, and acting upon threat data. The integration of artificial intelligence (AI) into these platforms significantly enhances their capabilities, providing more robust, adaptive, and timely threat intelligence. This section delves into how AI-driven threat intelligence platforms operate, their key features, benefits, and practical applications in modern cybersecurity.

1. Overview of AI-Driven Threat Intelligence Platforms

1.1. Definition and Purpose:

- **Definition**: AI-driven threat intelligence platforms are advanced systems that use artificial intelligence to collect, analyze, and provide actionable insights on cybersecurity threats.
- **Purpose**: These platforms aim to improve the accuracy and speed of threat detection and response by leveraging AI technologies to process vast amounts of data and identify potential threats more effectively.

1.2. Key Components:

- **Data Collection**: Aggregates data from various sources such as network traffic, endpoint logs, threat feeds, and open-source intelligence (OSINT).
- **Data Analysis**: Utilizes AI algorithms to analyze collected data, identify patterns, and detect anomalies that may indicate threats.
- **Threat Correlation**: Correlates data from different sources to build a comprehensive picture of the threat landscape.
- **Actionable Insights**: Provides actionable intelligence and recommendations for mitigating identified threats.

2. How AI Enhances Threat Intelligence Platforms

2.1. Advanced Data Processing:

Overview: AI enhances data processing capabilities by handling large volumes of data and extracting meaningful insights.

Techniques:

- **Natural Language Processing (NLP):** Analyzes textual data from threat feeds, security blogs, and incident reports to identify emerging threats and trends.
- **Machine Learning Algorithms**: Applies machine learning models to classify and predict threats based on historical data and known attack patterns.
- **Deep Learning**: Utilizes neural networks to recognize complex patterns and anomalies in large datasets.

2.2. Improved Threat Detection:

Overview: AI-driven platforms improve threat detection by analyzing data more accurately and rapidly than traditional methods.

Techniques:

- **Behavioral Analysis**: Monitors and analyzes the behavior of network traffic and user activities to identify deviations from normal patterns that may indicate malicious activity.
- **Anomaly Detection**: Uses AI algorithms to detect unusual patterns or anomalies that could signal a potential threat.

2.3. Enhanced Threat Correlation:

Overview: AI enhances the correlation of threat data from multiple sources to provide a more comprehensive view of the threat landscape.

Techniques:

- **Contextual Analysis**: Integrates context from various sources to improve the accuracy of threat correlation and analysis.
- **Pattern Recognition**: Identifies correlations between disparate data points to uncover complex attack scenarios and threat networks.

2.4. Real-Time Insights and Alerts:

Overview: AI-driven platforms provide real-time insights and alerts to enable timely response to emerging threats.

Techniques:

- **Automated Alerting**: Generates automated alerts based on AI analysis of data, reducing the time required to identify and respond to threats.
- **Dynamic Updates**: Continuously updates threat intelligence based on new data and evolving threat landscapes.

3. Key Benefits of AI-Driven Threat Intelligence Platforms

3.1. Faster Threat Detection and Response:

Overview: AI-driven platforms significantly reduce the time required to detect and respond to threats.

Benefits:

- **Rapid Analysis**: AI algorithms analyze large volumes of data quickly, enabling faster identification of threats.
- **Automated Response**: AI-driven automated response mechanisms can act on detected threats without human intervention, accelerating response times.

3.2. Improved Accuracy and Precision:

Overview: AI enhances the accuracy and precision of threat detection and analysis.

Benefits:

- **Reduced False Positives**: AI algorithms improve the accuracy of threat detection, reducing the number of false positives and enabling more focused responses.
- **Enhanced Insights**: Provides more precise and actionable insights into the nature and scope of threats.

3.3. Comprehensive Threat Visibility:

Overview: AI-driven platforms offer a more comprehensive view of the threat landscape by correlating data from multiple sources.

Benefits:

- **Holistic View**: Provides a unified view of threats across various data sources and systems.
- **Contextual Understanding**: Enhances understanding of threat contexts and relationships, improving overall threat assessment.

3.4. Scalable and Adaptable Solutions:

Overview: AI-driven threat intelligence platforms are scalable and adaptable to evolving threat landscapes.

Benefits:

- **Scalability**: Capable of handling increasing volumes of data and threats as organizations grow.
- **Adaptability**: Adapts to new threat patterns and trends, ensuring continuous relevance and effectiveness.

4. Practical Applications of AI-Driven Threat Intelligence Platforms

4.1. Proactive Threat Hunting:

Overview: AI-driven platforms support proactive threat hunting by providing insights and indicators of potential threats.

Applications:

- **Threat Indicators**: Identifies indicators of compromise (IOCs) and tactics, techniques, and procedures (TTPs) used by attackers.
- **Threat Scenarios**: Assists in constructing threat scenarios and simulations for proactive threat hunting.

4.2. Incident Response and Management:

Overview: AI-driven platforms enhance incident response by providing real-time alerts and actionable intelligence.

Applications:

- **Incident Prioritization**: Helps prioritize incidents based on severity and potential impact.

- **Response Coordination**: Provides insights and recommendations for coordinating incident response efforts.

4.3. Risk Assessment and Management:

Overview: AI-driven threat intelligence platforms support risk assessment and management by analyzing threat data and assessing potential risks.

Applications:

- **Risk Scoring**: Assigns risk scores to identified threats based on their potential impact and likelihood.
- **Risk Mitigation**: Provides recommendations for mitigating identified risks and vulnerabilities.

4.4. Threat Intelligence Sharing:

Overview: AI-driven platforms facilitate threat intelligence sharing among organizations and security communities.

Applications:

- **Collaborative Analysis**: Supports collaborative analysis and sharing of threat intelligence with partners and industry peers.
- **Community Insights**: Leverages insights from threat intelligence communities to enhance threat detection and response.

5. Best Practices for Implementing AI-Driven Threat Intelligence Platforms

5.1. Define Clear Objectives and Requirements:

Overview: Establish clear objectives and requirements for the AI-driven threat intelligence platform based on organizational needs.

Best Practices:

- **Objective Setting**: Define specific goals for threat intelligence, such as improving detection rates or reducing response times.
- **Requirements Analysis**: Identify key requirements, including data sources, integration needs, and performance metrics.

5.2. Integrate with Existing Security Infrastructure:

Overview: Ensure seamless integration of the AI-driven platform with existing security tools and infrastructure.

Best Practices:

- **Interoperability**: Choose platforms that are compatible with existing security tools and systems.
- **Data Integration**: Integrate threat intelligence data with existing security information and event management (SIEM) systems for comprehensive analysis.

5.3. Continuously Update and Train AI Models:

Overview: Regularly update and train AI models to ensure they remain effective and accurate.

Best Practices:

- **Model Training**: Continuously train AI models using up-to-date threat data and evolving threat patterns.
- **Performance Monitoring**: Monitor the performance of AI models and make adjustments as needed to improve accuracy and relevance.

5.4. Ensure Data Privacy and Compliance:

Overview: Implement measures to protect data privacy and ensure compliance with relevant regulations.

Best Practices:

- **Data Protection**: Apply encryption and access controls to protect sensitive threat intelligence data.
- **Regulatory Compliance**: Ensure that the platform adheres to data privacy and cybersecurity regulations.

5.5. Foster Collaboration and Information Sharing:

Overview: Encourage collaboration and information sharing with other organizations and industry groups to enhance threat intelligence.

Best Practices:

- **Information Sharing**: Participate in threat intelligence sharing communities and forums.
- **Collaborative Efforts**: Collaborate with partners and industry peers to share insights and improve threat detection.

AI-driven threat intelligence platforms represent a significant advancement in the field of cybersecurity, offering enhanced capabilities for threat detection, analysis, and response. By leveraging AI technologies such as machine learning, natural language processing, and deep learning, these platforms provide more accurate, timely, and actionable threat intelligence. Successful implementation of AI-driven threat intelligence platforms involves defining clear objectives, integrating with existing security infrastructure, continuously updating AI models, ensuring data privacy, and fostering collaboration. As the threat landscape continues to evolve, AI-driven platforms will play a crucial role in providing organizations with the tools and insights needed to stay ahead of emerging threats and maintain robust security postures.

8.2 Data Collection and Analysis

Effective threat intelligence relies heavily on robust data collection and analysis. AI-driven threat intelligence platforms leverage advanced techniques to gather and analyze vast amounts of data, providing actionable insights into potential threats. This section explores the methods and technologies used in data collection and analysis, highlighting their importance in enhancing cybersecurity.

1. Data Collection

1.1. Sources of Threat Data:

- **Network Traffic**: Captures data packets traversing the network to identify unusual patterns, potential intrusions, or malicious activities.
- **Endpoint Logs**: Collects logs from various endpoints (e.g., computers, mobile devices) to track user activities, system changes, and potential threats.
- **Threat Feeds**: Aggregates data from external threat intelligence feeds, including information on known threats, vulnerabilities, and attack signatures.

- **Open-Source Intelligence (OSINT):** Gathers publicly available information from sources like forums, social media, and news outlets to identify emerging threats and trends.
- **Dark Web Intelligence:** Monitors hidden parts of the internet (dark web) for discussions or activities related to potential threats or breaches.
- **Internal Incident Data:** Uses data from previous security incidents and historical attack patterns to identify recurring threats and vulnerabilities.

1.2. Data Collection Techniques:

- **Passive Data Collection:** Involves monitoring and recording data without actively interacting with the system or network. For example, capturing network traffic without altering it.
- **Active Data Collection:** Includes actively querying systems, performing scans, or using probes to gather information about network topology, vulnerabilities, and security configurations.
- **Automated Data Aggregation:** Employs automated tools and scripts to gather data from multiple sources, reducing manual effort and increasing efficiency.
- **API Integration:** Uses application programming interfaces (APIs) to connect with external threat intelligence sources and pull data into the platform.

1.3. Data Quality and Integrity:

- **Data Accuracy:** Ensures collected data is accurate and reflects the true state of the network or system. Implement data validation techniques to minimize errors.
- **Data Completeness:** Strives for completeness by gathering data from diverse sources to provide a comprehensive view of the threat landscape.
- **Data Timeliness:** Focuses on real-time or near-real-time data collection to ensure that threat intelligence remains relevant and up-to-date.
- **Data Privacy:** Adheres to privacy regulations and guidelines to protect sensitive information and ensure compliance.

2. Data Analysis

2.1. Data Preprocessing:

- **Data Cleaning:** Removes duplicates, irrelevant information, and errors from the collected data to improve the quality of the analysis.
- **Normalization:** Standardizes data formats and structures to ensure consistency and facilitate effective analysis.

- **Integration**: Combines data from different sources into a unified format or database to enable comprehensive analysis.

2.2. Analytical Techniques:

- **Statistical Analysis**: Uses statistical methods to identify patterns, trends, and anomalies in the data. For example, identifying unusual spikes in network traffic.
- **Machine Learning Algorithms**: Applies machine learning models to classify, predict, and detect threats based on historical data. Common algorithms include decision trees, clustering, and neural networks.
- **Natural Language Processing (NLP)**: Analyzes textual data from threat feeds, social media, or dark web sources to extract meaningful information and identify emerging threats.
- **Behavioral Analysis**: Monitors and analyzes user and system behavior to detect deviations from normal patterns that could indicate malicious activities.

2.3. Anomaly Detection:

- **Baseline Establishment**: Establishes a baseline of normal behavior for systems, networks, and users to identify deviations.
- **Anomaly Detection Algorithms**: Employs algorithms to detect anomalies by comparing current data against established baselines. Techniques include statistical thresholds, clustering, and machine learning models.
- **Real-Time Analysis**: Provides real-time analysis to detect and respond to anomalies as they occur, minimizing the impact of potential threats.

2.4. Threat Correlation:

- **Cross-Source Correlation**: Correlates data from multiple sources (e.g., network traffic, endpoint logs, threat feeds) to build a comprehensive picture of the threat landscape.
- **Event Correlation**: Analyzes and correlates individual security events to identify patterns or trends that may indicate a larger, coordinated attack.
- **Contextual Analysis**: Enhances threat correlation by incorporating context such as threat actor tactics, techniques, and procedures (TTPs) and attack vectors.

2.5. Visualization and Reporting:

- **Data Visualization**: Uses graphical representations such as charts, graphs, and dashboards to present analyzed data in an easily understandable format.

- **Threat Dashboards**: Provides real-time and historical views of threat data, enabling security teams to monitor and assess threats effectively.
- **Custom Reports**: Generates detailed reports on threat analysis, including insights, trends, and recommendations for action.

3. Challenges and Considerations

3.1. Data Overload:

- **Challenge**: Managing and analyzing large volumes of data can be overwhelming and may lead to information overload.
- **Solution**: Implement data filtering and prioritization techniques to focus on the most relevant and actionable information.

3.2. Data Integration:

- **Challenge**: Integrating data from diverse sources with varying formats and structures can be complex.
- **Solution**: Use data integration tools and techniques to standardize and combine data from different sources effectively.

3.3. Real-Time Analysis:

- **Challenge**: Ensuring real-time or near-real-time analysis can be resource-intensive and requires efficient processing capabilities.
- **Solution**: Employ scalable and high-performance analytics solutions to handle real-time data processing.

3.4. False Positives and Negatives:

- **Challenge**: AI-driven analysis may produce false positives (incorrectly identifying benign activities as threats) or false negatives (failing to detect actual threats).
- **Solution**: Continuously refine and train AI models to improve accuracy and reduce false positives and negatives.

3.5. Privacy and Compliance:

- **Challenge**: Balancing data collection and analysis with privacy regulations and compliance requirements.

- **Solution**: Implement data protection measures and ensure that data collection practices adhere to relevant regulations and standards.

4. Best Practices for Data Collection and Analysis

4.1. Define Clear Objectives:

Overview: Establish clear objectives for data collection and analysis to ensure that efforts are aligned with organizational goals and security needs.

Best Practices:

- **Objective Setting**: Define specific goals for threat intelligence, such as improving detection rates or understanding emerging threats.
- **Scope Definition**: Determine the scope of data collection and analysis based on these objectives.

4.2. Utilize Diverse Data Sources:

Overview: Collect data from a variety of sources to provide a comprehensive view of the threat landscape.

Best Practices:

- **Source Diversity**: Incorporate data from network traffic, endpoint logs, threat feeds, OSINT, and dark web intelligence.
- **Data Enrichment**: Enhance collected data with additional context and insights from multiple sources.

4.3. Implement Robust Data Processing Techniques:

Overview: Use effective data preprocessing and analytical techniques to ensure high-quality and actionable threat intelligence.

Best Practices:

- **Data Cleaning**: Regularly clean and validate data to maintain accuracy and relevance.
- **Advanced Analytics**: Apply machine learning, NLP, and other advanced techniques to extract valuable insights from data.

4.4. Ensure Real-Time Capabilities:

Overview: Implement solutions that provide real-time or near-real-time data collection and analysis to enable timely threat detection and response.

Best Practices:

- **Real-Time Monitoring**: Use real-time monitoring tools and dashboards to track and analyze threats as they occur.
- **Automated Alerts**: Set up automated alerts based on analysis to promptly address emerging threats.

4.5. Prioritize Data Privacy and Compliance:

Overview: Ensure that data collection and analysis practices adhere to privacy regulations and compliance requirements.

Best Practices:

- **Data Protection**: Implement encryption and access controls to protect sensitive data.
- **Regulatory Compliance**: Regularly review and update practices to comply with relevant data privacy and security regulations.

Data collection and analysis are foundational components of effective AI-driven threat intelligence platforms. By leveraging diverse data sources, employing advanced analytical techniques, and addressing challenges such as data overload and privacy concerns, organizations can enhance their ability to detect, understand, and respond to cyber threats. Implementing best practices in data collection and analysis ensures that threat intelligence remains accurate, actionable, and aligned with organizational security objectives, ultimately strengthening overall cybersecurity posture.

8.3 Predictive Analytics for Cyber Defense

Predictive analytics has become a transformative tool in the realm of cybersecurity, enabling organizations to anticipate and mitigate potential threats before they materialize. By analyzing historical data and employing advanced statistical and machine learning techniques, predictive analytics helps in forecasting future threats and vulnerabilities. This section explores the concept of predictive analytics in cyber defense, its methodologies, applications, and benefits.

1. Understanding Predictive Analytics

1.1. Definition and Scope:

- **Definition**: Predictive analytics involves using historical data, statistical algorithms, and machine learning techniques to identify the likelihood of future outcomes. n cybersecurity, it aims to predict potential security threats and vulnerabilities.
- **Scope**: Includes forecasting potential attack vectors, identifying emerging threats, and anticipating system weaknesses before they are exploited by malicious actors.

1.2. Key Components:

- **Data Collection**: Gathers historical and current data related to security incidents, system performance, and threat intelligence.
- **Data Processing**: Involves cleaning, normalizing, and integrating data to prepare it for analysis.
- **Model Building**: Uses statistical and machine learning models to analyze data and generate predictions.
- **Prediction and Analysis**: Provides forecasts and actionable insights based on the analysis.

2. Methodologies in Predictive Analytics

2.1. Statistical Techniques:

- **Time Series Analysis**: Analyzes data points collected or recorded at specific time intervals to identify patterns and trends over time. Useful for forecasting recurring attack patterns and seasonal threats.
- **Regression Analysis**: Examines the relationship between variables to predict outcomes. For example, it can be used to predict the likelihood of a security breach based on historical incident data.
- **Survival Analysis**: Estimates the time until an event occurs, such as the time until a system vulnerability is exploited.

2.2. Machine Learning Models:

- **Supervised Learning**: Uses labeled data to train models that can predict future events. Techniques include decision trees, random forests, and support vector machines.
- **Example**: A supervised model trained on historical attack data can predict the likelihood of a similar attack occurring.

- **Unsupervised Learning**: Analyzes unlabeled data to identify patterns and anomalies without predefined categories. Techniques include clustering and anomaly detection.
- **Example**: Unsupervised learning can identify unusual patterns in network traffic that may indicate emerging threats.

- **Deep Learning**: Utilizes neural networks with multiple layers to analyze complex patterns and relationships in large datasets.
- **Example**: Deep learning models can detect sophisticated malware by analyzing its behavior and characteristics.

2.3. Predictive Modeling Techniques:

- **Scenario Analysis**: Evaluates different threat scenarios and their potential impacts to prepare for various contingencies.
- **Example**: Analyzing scenarios where different attack vectors are used to predict the impact on organizational assets.

- **Risk Assessment Models**: Quantifies and prioritizes risks based on their likelihood and potential impact.
- **Example**: Risk assessment models can prioritize vulnerabilities based on their potential to be exploited and the severity of potential damage.

3. Applications of Predictive Analytics in Cyber Defense

3.1. Threat Forecasting:

Overview: Predictive analytics helps in forecasting potential threats by analyzing historical data and identifying emerging patterns.

Applications:

- **Attack Vector Prediction**: Identifies potential attack vectors based on past incidents and current threat intelligence.
- **Emerging Threat Identification**: Detects new and evolving threats by analyzing trends and patterns in threat data.

3.2. Vulnerability Management:

Overview: Helps in anticipating vulnerabilities that may be exploited by attackers, allowing for proactive remediation.

Applications:

- **Vulnerability Assessment**: Predicts which vulnerabilities are likely to be targeted based on historical data and threat intelligence.
- **Patch Management**: Forecasts the impact of vulnerabilities and prioritizes patching efforts based on potential risk.

3.3. Incident Response:

Overview: Enhances incident response by predicting potential incidents and providing insights for effective response strategies.

Applications:

- **Incident Prediction**: Forecasts potential security incidents based on historical patterns and current threat intelligence.
- **Response Planning**: Provides insights into potential incident scenarios, enabling organizations to develop effective response plans.

3.4. Fraud Detection:

Overview: Utilizes predictive analytics to identify and prevent fraudulent activities by analyzing transaction patterns and user behaviors.

Applications:

- **Transaction Monitoring**: Detects anomalous transaction patterns that may indicate fraudulent activities.
- **Behavioral Analysis**: Identifies unusual user behavior that could signal fraud or account compromise.

4. Benefits of Predictive Analytics for Cyber Defense

4.1. Proactive Threat Management:

Overview: Enables organizations to anticipate and address potential threats before they materialize, reducing the impact of security incidents.

Benefits:

- **Early Detection**: Identifies potential threats early, allowing for timely intervention and mitigation.
- **Preventive Measures**: Implements preventive measures based on predicted threats, reducing the likelihood of successful attacks.

4.2. Enhanced Risk Management:

Overview: Improves risk management by providing insights into potential vulnerabilities and threats, allowing for more effective risk assessment and mitigation.

Benefits:

- **Prioritized Risk Mitigation**: Focuses resources on the most critical risks and vulnerabilities.
- **Informed Decision-Making**: Provides data-driven insights for making informed decisions about risk management and resource allocation.

4.3. Improved Incident Response:

Overview: Enhances incident response capabilities by providing forecasts and insights into potential incidents and their impact.

Benefits:

- **Faster Response**: Enables quicker response to predicted incidents, minimizing damage and recovery time.
- **Effective Planning**: Assists in developing effective response plans based on predicted incident scenarios.

4.4. Cost Efficiency:

Overview: Reduces the costs associated with security incidents by enabling proactive threat management and risk mitigation.

Benefits:

- **Reduced Incident Costs:** Minimizes the financial impact of security incidents through early detection and prevention.
- **Resource Optimization**: Optimizes the allocation of resources by focusing on high-priority threats and vulnerabilities.

5. Challenges and Considerations

5.1. Data Quality and Accuracy:

- **Challenge**: The effectiveness of predictive analytics relies on the quality and accuracy of the data used.
- **Solution**: Ensure data accuracy through regular validation, cleaning, and integration from reliable sources.

5.2. Model Complexity and Interpretability:

- **Challenge**: Complex machine learning models may be difficult to interpret and understand.
- **Solution**: Use explainable AI techniques to provide insights into model decisions and enhance interpretability.

5.3. Evolving Threat Landscape:

- **Challenge**: The threat landscape is constantly evolving, which can impact the effectiveness of predictive models.
- **Solution**: Continuously update and retrain predictive models to reflect changes in the threat landscape and emerging trends.

5.4. Privacy and Compliance:

- **Challenge**: Ensuring that predictive analytics practices adhere to privacy regulations and compliance requirements.
- **Solution**: Implement data protection measures and ensure compliance with relevant regulations and standards.

5.5. Resource and Expertise Requirements:

- **Challenge**: Predictive analytics requires specialized skills and resources for model development and implementation.
- **Solution**: Invest in training and hiring skilled personnel or collaborate with external experts to leverage predictive analytics effectively.

6. Best Practices for Implementing Predictive Analytics

6.1. Define Clear Objectives:

Overview: Establish clear objectives for predictive analytics to align with organizational goals and security needs.

Best Practices:

- **Objective Setting**: Define specific goals for predictive analytics, such as improving threat forecasting or enhancing vulnerability management.
- **Scope Definition**: Determine the scope of predictive analytics based on these objectives.

6.2. Leverage High-Quality Data:

Overview: Use high-quality, relevant data to ensure the accuracy and effectiveness of predictive models.

Best Practices:

- **Data Collection**: Collect data from diverse sources, including network traffic, endpoint logs, and threat intelligence.
- **Data Integration**: Integrate data from different sources to provide a comprehensive view of potential threats and vulnerabilities.

6.3. Choose Appropriate Modeling Techniques:

Overview: Select and implement appropriate statistical and machine learning techniques for predictive modeling.

Best Practices:

- **Model Selection**: Choose modeling techniques based on the specific objectives and characteristics of the data.
- **Model Evaluation**: Regularly evaluate and validate predictive models to ensure their accuracy and relevance.

6.4. Ensure Continuous Monitoring and Updates:

Overview: Continuously monitor and update predictive models to reflect changes in the threat landscape and emerging trends.

Best Practices:

- **Model Updating**: Regularly update models with new data and retrain them to maintain accuracy and effectiveness.
- **Threat Intelligence Integration**: Integrate current threat intelligence into predictive models to enhance their predictive capabilities.

6.5. Balance Privacy and Security:

Overview: Ensure that predictive analytics practices balance privacy considerations with security needs.

Best Practices:

- **Data Protection**: Implement measures to protect sensitive data and ensure compliance with privacy regulations.
- **Compliance**: Regularly review practices to ensure adherence to relevant regulations and standards.

Predictive analytics plays a crucial role in modern cybersecurity by enabling organizations to anticipate and mitigate potential threats before they occur. By leveraging advanced statistical and machine learning techniques, organizations can forecast emerging threats, identify vulnerabilities, and enhance their overall security posture. Effective implementation of predictive analytics involves defining clear objectives, leveraging high-quality data, selecting appropriate modeling techniques, and ensuring continuous monitoring and updates. Balancing privacy and security considerations is also essential to ensure that predictive analytics practices align with regulatory requirements and organizational goals. Ultimately, predictive analytics empowers organizations to stay ahead of evolving threats and proactively manage their cybersecurity risks.

8.4 Integrating AI with Existing Threat Feeds

Integrating AI with existing threat feeds is a strategic approach to enhance cybersecurity by leveraging the power of artificial intelligence to process and analyze threat intelligence more effectively. This integration can significantly improve threat detection, response, and overall security posture. This section explores the integration of AI with threat feeds, including the methods, benefits, challenges, and best practices.

1. Understanding Threat Feeds

1.1. Definition and Purpose:

- **Definition**: Threat feeds are data sources that provide information about current and emerging cyber threats, including indicators of compromise (IOCs), tactics, techniques, and procedures (TTPs) used by attackers, and other relevant threat intelligence.
- **Purpose**: To offer actionable insights and data that help organizations detect, prevent, and respond to cyber threats.

1.2. Types of Threat Feeds:

- **Commercial Feeds**: Provided by cybersecurity vendors and offer curated, high-quality threat intelligence data.
- **Open-Source Feeds**: Publicly available threat intelligence data from various sources such as forums, social media, and research publications.
- **Internal Feeds**: Data collected from within an organization, including historical incident data, log files, and internal threat intelligence.

2. Integrating AI with Threat Feeds

2.1. Data Aggregation:

Overview: Aggregating data from multiple threat feeds and other sources into a centralized platform where AI can process and analyze it.

Methods:

- **API Integration**: Connects threat feeds to security platforms using APIs to automate data ingestion and updates.
- **Data Parsing**: Extracts relevant information from raw threat feed data and normalizes it for analysis.

2.2. Data Enrichment:

Overview: Enhancing threat feed data with additional context to improve its value and relevance.

Methods:

- **Contextual Analysis**: AI algorithms analyze and contextualize threat feed data, such as associating IOCs with specific threat actors or attack campaigns.
- **Cross-Referencing**: Integrates threat feed data with internal data sources and other threat intelligence to provide a more comprehensive view.

2.3. Threat Detection and Analysis:

Overview: Using AI to analyze aggregated and enriched threat feed data to identify potential threats and anomalies.

Methods:

- **Machine Learning Models**: Applies machine learning models to identify patterns and trends in threat feed data that may indicate potential threats.
- **Behavioral Analysis**: AI analyzes behavioral patterns and compares them with threat feed data to detect anomalies.

2.4. Incident Response and Automation:

Overview: Leveraging AI to automate responses and actions based on insights derived from threat feeds.

Methods:

- **Automated Alerts**: AI generates alerts and notifications based on analysis of threat feed data and predefined thresholds.

- **Response Automation**: AI-driven systems can trigger automated responses, such as blocking IP addresses or isolating affected systems, based on threat feed intelligence.

3. Benefits of Integrating AI with Threat Feeds

3.1. Enhanced Threat Detection:

Overview: AI improves the accuracy and speed of threat detection by analyzing large volumes of threat feed data and identifying potential threats more effectively.

Benefits:

- **Early Detection**: AI can identify emerging threats and anomalies early, allowing for proactive mitigation.
- **Improved Accuracy**: Reduces false positives and false negatives by analyzing threat data in context and identifying patterns.

3.2. Increased Efficiency:

Overview: Automates the processing and analysis of threat feed data, reducing the manual effort required and speeding up the response process.

Benefits:

- **Faster Analysis**: AI can process and analyze threat data much faster than manual methods.
- **Reduced Workload**: Frees up security teams from manual data analysis tasks, allowing them to focus on more strategic activities.

3.3. Better Contextual Understanding:

Overview: AI provides additional context to threat feed data, improving the relevance and usefulness of the information.

Benefits:

- **Comprehensive View**: Offers a more complete understanding of threats by integrating and contextualizing data from multiple sources.

- **Enhanced Decision-Making**: Provides actionable insights that help security teams make informed decisions.

3.4. Proactive Threat Mitigation:

Overview: Enables organizations to take proactive measures based on predictive insights and automated responses derived from threat feeds.

Benefits:

- **Preventative Actions**: Allows for the implementation of preventive measures before threats can cause significant damage.
- **Automated Defense**: Enhances defensive capabilities through automated actions based on threat intelligence.

4. Challenges and Considerations

4.1. Data Quality and Reliability:

- **Challenge**: Ensuring that the threat feed data is accurate, up-to-date, and reliable.
- **Solution**: Use reputable threat feeds and regularly validate and update data to maintain accuracy.

4.2. Integration Complexity:

- **Challenge**: Integrating AI with multiple threat feeds and existing security systems can be complex and resource-intensive.
- **Solution**: Use standardized APIs and data formats to streamline integration and minimize complexity.

4.3. False Positives and Noise:

- **Challenge**: Managing false positives and irrelevant data that may overwhelm the system and reduce effectiveness.
- **Solution**: Implement AI models that refine and filter data to focus on relevant threats and reduce noise.

4.4. Privacy and Compliance:

- **Challenge**: Balancing the use of threat feed data with privacy regulations and compliance requirements.
- **Solution**: Ensure that data collection and analysis practices adhere to privacy regulations and implement data protection measures.

4.5. Resource and Expertise Requirements:

- **Challenge**: Implementing and managing AI-driven threat feed integration requires specialized skills and resources.
- **Solution**: Invest in training and hiring skilled personnel or collaborate with external experts to effectively leverage AI.

5. Best Practices for Integrating AI with Threat Feeds

5.1. Define Clear Objectives:

Overview: Establish clear objectives for integrating AI with threat feeds to ensure alignment with organizational goals and security needs.

Best Practices:

- **Objective Setting**: Define specific goals for threat feed integration, such as improving threat detection or enhancing incident response.
- **Scope Definition**: Determine the scope of integration based on these objectives.

5.2. Choose the Right Threat Feeds:

Overview: Select high-quality and relevant threat feeds that align with the organization's security needs and objectives.

Best Practices:

- **Feed Selection**: Evaluate and choose threat feeds based on their reputation, accuracy, and relevance to your organization.
- **Feed Integration**: Ensure that selected threat feeds are compatible with your AI and security platforms.

5.3. Implement Robust Data Processing:

Overview: Use effective data processing techniques to prepare threat feed data for analysis by AI systems.

Best Practices:

- **Data Normalization**: Normalize data from different threat feeds to ensure consistency and facilitate analysis.
- **Data Enrichment**: Enhance threat feed data with additional context to improve its usefulness.

5.4. Continuously Monitor and Update:

Overview: Regularly monitor and update AI models and threat feeds to reflect changes in the threat landscape and emerging trends.

Best Practices:

- **Model Updating**: Continuously retrain and update AI models to maintain accuracy and effectiveness.
- **Feed Refreshing**: Regularly review and update threat feeds to ensure they provide relevant and current information.

5.5. Balance Privacy and Security:

Overview: Ensure that threat feed integration practices balance privacy considerations with security needs.

Best Practices:

- **Data Protection**: Implement measures to protect sensitive data and ensure compliance with privacy regulations.
- **Regulatory Compliance**: Regularly review practices to ensure adherence to relevant regulations and standards.

Integrating AI with existing threat feeds offers significant advantages for enhancing cybersecurity by improving threat detection, analysis, and response capabilities. By aggregating and enriching threat feed data, leveraging advanced AI techniques for analysis, and automating responses, organizations can proactively manage and mitigate cyber threats. Effective integration requires careful consideration of data quality, system complexity, and privacy regulations, as well as ongoing monitoring and updates. By following best practices and addressing challenges, organizations can optimize their use of AI-driven threat intelligence and strengthen their overall security posture.

8.5 Case Studies and Applications

Incorporating AI into cybersecurity practices has led to numerous successful implementations and innovations. Case studies provide valuable insights into how AI is applied in real-world scenarios to address specific challenges and enhance security. This section explores various case studies and applications of AI in the context of threat intelligence and cybersecurity.

1. Case Study 1: Enhancing Threat Detection with AI

1.1. Background:

A large financial institution faced challenges with detecting and mitigating advanced threats due to the volume and complexity of network traffic and threat data. Traditional methods struggled to keep up with evolving attack techniques and patterns.

1.2. AI Solution:

The institution implemented an AI-driven threat detection system that utilized machine learning models to analyze network traffic and detect anomalies. The system integrated with existing threat feeds to enhance its detection capabilities.

1.3. Implementation:

- **Data Integration**: Aggregated data from multiple sources, including internal network logs and external threat feeds.
- **Model Training**: Trained machine learning models on historical attack data to recognize patterns and anomalies.
- **Real-Time Analysis**: AI models continuously analyzed network traffic in real-time, comparing it with threat feed data to identify potential threats.

1.4. Results:

- **Improved Detection Rates**: The AI system significantly improved the detection rate of advanced threats, reducing false positives and identifying previously undetected attack patterns.
- **Faster Response**: Enabled quicker identification and response to threats, minimizing potential damage.

1.5. Lessons Learned:

- **Data Quality**: Ensuring high-quality and relevant data is crucial for effective AI-driven threat detection.
- **Continuous Monitoring**: Regular updates and monitoring of AI models are necessary to adapt to evolving threat landscapes.

2. Case Study 2: Automating Incident Response

2.1. Background:

A global technology company experienced frequent security incidents that required rapid response to minimize impact. Manual incident response processes were slow and prone to human error.

2.2. AI Solution:

The company adopted an AI-powered incident response platform that automated incident detection, analysis, and response actions. The platform integrated with threat feeds to enhance its decision-making capabilities.

2.3. Implementation:

- **Automated Alerting**: AI algorithms generated alerts based on real-time analysis of threat feed data and internal security events.
- **Response Automation**: Implemented automated response actions, such as isolating affected systems and blocking malicious IP addresses, based on predefined rules and threat intelligence.

2.4. Results:

- **Reduced Response Time**: The automated platform reduced incident response times from hours to minutes, significantly improving overall security posture.

- **Increased Efficiency**: Freed up security teams to focus on strategic tasks by automating routine response actions.

2.5. Lessons Learned:

- **Rule Tuning**: Regularly fine-tune automation rules to balance responsiveness with accuracy and prevent over-reliance on automated systems.
- **Integration**: Ensure seamless integration with existing security tools and workflows for effective incident management.

3. Case Study 3: Securing IoT Devices with AI

3.1. Background:

A smart city project faced challenges securing a vast network of Internet of Things (IoT) devices. The diverse and distributed nature of IoT devices made traditional security measures insufficient.

3.2. AI Solution:

An AI-driven security solution was deployed to monitor and secure IoT devices across the smart city network. The system used machine learning to analyze device behavior and detect anomalies.

3.3. Implementation:

- **Behavioral Monitoring**: AI models monitored device behavior, analyzing patterns and identifying deviations from normal operations.
- **Threat Intelligence Integration**: Integrated threat feeds to enhance the detection of known IoT-specific threats and vulnerabilities.

3.4. Results:

- **Enhanced Security**: Improved detection of anomalous behavior and potential threats specific to IoT devices.
- **Proactive Defense**: Enabled proactive security measures and timely responses to emerging threats.

3.5. Lessons Learned:

- **Adaptability**: AI solutions must be adaptable to the specific characteristics and behavior of IoT devices.
- **Scalability**: Ensure that the solution can scale to accommodate the growing number of IoT devices.

4. Case Study 4: Predictive Analytics for Cyber Threat Intelligence

4.1. Background:

A multinational corporation sought to enhance its threat intelligence capabilities by predicting future threats based on historical data and threat feed information.

4.2. AI Solution:

The corporation implemented a predictive analytics platform that used AI to forecast potential threats and vulnerabilities. The platform combined historical incident data with real-time threat feeds.

4.3. Implementation:

- **Data Aggregation**: Collected and integrated data from historical incidents, threat feeds, and other relevant sources.
- **Predictive Modeling**: Developed machine learning models to analyze trends and predict future threats based on historical patterns and current intelligence.

4.4. Results:

- **Proactive Threat Management**: Enabled the corporation to anticipate and mitigate potential threats before they materialized.
- **Strategic Planning**: Improved strategic planning and resource allocation based on predictive insights.

4.5. Lessons Learned:

- **Model Accuracy**: Continuously validate and update predictive models to ensure accuracy and relevance.
- **Integration**: Ensure that predictive analytics seamlessly integrates with existing threat intelligence and security operations.

5. Case Study 5: Cloud Security with AI

5.1. Background:

A leading cloud service provider faced challenges securing its cloud infrastructure against increasingly sophisticated attacks and vulnerabilities.

5.2. AI Solution:

The provider implemented an AI-driven cloud security platform that analyzed cloud infrastructure and application behavior to detect and respond to threats.

5.3. Implementation:

- **Behavioral Analysis**: AI models monitored cloud resource usage and application behavior, identifying deviations that could indicate security issues.
- **Threat Intelligence Integration**: Integrated external threat feeds to enhance threat detection and response capabilities.

5.4. Results:

- **Improved Visibility**: Enhanced visibility into cloud infrastructure and application behavior, leading to better threat detection.
- **Automated Response**: Enabled automated responses to detected threats, reducing the need for manual intervention.

5.5. Lessons Learned:

- **Cloud-Specific Challenges**: Address the unique security challenges associated with cloud environments and applications.
- **Collaboration**: Collaborate with cloud service providers to ensure effective integration and security management.

6. Best Practices for Implementing AI in Cybersecurity

6.1. Define Clear Objectives:

Overview: Establish clear objectives for AI implementation to align with organizational goals and security needs.

Best Practices:

- **Objective Setting**: Define specific goals for AI applications, such as improving threat detection or automating responses.
- **Scope Definition**: Determine the scope of AI implementation based on these objectives.

6.2. Ensure Data Quality:

Overview: Use high-quality, relevant data for training AI models and enhancing threat intelligence.

Best Practices:

- **Data Validation**: Regularly validate and clean data to ensure accuracy and reliability.
- **Data Integration**: Integrate data from diverse sources to provide a comprehensive view of threats.

6.3. Continuously Monitor and Update:

Overview: Regularly monitor and update AI models and security systems to adapt to evolving threats and trends.

Best Practices:

- **Model Updating**: Continuously retrain and update AI models to maintain effectiveness.
- **Threat Intelligence**: Keep threat feeds and intelligence up-to-date to reflect current threat landscapes.

6.4. Balance Automation and Human Oversight:

Overview: Combine automated AI-driven actions with human oversight to ensure effective and accurate security management.

Best Practices:

- **Automation Tuning**: Fine-tune automation rules to balance responsiveness with accuracy.

- **Human Review**: Implement processes for human review and intervention where necessary.

6.5. Address Privacy and Compliance:

Overview: Ensure that AI implementation adheres to privacy regulations and compliance requirements.

Best Practices:

- **Data Protection**: Implement measures to protect sensitive data and ensure compliance with relevant regulations.
- **Regulatory Compliance**: Regularly review and update practices to adhere to privacy and security standards.

Case studies demonstrate the transformative impact of AI on cybersecurity, showcasing successful implementations across various sectors and applications. By leveraging AI to enhance threat detection, automate responses, and improve threat intelligence, organizations can significantly strengthen their security posture. Best practices, including defining clear objectives, ensuring data quality, and balancing automation with human oversight, are crucial for effective AI integration. As cybersecurity threats continue to evolve, AI will play an increasingly critical role in safeguarding digital assets and ensuring robust security measures.

Chapter 9: Ethical and Legal Considerations

Chapter 9 addresses the critical ethical and legal considerations associated with integrating artificial intelligence (AI) into cybersecurity practices. As AI technologies become more prevalent in the field of cyber defense, it is essential to navigate the complex landscape of ethics, privacy, and regulation to ensure responsible and effective use.

We start by discussing the ethical implications of using AI in cybersecurity. This includes considerations around transparency, accountability, and the potential for bias in AI algorithms. We explore how biased data or flawed algorithms can lead to unfair or ineffective security measures, and the importance of ensuring that AI systems are designed and implemented ethically.

Next, we examine legal and regulatory frameworks governing the use of AI in cybersecurity. Different regions and countries have varying laws and regulations regarding data protection, privacy, and the use of AI technologies. We discuss key regulations such as the General Data Protection Regulation (GDPR) in Europe and the California Consumer Privacy Act (CCPA) in the United States, and how they impact the deployment of AI in cybersecurity.

Privacy concerns are also a major focus. AI-driven security systems often require access to vast amounts of data, including personal and sensitive information. We discuss the importance of safeguarding this data and ensuring that AI systems comply with privacy laws and ethical standards.

The chapter also addresses the challenges of ensuring fairness and avoiding discriminatory practices in AI-driven security solutions. We explore strategies for mitigating biases and ensuring that AI systems are designed to be fair and equitable.

Finally, we cover the importance of ongoing oversight and governance. Establishing clear guidelines and monitoring the impact of AI systems is essential for maintaining ethical standards and legal compliance.

By the end of this chapter, you will have a comprehensive understanding of the ethical and legal dimensions of AI in cybersecurity. Navigating these considerations is crucial for implementing AI solutions responsibly and effectively, ensuring that they enhance security while respecting legal and ethical boundaries.

9.1 Ethics of AI in Cybersecurity

The integration of artificial intelligence (AI) into cybersecurity has introduced numerous advancements and efficiencies, but it also raises important ethical considerations. As organizations leverage AI to enhance their security measures, they must address various ethical issues to ensure responsible and fair use of these technologies. This section explores the key ethical concerns associated with AI in cybersecurity and provides guidance on addressing these issues.

1. Privacy Concerns

1.1. Data Collection and Surveillance:

Overview: AI-driven cybersecurity systems often require extensive data collection and monitoring to function effectively. This can include monitoring network traffic, user behavior, and other sensitive information.

Ethical Considerations:

- **Informed Consent**: Organizations must obtain informed consent from users and stakeholders before collecting and analyzing their data.
- **Transparency**: Clearly communicate data collection practices and the purpose of data use to all relevant parties.
- **Minimization**: Collect only the data necessary for achieving security objectives and avoid excessive monitoring.

1.2. Data Protection:

Overview: Ensuring that collected data is protected from unauthorized access and breaches is critical.

Ethical Considerations:

- **Data Security**: Implement robust security measures to protect collected data from breaches and misuse.
- **Anonymization**: Use anonymization techniques to protect individual privacy and prevent the identification of individuals from data sets.

2. Bias and Fairness

2.1. Algorithmic Bias:

Overview: AI systems can inadvertently perpetuate or amplify biases present in training data, leading to unfair or discriminatory outcomes.

Ethical Considerations:

- **Bias Detection**: Regularly assess AI algorithms for potential biases and take corrective actions as needed.
- **Diverse Data**: Use diverse and representative data sets for training AI models to minimize bias and ensure fairness.

2.2. Fairness in Decision-Making:

Overview: AI-driven decision-making processes must be fair and unbiased to avoid discrimination against specific groups or individuals.

Ethical Considerations:

- **Equitable Treatment**: Ensure that AI systems do not unfairly target or disadvantage certain groups.
- **Transparency**: Provide transparency in decision-making processes and criteria used by AI systems.

3. Accountability and Responsibility

3.1. Accountability for AI Actions:

Overview: Determining who is responsible for the actions and decisions made by AI systems is crucial.

Ethical Considerations:

- **Clear Accountability**: Establish clear lines of accountability for AI-driven actions and decisions.
- **Human Oversight**: Ensure that AI systems operate under human supervision to maintain accountability and address any potential issues.

3.2. Responsibility for Errors:

Overview: Addressing the consequences of errors or failures in AI systems is essential.

Ethical Considerations:

- **Error Management**: Implement mechanisms to detect and correct errors in AI systems promptly.
- **Responsibility**: Define responsibilities and protocols for addressing the impact of AI system errors on individuals and organizations.

4. Transparency and Explainability

4.1. Explainable AI:

Overview: AI systems should be transparent and provide explanations for their decisions and actions.

Ethical Considerations:

- **Explainability**: Develop AI models that offer clear explanations for their outputs and decision-making processes.
- **User Understanding**: Ensure that users and stakeholders can understand and interpret the results and actions of AI systems.

4.2. Transparency in AI Development:

Overview: Transparency in the development and deployment of AI systems is important for ethical practices.

Ethical Considerations:

- **Development Processes**: Share information about the development processes, data sources, and algorithms used in AI systems.
- **Disclosure**: Disclose any potential limitations, biases, or risks associated with AI systems to stakeholders.

5. Security and Misuse

5.1. AI Security Risks:

Overview: AI systems themselves can be vulnerable to attacks and misuse, leading to potential security risks.

Ethical Considerations:

- **Robust Security**: Implement strong security measures to protect AI systems from adversarial attacks and misuse.
- **Ethical Use**: Ensure that AI systems are used ethically and do not facilitate malicious activities or breaches.

5.2. Responsible AI Use:

Overview: Responsible use of AI involves adhering to ethical guidelines and preventing misuse.

Ethical Considerations:

- **Usage Policies**: Develop and enforce policies for the ethical use of AI systems in cybersecurity.
- **Compliance**: Ensure compliance with relevant laws, regulations, and ethical standards.

6. Human Impact and Employment

6.1. Impact on Employment:

Overview: The implementation of AI in cybersecurity may impact employment and job roles within the industry.

Ethical Considerations:

- **Job Transition**: Support employees in transitioning to new roles or acquiring new skills as AI technologies change job requirements.
- **Education and Training**: Provide education and training opportunities to help employees adapt to evolving technological landscapes.

6.2. Human Oversight:

Overview: Maintaining human oversight in AI-driven cybersecurity processes is essential for ethical practices.

Ethical Considerations:

- **Human Control**: Ensure that human decision-makers retain control over critical security decisions and actions.
- **Supervision**: Implement supervision mechanisms to oversee AI systems and address any ethical concerns.

7. Best Practices for Ethical AI in Cybersecurity

7.1. Establish Ethical Guidelines:

Overview: Develop and implement ethical guidelines and principles for AI use in cybersecurity.

Best Practices:

- **Ethical Frameworks**: Create frameworks that outline ethical considerations and practices for AI in cybersecurity.
- **Regular Review**: Regularly review and update ethical guidelines to reflect evolving technologies and practices.

7.2. Engage Stakeholders:

Overview: Involve stakeholders in discussions about the ethical implications of AI in cybersecurity.

Best Practices:

- **Consultation**: Consult with stakeholders, including users, regulators, and experts, to address ethical concerns and ensure responsible AI use.
- **Feedback Mechanisms**: Implement mechanisms for receiving and addressing feedback on ethical practices and concerns.

7.3. Promote Ethical Awareness:

Overview: Foster awareness of ethical issues related to AI among cybersecurity professionals and organizations.

Best Practices:

- **Training**: Provide training on ethical considerations and best practices for AI use in cybersecurity.
- **Awareness Campaigns**: Promote awareness of ethical issues and responsible AI practices within the cybersecurity community.

The ethical use of AI in cybersecurity requires careful consideration of privacy, bias, accountability, transparency, security, and human impact. By addressing these ethical concerns and implementing best practices, organizations can ensure that AI technologies are used responsibly and effectively to enhance cybersecurity while maintaining fairness and respect for individual rights. Ethical considerations should be an integral part of AI development and deployment processes, ensuring that AI-driven solutions contribute positively to the security landscape.

9.2 Legal and Regulatory Frameworks

As artificial intelligence (AI) becomes increasingly integrated into cybersecurity practices, understanding the legal and regulatory frameworks governing its use is crucial. These frameworks help ensure that AI technologies are employed responsibly and within legal boundaries, addressing issues related to privacy, data protection, and accountability. This section explores the key legal and regulatory considerations for AI in cybersecurity and provides an overview of relevant frameworks and compliance requirements.

1. Data Protection and Privacy Laws

1.1. General Data Protection Regulation (GDPR):

Overview: The GDPR is a comprehensive data protection regulation enforced in the European Union (EU) that establishes guidelines for the collection, storage, and processing of personal data.

Key Provisions:

- **Data Subject Rights**: Individuals have the right to access, correct, and delete their personal data.
- **Data Protection Impact Assessments (DPIAs):** Organizations must conduct DPIAs when processing data that may impact privacy.

- **Data Breach Notification**: Organizations must notify relevant authorities and affected individuals of data breaches within 72 hours.

1.2. California Consumer Privacy Act (CCPA):

Overview: The CCPA is a data privacy law that provides California residents with rights regarding their personal information.

Key Provisions:

- **Consumer Rights**: Includes the right to access, delete, and opt out of the sale of personal information.
- **Business Obligations**: Requires businesses to disclose data collection practices and provide mechanisms for consumers to exercise their rights.

1.3. Health Insurance Portability and Accountability Act (HIPAA):

Overview: HIPAA is a U.S. law that protects the privacy and security of individuals' health information.

Key Provisions:

- **Privacy Rule**: Regulates the use and disclosure of protected health information (PHI).
- **Security Rule**: Establishes standards for safeguarding electronic PHI.

2. AI-Specific Regulations and Guidelines

2.1. AI Act (European Union):

Overview: The AI Act is a proposed regulation by the European Commission aimed at regulating AI technologies based on their risk levels.

Key Provisions:

- **Risk-Based Classification**: AI systems are classified into different risk categories, with stricter requirements for higher-risk applications.
- **Transparency and Accountability**: Requires transparency in AI systems' functioning and clear accountability for their decisions.

2.2. Algorithmic Accountability Act (United States):

Overview: The Algorithmic Accountability Act is a proposed U.S. legislation aimed at increasing transparency and accountability in algorithmic decision-making.

Key Provisions:

- **Algorithmic Audits**: Requires companies to conduct audits of their algorithms to assess and mitigate risks related to bias and fairness.
- **Disclosure Requirements**: Mandates disclosure of information about algorithmic decision-making processes.

2.3. OECD AI Principles:

Overview: The Organisation for Economic Co-operation and Development (OECD) has established principles for the responsible development and use of AI.

Key Provisions:

- **Human-Centered Values**: Emphasizes that AI should respect human rights, democratic values, and societal well-being.
- **Transparency**: Calls for transparency in AI systems to enable understanding and accountability.

3. Cybersecurity-Specific Regulations

3.1. Cybersecurity Information Sharing Act (CISA):

Overview: CISA is a U.S. law that facilitates information sharing between the government and private sector to improve cybersecurity.

Key Provisions:

- **Information Sharing**: Encourages sharing of cyber threat information and defensive measures.
- **Liability Protection**: Provides liability protection for organizations sharing cybersecurity information.

3.2. NIST Cybersecurity Framework:

Overview: The National Institute of Standards and Technology (NIST) Cybersecurity Framework provides guidelines for managing cybersecurity risks.

Key Provisions:

- **Core Functions**: Includes Identify, Protect, Detect, Respond, and Recover functions for managing cybersecurity.
- **Flexibility**: Offers a flexible approach that can be adapted to various organizational needs and risk profiles.

3.3. Payment Card Industry Data Security Standard (PCI DSS):

Overview: PCI DSS is a set of security standards designed to protect payment card information.

Key Provisions:

- **Data Protection**: Requires measures for securing payment card data during transmission and storage.
- **Compliance**: Organizations handling payment card information must comply with PCI DSS requirements.

4. International Considerations

4.1. Cross-Border Data Transfers:

Overview: Legal frameworks often address the transfer of personal data across borders, which is relevant for multinational organizations using AI in cybersecurity.

Key Provisions:

- **Adequacy Decisions**: Some jurisdictions, like the EU, may require that data transfers are made to countries with adequate data protection standards.
- **Standard Contractual Clauses (SCCs):** SCCs are used to ensure that data transfers comply with data protection laws.

4.2. Global Cooperation on Cybersecurity:

Overview: International cooperation and agreements play a role in addressing global cybersecurity challenges.

Key Provisions:

- **Bilateral Agreements**: Countries may enter into agreements to enhance cybersecurity collaboration and information sharing.
- **International Standards**: Adherence to international standards and best practices for cybersecurity can support global efforts.

5. Compliance and Enforcement

5.1. Compliance Strategies:

Overview: Organizations must develop strategies to ensure compliance with legal and regulatory requirements related to AI in cybersecurity.

Strategies:

- **Regular Audits**: Conduct regular audits to assess compliance with data protection laws and AI regulations.
- **Training and Awareness**: Provide training to employees on legal and regulatory requirements related to AI and cybersecurity.

5.2. Enforcement and Penalties:

Overview: Non-compliance with legal and regulatory frameworks can result in penalties and enforcement actions.

Enforcement Actions:

- **Fines and Sanctions**: Regulatory bodies may impose fines or sanctions for violations of data protection and cybersecurity laws.
- **Legal Actions**: Organizations may face legal actions or litigation related to non-compliance.

6. Best Practices for Legal and Regulatory Compliance

6.1. Stay Informed:

Overview: Keeping up-to-date with changes in legal and regulatory frameworks is essential for compliance.

Best Practices:

- **Monitor Legislation**: Regularly monitor changes in data protection and AI regulations.
- **Engage Legal Experts**: Consult with legal experts to understand and address regulatory requirements.

6.2. Implement Governance Frameworks:

Overview: Establish governance frameworks to oversee compliance with legal and regulatory requirements.

Best Practices:

- **Compliance Teams**: Form dedicated teams responsible for managing legal and regulatory compliance.
- **Policies and Procedures**: Develop and implement policies and procedures for adhering to legal and regulatory requirements.

6.3. Promote Transparency and Accountability:

Overview: Ensure transparency and accountability in AI systems and cybersecurity practices.

Best Practices:

- **Documentation**: Maintain comprehensive documentation of data processing activities and AI system operations.
- **Stakeholder Communication**: Communicate openly with stakeholders about compliance efforts and regulatory adherence.

Navigating the legal and regulatory frameworks related to AI in cybersecurity is essential for ensuring responsible and compliant use of these technologies. By understanding and adhering to data protection laws, AI-specific regulations, and cybersecurity standards, organizations can effectively manage legal risks and contribute to a secure and ethical digital environment. Ongoing compliance efforts, coupled with transparency and accountability, will support the responsible integration of AI into cybersecurity practices and help address emerging challenges.

9.3 Privacy Concerns and Data Protection

As artificial intelligence (AI) increasingly integrates into cybersecurity, it brings with it significant privacy and data protection concerns. AI systems rely on vast amounts of data to function effectively, and managing this data in a way that respects individuals' privacy and adheres to data protection regulations is critical. This section explores the privacy concerns and data protection issues associated with AI in cybersecurity, highlighting best practices and strategies for addressing these challenges.

1. Data Collection and Usage

1.1. Scope of Data Collection:

Overview: AI systems in cybersecurity often require extensive data collection to detect threats and anomalies. This can include data from network traffic, user behavior, and system logs.

Privacy Concerns:

- **Data Minimization**: Collecting only the data necessary for achieving security objectives helps minimize privacy risks.
- **User Awareness**: Users should be informed about what data is being collected and how it will be used.

1.2. Data Usage and Processing:

Overview: The way data is processed and used by AI systems can impact privacy. Data used for training models must be handled with care to avoid misuse.

Privacy Concerns:

- **Purpose Limitation**: Data should be used only for the purposes for which it was collected and should not be repurposed without consent.
- **Data Anonymization**: Anonymizing data helps protect individual privacy while still enabling effective AI analysis.

2. Data Security

2.1. Data Protection Measures:

Overview: Protecting data from unauthorized access and breaches is essential for maintaining privacy and compliance with data protection laws.

Best Practices:

- **Encryption**: Use strong encryption methods to secure data both at rest and in transit.
- **Access Controls**: Implement strict access controls to limit data access to authorized personnel only.
- **Regular Audits**: Conduct regular security audits to identify and address potential vulnerabilities.

2.2. Breach Management:

Overview: In the event of a data breach, swift and effective management is crucial to minimize harm and comply with legal requirements.

Best Practices:

- **Incident Response Plan**: Develop and maintain an incident response plan to address data breaches promptly.
- **Notification Requirements**: Comply with legal requirements for notifying affected individuals and regulatory authorities about data breaches.

3. Compliance with Data Protection Laws

3.1. General Data Protection Regulation (GDPR):

Overview: The GDPR provides comprehensive data protection standards for handling personal data within the EU.

Key Requirements:

- **Data Subject Rights**: Respect individuals' rights to access, correct, and delete their personal data.
- **Data Protection Impact Assessments (DPIAs):** Conduct DPIAs to assess and mitigate privacy risks associated with data processing.

3.2. California Consumer Privacy Act (CCPA):

Overview: The CCPA grants California residents specific rights regarding their personal data.

Key Requirements:

- **Consumer Rights**: Provide mechanisms for consumers to access, delete, and opt out of the sale of their personal information.
- **Disclosure**: Clearly disclose data collection practices and purposes.

3.3. Health Insurance Portability and Accountability Act (HIPAA):

Overview: HIPAA regulates the handling of protected health information (PHI) in the U.S.

Key Requirements:

- **Privacy Rule**: Ensure compliance with the Privacy Rule to safeguard PHI.
- **Security Rule**: Implement security measures to protect electronic PHI.

4. Ethical Considerations

4.1. Informed Consent:

Overview: Obtaining informed consent from individuals before collecting or processing their data is an ethical and legal obligation.

Best Practices:

- **Transparency**: Clearly inform individuals about data collection practices, purposes, and potential risks.
- **Consent Mechanisms**: Provide clear and accessible mechanisms for individuals to give or withdraw consent.

4.2. Data Minimization:

Overview: Data minimization involves collecting only the data necessary for specific purposes, which helps reduce privacy risks.

Best Practices:

- **Purpose Limitation**: Define and adhere to specific purposes for data collection and processing.
- **Data Retention**: Implement policies for retaining data only as long as necessary and securely deleting it when no longer needed.

5. AI-Specific Privacy Concerns

5.1. Algorithmic Transparency:

Overview: Ensuring transparency in how AI algorithms process and analyze data is crucial for maintaining trust and addressing privacy concerns.

Best Practices:

- **Explainability**: Develop AI systems that provide clear explanations for their decisions and data processing methods.
- **Documentation**: Maintain documentation on the design and functioning of AI systems to facilitate transparency.

5.2. Bias and Fairness:

Overview: AI systems can perpetuate or amplify biases present in training data, leading to unfair treatment of individuals.

Best Practices:

- **Bias Detection**: Regularly assess and mitigate biases in AI algorithms and data sets.
- **Fairness**: Ensure that AI systems do not unfairly target or disadvantage specific groups.

5.3. Anonymization and De-identification:

Overview: Anonymizing and de-identifying data helps protect individual privacy while still enabling useful analysis.

Best Practices:

- **Techniques**: Use techniques such as data masking and aggregation to anonymize data.

- **Limitations**: Be aware of the limitations of anonymization and implement additional safeguards as needed.

6. Practical Strategies for Privacy Protection

6.1. Privacy-By-Design:

Overview: Integrate privacy considerations into the design and development of AI systems from the outset.

Best Practices:

- **Design Principles**: Adopt privacy-by-design principles to ensure that data protection is built into the AI system's architecture and processes.
- **Regular Reviews**: Conduct regular reviews to ensure that privacy measures remain effective and up-to-date.

6.2. Data Governance:

Overview: Implement strong data governance practices to manage and protect data throughout its lifecycle.

Best Practices:

- **Policies and Procedures**: Develop and enforce policies and procedures for data management and protection.
- **Training**: Provide training for employees on data protection and privacy practices.

6.3. Vendor Management:

Overview: Ensure that third-party vendors handling data comply with privacy and data protection standards.

Best Practices:

- **Due Diligence**: Perform due diligence when selecting vendors and assess their data protection practices.
- **Contractual Agreements**: Include data protection requirements in contracts with third-party vendors.

7. Future Considerations

7.1. Evolving Regulations:

Overview: Data protection and privacy regulations are continuously evolving, and organizations must stay informed about changes.

Best Practices:

- **Monitoring**: Regularly monitor regulatory updates and adjust practices to comply with new requirements.
- **Engagement**: Engage with regulatory bodies and industry groups to stay abreast of emerging trends and best practices.

7.2. Technological Advancements:

Overview: Advances in technology may introduce new privacy challenges and opportunities for enhancing data protection.

Best Practices:

- **Innovation**: Stay informed about technological advancements and explore innovative solutions for improving privacy and data protection.
- **Adaptation**: Adapt privacy practices to address new challenges and leverage emerging technologies responsibly.

Addressing privacy concerns and ensuring data protection are critical aspects of integrating AI into cybersecurity practices. By implementing robust data protection measures, adhering to legal and regulatory requirements, and adopting ethical principles, organizations can manage privacy risks effectively and maintain trust with users and stakeholders. As technology continues to evolve, ongoing attention to privacy and data protection will be essential for ensuring that AI systems contribute positively to cybersecurity while respecting individual rights and privacy.

9.4 Bias and Fairness in AI Models

Bias and fairness in AI models are critical concerns, particularly as these systems increasingly influence decision-making processes across various domains, including cybersecurity. Ensuring that AI models operate fairly and without bias is essential for maintaining trust, legality, and ethical standards. This section explores the concepts of bias and fairness in AI, how they impact AI systems, and strategies to address these issues effectively.

1. Understanding Bias in AI Models

1.1. Definition of Bias:

Overview: Bias in AI refers to systematic favoritism or prejudice that leads to unfair treatment of individuals or groups. It often arises from the data used to train models, the algorithms themselves, or the interactions between these elements.

Types of Bias:

- **Data Bias:** Arises when training data is not representative of the population or contains inherent prejudices.
- **Algorithmic Bias**: Occurs when algorithms perpetuate or amplify biases present in the data or are designed in a way that leads to discriminatory outcomes.
- **Human Bias**: Introduced by the developers' or users' unconscious biases, affecting how AI systems are designed or used.

1.2. Sources of Bias:

- **Data Collection**: Biases can be introduced during data collection if the data is unrepresentative or skewed. For example, underrepresentation of certain groups in training data can lead to biased outcomes.
- **Data Annotation**: Biases in labeling or annotation of data can affect the quality and fairness of the AI model. Mislabeling or subjective interpretations can introduce systemic biases.
- **Model Design**: The choice of features, algorithms, and model parameters can introduce bias if not carefully considered. For instance, models trained with features correlated with protected attributes (like race or gender) can inadvertently perpetuate discrimination.

2. Impact of Bias on AI Systems

2.1. Consequences of Bias:

- **Discriminatory Outcomes**: Bias in AI models can lead to unfair treatment of individuals, such as unequal access to services, discriminatory decision-making, and reinforcement of existing social inequalities.
- **Loss of Trust**: When AI systems exhibit bias, it erodes trust in the technology and its developers, potentially leading to reluctance or resistance to adopting AI solutions.
- **Legal and Regulatory Risks**: Bias in AI systems can result in legal and regulatory challenges, including violations of anti-discrimination laws and data protection regulations.

2.2. Examples of Bias in AI:

- **Hiring Algorithms**: AI-based hiring tools have been found to favor certain demographic groups over others, leading to discriminatory hiring practices.
- **Credit Scoring**: Bias in credit scoring models can result in unfair lending practices, disproportionately affecting marginalized communities.
- **Facial Recognition**: Facial recognition systems have demonstrated higher error rates for individuals with darker skin tones, leading to concerns about racial bias and inaccuracy.

3. Ensuring Fairness in AI Models

3.1. Defining Fairness:

- **Overview**: Fairness in AI refers to the principle that AI systems should treat individuals and groups equitably, without discrimination or bias. There are different definitions of fairness, including:
- **Equal Opportunity**: Ensures that individuals have equal chances of favorable outcomes regardless of their group membership.
- **Disparate Impact**: Aims to prevent AI systems from disproportionately impacting specific groups in a way that is not justifiable.
- **Fairness Through Unawareness**: Involves designing AI models to ignore protected attributes (e.g., race, gender) to avoid biased decisions.

3.2. Techniques for Mitigating Bias:

Data Preprocessing:

- **Data Augmentation**: Enhance underrepresented groups in the training data to improve model fairness.

- **Bias Detection**: Use statistical methods to detect and quantify bias in the data before training.

Algorithmic Adjustments:

- **Fairness Constraints**: Incorporate fairness constraints during model training to ensure equitable outcomes.
- **Bias Mitigation Algorithms**: Apply algorithms designed to reduce bias, such as re-weighting or re-sampling techniques.

Post-Processing:

- **Outcome Analysis**: Evaluate the model's predictions to identify and correct biased outcomes.
- **Fairness Metrics**: Use metrics such as demographic parity, equalized odds, and predictive parity to assess and improve fairness.

3.3. Evaluating Fairness:

Overview: Regular evaluation of AI models for fairness is essential for identifying and addressing biases.

Evaluation Metrics:

- **Disparate Impact Ratio**: Measures the ratio of favorable outcomes for different groups to assess if certain groups are disadvantaged.
- **Equal Opportunity Difference**: Compares the true positive rates across different groups to ensure fairness in positive outcomes.
- **Fairness Audits**: Conduct audits of AI systems to assess their compliance with fairness principles and identify areas for improvement.

4. Ethical and Legal Considerations

4.1. Ethical Responsibility:

Overview: Developers and organizations have an ethical responsibility to ensure that AI systems are fair and unbiased. This includes:

- **Transparency**: Being transparent about how AI systems are designed, trained, and evaluated for fairness.

- **Accountability**: Holding developers and organizations accountable for the outcomes of their AI systems, including addressing any identified biases.

4.2. Legal Frameworks:

- **Anti-Discrimination Laws**: Ensure that AI systems comply with anti-discrimination laws, such as the Civil Rights Act and Fair Housing Act, which prohibit discrimination based on race, gender, or other protected characteristics.
- **Regulatory Guidelines**: Follow regulatory guidelines and standards related to fairness and bias in AI, including emerging regulations and industry best practices.

5. Best Practices for Addressing Bias and Fairness

5.1. Diverse Teams:

Overview: Assemble diverse teams of developers, data scientists, and domain experts to provide different perspectives and reduce the risk of biased outcomes.

Best Practices:

- **Inclusive Hiring**: Recruit team members from diverse backgrounds to ensure a range of viewpoints and experiences.
- **Collaborative Approaches**: Foster collaboration between technical and non-technical experts to address bias and fairness comprehensively.

5.2. Continuous Monitoring and Improvement:

Overview: Implement ongoing monitoring and improvement processes to ensure that AI systems remain fair and unbiased over time.

Best Practices:

- **Feedback Loops**: Establish mechanisms for receiving and addressing feedback from users and stakeholders regarding fairness.
- **Regular Updates**: Continuously update and refine AI models and data to address emerging biases and changing societal norms.

5.3. User Involvement:

Overview: Involve users and affected parties in the development and evaluation of AI systems to ensure that their perspectives are considered.

Best Practices:

- **User Testing**: Conduct user testing with diverse groups to identify and address potential biases.
- **Stakeholder Engagement**: Engage with stakeholders, including advocacy groups and affected communities, to gain insights into fairness concerns.

6. Future Directions

6.1. Advancements in Fairness Research:

Overview: Ongoing research in AI fairness aims to develop new methods and tools for detecting and mitigating bias.

Future Directions:

- **Fairness-aware Algorithms**: Explore advancements in algorithms designed to enhance fairness and reduce bias.
- **Cross-disciplinary Approaches**: Integrate insights from fields such as social science, ethics, and law to address fairness in AI.

6.2. Evolving Regulatory Standards:

Overview: Regulatory standards related to fairness and bias in AI are evolving, and organizations must stay informed about new developments.

Future Directions:

- **Adapting to Regulations**: Adjust practices to comply with emerging regulations and industry standards related to AI fairness.
- **Influencing Policy**: Contribute to policy discussions and initiatives aimed at promoting fairness and reducing bias in AI systems.

Addressing bias and ensuring fairness in AI models are essential for the responsible and ethical deployment of AI technologies. By understanding the sources and impacts of bias, implementing effective mitigation strategies, and adhering to ethical and legal standards, organizations can develop AI systems that promote equitable outcomes and maintain public trust. Continuous monitoring, research, and collaboration will be key to advancing fairness in AI and ensuring that these systems contribute positively to society.

9.5 Navigating Ethical Dilemmas

As AI technologies become more integrated into cybersecurity, they present a range of ethical dilemmas that need to be addressed to ensure responsible and fair use. Navigating these ethical challenges is crucial for maintaining public trust, ensuring compliance with laws and regulations, and fostering an environment where AI systems contribute positively to society. This section explores key ethical dilemmas in AI, provides frameworks for addressing these challenges, and offers strategies for ethical decision-making in cybersecurity contexts.

1. Ethical Dilemmas in AI

1.1. Privacy vs. Security:

Overview: One of the primary ethical dilemmas is balancing privacy with security. AI systems designed to enhance security often involve extensive data collection and analysis, which can conflict with individuals' right to privacy.

Considerations:

- **Surveillance vs. Privacy**: Implementing AI for surveillance purposes may lead to intrusive monitoring, raising concerns about individual privacy rights.
- **Data Collection**: Collecting and analyzing large amounts of personal data for security purposes must be balanced against the potential for misuse and privacy infringements.

1.2. Accountability and Transparency:

Overview: AI systems can make complex decisions that affect individuals' lives, raising questions about accountability and transparency. When decisions made by AI systems lead to adverse outcomes, determining who is responsible can be challenging.

Considerations:

- **Algorithmic Transparency**: Ensuring that AI systems are transparent and explainable helps build trust and accountability by allowing stakeholders to understand how decisions are made.
- **Responsibility**: Identifying who is accountable for decisions made by AI systems—whether it's the developers, users, or organizations—can be complex and needs to be addressed clearly.

1.3. Bias and Fairness:

Overview: As discussed in previous sections, bias and fairness in AI systems are critical ethical concerns. Bias in AI models can lead to unfair treatment and discrimination, impacting marginalized groups disproportionately.

Considerations:

- **Mitigating Bias**: Developing strategies to detect and reduce bias in AI systems is essential to ensure fairness and prevent discrimination.
- **Ethical Implications**: Addressing bias involves considering the broader ethical implications of how AI systems affect different demographic groups and ensuring equitable outcomes.

1.4. Autonomy and Human Oversight:

Overview: The autonomy of AI systems in making decisions poses ethical questions about human oversight and control. Ensuring that AI systems do not operate in ways that undermine human decision-making authority is crucial.

Considerations:

- **Human-in-the-Loop**: Implementing human-in-the-loop approaches allows for human oversight and intervention in AI decision-making processes.
- **Autonomy Limits**: Setting boundaries on the autonomy of AI systems to ensure that critical decisions remain under human control is essential for maintaining ethical standards.

2. Frameworks for Ethical Decision-Making

2.1. Ethical Guidelines and Principles:

Overview: Developing and adhering to ethical guidelines and principles can provide a framework for navigating ethical dilemmas in AI.

Key Principles:

- **Transparency**: Ensure that AI systems are transparent in their operations and decision-making processes.
- **Accountability**: Establish clear accountability for decisions made by AI systems and ensure that there are mechanisms for addressing issues that arise.
- **Fairness**: Strive to eliminate bias and ensure fairness in AI systems to prevent discrimination and ensure equitable outcomes.

2.2. Ethical Review Boards:

Overview: Establishing ethical review boards or committees can help organizations assess and address ethical concerns related to AI projects.

Functions:

- **Review Processes**: Review AI projects and applications to evaluate their adherence to ethical guidelines and identify potential ethical issues.
- **Advisory Role**: Provide guidance and recommendations on ethical practices and decision-making in AI development and deployment.

2.3. Ethical Impact Assessments:

Overview: Conducting ethical impact assessments helps organizations evaluate the potential ethical implications of AI systems before deployment.

Components:

- **Risk Assessment**: Identify and assess potential risks related to privacy, bias, and fairness associated with AI systems.
- **Stakeholder Engagement**: Engage with stakeholders, including affected communities and experts, to gather input and address ethical concerns.

3. Strategies for Addressing Ethical Dilemmas

3.1. Implementing Ethical AI Practices:

Overview: Organizations should adopt practices that align with ethical standards and address potential ethical dilemmas in AI.

Strategies:

- **Ethical AI Frameworks**: Develop and implement frameworks for ethical AI development and deployment, including guidelines for privacy, fairness, and accountability.
- **Training and Awareness**: Provide training for developers, data scientists, and decision-makers on ethical AI practices and the importance of addressing ethical dilemmas.

3.2. Engaging Stakeholders:

Overview: Engaging with stakeholders is crucial for understanding diverse perspectives and addressing ethical concerns.

Strategies:

- **Public Consultation**: Conduct public consultations and forums to gather input from individuals and communities affected by AI systems.
- **Collaboration**: Collaborate with academic institutions, industry groups, and advocacy organizations to address ethical challenges and develop best practices.

3.3. Continuous Monitoring and Evaluation:

Overview: Regularly monitoring and evaluating AI systems is essential for identifying and addressing ethical issues as they arise.

Strategies:

- **Performance Monitoring**: Monitor the performance of AI systems to detect any unintended consequences or ethical issues.
- **Feedback Mechanisms**: Establish feedback mechanisms for users and stakeholders to report ethical concerns and suggest improvements.

4. Case Studies and Examples

4.1. Ethical Challenges in Surveillance:

- **Overview**: Surveillance systems powered by AI raise significant ethical concerns related to privacy and civil liberties.
- **Example**: The use of facial recognition technology for public surveillance has led to debates about privacy invasion and potential misuse by authorities.

4.2. Bias in Hiring Algorithms:

- **Overview**: AI-driven hiring tools have faced criticism for perpetuating bias and discrimination in recruitment processes.
- **Example**: AI systems used for screening resumes have been found to favor candidates from certain demographic groups, leading to biased hiring practices.

4.3. Ethical Issues in Predictive Policing:

- **Overview**: Predictive policing systems that use AI to forecast criminal activity have raised concerns about bias and fairness.
- **Example**: Predictive policing algorithms have been criticized for disproportionately targeting certain communities, leading to ethical debates about fairness and accountability.

5. Future Considerations

5.1. Evolving Ethical Standards:

Overview: Ethical standards for AI are continually evolving as technology advances and societal values shift.

Future Directions:

- **Adaptive Frameworks**: Develop adaptive ethical frameworks that can evolve with emerging technologies and changing societal norms.
- **Global Collaboration**: Foster global collaboration to address ethical challenges in AI and develop international standards and best practices.

5.2. Integrating Ethics into AI Development:

Overview: Incorporating ethical considerations into every stage of AI development is essential for responsible AI deployment.

Future Directions:

- **Ethics by Design**: Implement ethics by design principles to ensure that ethical considerations are integrated into the design and development of AI systems.
- **Holistic Approaches**: Adopt holistic approaches that consider the ethical implications of AI systems from technical, societal, and regulatory perspectives.

Navigating ethical dilemmas in AI requires a thoughtful and proactive approach to address privacy, accountability, bias, and fairness concerns. By implementing ethical frameworks, engaging stakeholders, and continuously monitoring AI systems, organizations can navigate these challenges responsibly and ensure that AI technologies contribute positively to society. As AI continues to evolve, ongoing attention to ethical considerations will be essential for maintaining trust, compliance, and ethical integrity in the deployment of AI systems.

Chapter 10: Building an AI-Driven Security Strategy

Chapter 10 provides a practical guide to developing and implementing an AI-driven security strategy. As organizations increasingly adopt artificial intelligence to enhance their cybersecurity posture, it is crucial to approach this integration thoughtfully and strategically. This chapter offers a step-by-step framework for building an effective AI-driven security strategy that aligns with your organization's goals and requirements.

We begin by outlining the steps to integrate AI into existing cybersecurity infrastructures. This includes assessing your current security landscape, identifying gaps, and determining how AI can address these deficiencies. We discuss how to select the right AI tools and technologies based on your specific needs and security objectives.

Next, we focus on choosing the appropriate AI tools and technologies. With a wide range of AI solutions available, selecting the right ones requires careful consideration of their capabilities, compatibility, and potential benefits. We provide criteria for evaluating AI tools, including performance, scalability, and ease of integration.

Training and upskilling your security team is a critical component of successfully implementing AI. We explore strategies for equipping your team with the necessary knowledge and skills to work effectively with AI-driven solutions. This includes providing training on AI technologies, data analysis, and interpreting AI-generated insights.

We then discuss how to measure the effectiveness of AI solutions. Establishing clear metrics and benchmarks allows you to evaluate the performance of your AI-driven security strategy and make data-driven adjustments. We cover key performance indicators (KPIs) and methods for assessing the impact of AI on your overall security posture.

Finally, we emphasize the importance of continual improvement and adaptation. The cybersecurity landscape is dynamic, and so are AI technologies. Regularly reviewing and updating your AI strategy ensures that it remains effective in addressing evolving threats and leveraging the latest advancements in AI.

By the end of this chapter, you will have a clear roadmap for building and implementing a robust AI-driven security strategy. From integration and tool selection to training and performance measurement, this chapter equips you with the knowledge and practical steps needed to harness the full potential of AI in your cybersecurity efforts.

10.1 Steps to Integrate AI into Cybersecurity Infrastructure

Integrating AI into cybersecurity infrastructure can significantly enhance threat detection, response, and overall security posture. However, the integration process involves careful planning, execution, and ongoing management to ensure that AI systems are effectively utilized and aligned with organizational goals. This section outlines a structured approach to integrating AI into cybersecurity infrastructure, covering key steps from assessment to deployment and maintenance.

1. Assessing Current Cybersecurity Infrastructure

1.1. Evaluate Existing Systems:

Overview: Begin by assessing the current cybersecurity infrastructure to understand its strengths, weaknesses, and integration points for AI technologies.

Actions:

- **Inventory Assessment**: Document existing security tools, platforms, and processes.
- **Performance Review**: Evaluate the effectiveness and limitations of current systems in addressing threats and vulnerabilities.
- **Integration Points**: Identify areas where AI can enhance or complement existing systems.

1.2. Identify Security Needs and Objectives:

Overview: Determine specific security needs and objectives that AI integration aims to address.

Actions:

- **Threat Analysis**: Conduct a thorough analysis of current and emerging threats to identify areas where AI can add value.
- **Goal Setting**: Define clear objectives for AI integration, such as improving threat detection, automating response, or enhancing threat intelligence.

2. Selecting the Right AI Technologies

2.1. Evaluate AI Solutions:

Overview: Assess various AI technologies and solutions to find those best suited for your organization's cybersecurity needs.

Actions:

- **Vendor Research**: Research and evaluate different AI vendors and solutions, considering their capabilities, reputation, and alignment with your security needs.
- **Technology Assessment**: Analyze the features and functionalities of AI solutions, such as machine learning models, behavioral analysis, and threat intelligence platforms.

2.2. Consider Integration Compatibility:

Overview: Ensure that selected AI technologies can seamlessly integrate with existing cybersecurity infrastructure.

Actions:

- **Compatibility Check**: Verify compatibility with current security tools, platforms, and data sources.
- **Interoperability**: Assess the ability of AI solutions to work in conjunction with existing systems and workflows.

2.3. Evaluate Costs and ROI:

Overview: Consider the costs associated with AI integration and the potential return on investment (ROI).

Actions:

- **Cost Analysis**: Estimate the costs of acquiring, implementing, and maintaining AI technologies.
- **ROI Evaluation**: Evaluate the potential benefits, such as improved threat detection rates and reduced response times, to determine the expected ROI.

3. Designing and Planning Integration

3.1. Develop an Integration Plan:

Overview: Create a comprehensive plan for integrating AI technologies into your cybersecurity infrastructure.

Actions:

- **Roadmap**: Develop a roadmap outlining key milestones, timelines, and resources required for integration.
- **Resource Allocation**: Allocate necessary resources, including budget, personnel, and technology, for successful integration.

3.2. Define Integration Points and Use Cases:

Overview: Identify specific use cases and integration points for AI technologies within your cybersecurity framework.

Actions:

- **Use Case Identification**: Define how AI will be applied, such as in threat detection, incident response, or network security.
- **Integration Points**: Determine where AI solutions will be integrated, such as security information and event management (SIEM) systems, intrusion detection systems (IDS), or endpoint protection platforms.

3.3. Plan for Data Management and Security:

Overview: Address data management and security considerations related to AI integration.

Actions:

- **Data Collection**: Plan for the collection and storage of data required for training and operating AI models.
- **Data Privacy**: Ensure compliance with data privacy regulations and implement measures to protect sensitive information.

4. Implementing AI Solutions

4.1. Deploy AI Technologies:

Overview: Begin the deployment of selected AI technologies according to the integration plan.

Actions:

- **Installation**: Install and configure AI solutions, ensuring proper setup and functionality.
- **Integration**: Integrate AI technologies with existing systems and workflows, following the defined integration points.

4.2. Train and Test AI Models:

Overview: Train and test AI models to ensure they perform effectively in detecting and responding to cybersecurity threats.

Actions:

- **Training**: Use relevant data to train AI models, ensuring they are capable of identifying and addressing various threats.
- **Testing**: Conduct thorough testing to validate the performance and accuracy of AI models, adjusting parameters as needed.

4.3. Monitor and Optimize Performance:

Overview: Continuously monitor the performance of AI technologies and optimize them for improved effectiveness.

Actions:

- **Performance Monitoring**: Track the performance of AI systems, including their accuracy in detecting threats and efficiency in response.
- **Optimization**: Make necessary adjustments to enhance the performance and accuracy of AI models based on monitoring results.

5. Training and Change Management

5.1. Provide Training for Security Teams:

Overview: Ensure that cybersecurity teams are trained to work effectively with AI technologies.

Actions:

- **Training Programs**: Develop and deliver training programs to familiarize security teams with AI tools and their functionalities.
- **Hands-on Experience**: Provide hands-on experience and simulations to help teams practice using AI technologies in real-world scenarios.

5.2. Manage Organizational Change:

Overview: Address organizational change management aspects related to the integration of AI technologies.

Actions:

- **Communication**: Communicate the benefits and goals of AI integration to all stakeholders, including security teams and management.
- **Support**: Offer ongoing support and resources to help teams adapt to new workflows and technologies.

6. Continuous Evaluation and Improvement

6.1. Conduct Regular Reviews:

Overview: Regularly review the performance and impact of AI technologies within the cybersecurity infrastructure.

Actions:

- **Performance Reviews**: Schedule periodic reviews to assess the effectiveness of AI solutions and their contribution to security objectives.
- **Feedback Collection**: Gather feedback from security teams and other stakeholders to identify areas for improvement.

6.2. Update and Refine AI Models:

Overview: Continuously update and refine AI models to address evolving threats and changing cybersecurity needs.

Actions:

- **Model Updates**: Update AI models with new data and algorithms to improve their performance and accuracy.
- **Adaptation**: Adapt AI solutions to emerging threats and changes in the cybersecurity landscape.

6.3. Stay Informed on AI Advancements:

Overview: Stay informed about advancements in AI technologies and cybersecurity trends to ensure that your AI integration remains effective and current.

Actions:

- **Industry Research**: Keep up with industry research and developments in AI and cybersecurity.
- **Technology Upgrades**: Explore opportunities to incorporate new AI technologies and improvements into your cybersecurity infrastructure.

Integrating AI into cybersecurity infrastructure requires a well-structured approach that encompasses assessment, selection, planning, implementation, and continuous evaluation. By following these steps, organizations can effectively leverage AI technologies to enhance their security posture, improve threat detection and response, and stay ahead of evolving cyber threats. Successful integration of AI not only strengthens cybersecurity defenses but also positions organizations to adapt to future challenges and opportunities in the rapidly evolving landscape of cybersecurity.

10.2 Choosing the Right AI Tools and Technologies

Selecting the appropriate AI tools and technologies for cybersecurity is crucial to maximizing their effectiveness and ensuring they align with your organization's specific needs and objectives. The right choices can enhance threat detection, automate responses, and improve overall security posture. This section outlines a structured approach to choosing AI tools and technologies, including key considerations, evaluation criteria, and practical steps.

1. Identifying Needs and Objectives

1.1. Define Security Goals:

Overview: Start by defining the security goals and challenges that AI tools should address.

Actions:

- **Threat Landscape Analysis**: Identify the types of threats your organization faces, such as malware, phishing, or advanced persistent threats (APTs).
- **Objective Setting**: Establish clear objectives for AI tools, such as improving detection accuracy, reducing response time, or enhancing threat intelligence.

1.2. Assess Current Capabilities:

Overview: Evaluate your existing cybersecurity tools and processes to understand where AI can provide the most value.

Actions:

- **Capability Assessment**: Review current security technologies, including intrusion detection systems (IDS), endpoint protection platforms, and threat intelligence feeds.
- **Gap Analysis**: Identify gaps or limitations in existing capabilities that AI tools could address.

2. Evaluating AI Tools and Technologies

2.1. Consider Technology Types:

Overview: Understand the different types of AI technologies and tools available for cybersecurity and their respective functionalities.

Actions:

- **Machine Learning Models**: Evaluate models for threat detection, anomaly detection, and behavioral analysis.
- **Natural Language Processing (NLP):** Consider tools for analyzing and understanding textual data from logs, threat feeds, and reports.
- **Automated Response Systems**: Explore solutions for automating incident response and remediation.

2.2. Assess Vendor Offerings:

Overview: Research and evaluate AI tools from different vendors based on their features, performance, and alignment with your needs.

Actions:

- **Vendor Analysis**: Review vendor offerings, including their reputation, expertise, and customer support.
- **Feature Comparison**: Compare features such as detection capabilities, integration options, scalability, and ease of use.

2.3. Evaluate Performance and Accuracy:

Overview: Assess the performance and accuracy of AI tools to ensure they meet your security needs.

Actions:

- **Accuracy Testing**: Test tools for their accuracy in detecting and responding to threats based on historical data and real-world scenarios.
- **Performance Metrics**: Evaluate metrics such as false positive rates, detection speed, and response efficiency.

3. Integration and Compatibility

3.1. Check Integration Capabilities:

Overview: Ensure that selected AI tools can integrate seamlessly with your existing cybersecurity infrastructure.

Actions:

- **Integration Points**: Identify integration points with existing systems such as security information and event management (SIEM) platforms, intrusion prevention systems (IPS), and network monitoring tools.
- **APIs and Connectors**: Evaluate the availability and compatibility of APIs and connectors for integration.

3.2. Consider Scalability:

Overview: Choose AI tools that can scale with your organization's growth and evolving security needs.

Actions:

- **Scalability Assessment**: Assess the ability of tools to handle increasing volumes of data and traffic as your organization grows.
- **Resource Requirements**: Evaluate the hardware and software resources required for scaling the AI solutions.

4. Cost and ROI Analysis

4.1. Analyze Costs:

Overview: Consider the costs associated with acquiring, implementing, and maintaining AI tools.

Actions:

- **Cost Breakdown**: Review the cost components, including licensing fees, subscription models, hardware requirements, and ongoing maintenance.
- **Budget Alignment**: Ensure that the costs align with your budget and financial constraints.

4.2. Evaluate Return on Investment (ROI):

Overview: Assess the potential ROI of AI tools based on their impact on your cybersecurity posture.

Actions:

- **Benefit Analysis**: Evaluate the benefits, such as improved threat detection rates, reduced response times, and enhanced operational efficiency.
- **ROI Calculation**: Calculate the expected ROI by comparing the costs of implementation with the anticipated benefits and improvements.

5. Testing and Validation

5.1. Conduct Pilot Testing:

Overview: Perform pilot testing to evaluate the effectiveness of AI tools in a controlled environment before full deployment.

Actions:

- **Pilot Deployment**: Deploy AI tools in a test environment to assess their performance and compatibility with existing systems.
- **Performance Evaluation**: Monitor and evaluate the performance of AI tools during the pilot phase, including their impact on detection and response.

5.2. Gather Feedback:

Overview: Collect feedback from users and stakeholders involved in the pilot testing phase.

Actions:

- **User Feedback**: Obtain feedback from cybersecurity teams and end-users on the usability, effectiveness, and impact of the AI tools.
- **Adjustments**: Make necessary adjustments based on feedback to improve the tools' performance and integration.

6. Implementation and Deployment

6.1. Develop an Implementation Plan:

Overview: Create a detailed plan for implementing AI tools, including deployment strategies, timelines, and resource allocation.

Actions:

- **Deployment Strategy**: Outline the steps for deploying AI tools across your cybersecurity infrastructure.
- **Resource Allocation**: Allocate resources, including personnel, hardware, and software, for the implementation process.

6.2. Monitor and Optimize:

Overview: Continuously monitor the performance of AI tools and optimize them for improved effectiveness.

Actions:

- **Performance Monitoring**: Track the performance of AI tools and their impact on cybersecurity operations.
- **Optimization**: Make necessary adjustments to enhance the tools' performance and address any issues that arise.

7. Documentation and Training

7.1. Document Integration Processes:

Overview: Maintain comprehensive documentation of the integration processes, configurations, and settings for AI tools.

Actions:

- **Configuration Records**: Document the configurations, settings, and integration points of AI tools.
- **Operational Procedures**: Develop and maintain operational procedures and guidelines for using and managing AI tools.

7.2. Provide Training:

Overview: Train cybersecurity teams and stakeholders on how to effectively use and manage AI tools.

Actions:

- **Training Programs**: Develop training programs to educate users on the functionalities and best practices for using AI tools.
- **Ongoing Support**: Offer ongoing support and resources to address any questions or issues that arise during tool usage.

8. Future Considerations

8.1. Stay Updated on AI Advancements:

Overview: Keep abreast of advancements in AI technologies and cybersecurity trends to ensure your tools remain effective and relevant.

Actions:

- **Industry Research**: Follow industry research and developments in AI and cybersecurity.
- **Technology Upgrades**: Explore opportunities to upgrade or incorporate new AI technologies as they become available.

8.2. Plan for Continuous Improvement:

Overview: Develop a plan for continuous improvement and optimization of AI tools based on evolving threats and organizational needs.

Actions:

- **Feedback Integration**: Integrate feedback from users and stakeholders to drive improvements in AI tools.
- **Innovation Adoption**: Stay open to adopting innovative solutions and technologies that can enhance your cybersecurity capabilities.

Choosing the right AI tools and technologies for cybersecurity involves a comprehensive approach that considers security needs, technology capabilities, integration requirements, and cost considerations. By following a structured process for evaluation, testing, and deployment, organizations can effectively integrate AI solutions into their cybersecurity infrastructure, enhance threat detection and response, and improve overall security posture. Continuous monitoring, optimization, and staying informed about advancements will ensure that AI tools remain effective and aligned with evolving cybersecurity challenges.

10.3 Training and Upskilling the Security Team

Effective integration of AI tools into cybersecurity infrastructure is not solely about selecting the right technologies; it also requires ensuring that your security team is adequately trained and skilled to leverage these tools effectively. Training and upskilling are critical to maximizing the benefits of AI in cybersecurity and ensuring that your team can respond to new threats efficiently. This section outlines a comprehensive approach to training and upskilling your security team, including key considerations and practical steps.

1. Assessing Training Needs

1.1. Evaluate Current Skill Levels:

Overview: Begin by assessing the current skill levels of your security team to identify gaps and areas for improvement.

Actions:

- **Skill Assessment**: Conduct a skills assessment to evaluate the knowledge and expertise of team members in AI and cybersecurity.
- **Gap Analysis**: Identify gaps between current skills and the skills needed to effectively use AI tools and technologies.

1.2. Define Training Objectives:

Overview: Set clear training objectives based on the identified skill gaps and organizational goals.

Actions:

- **Objective Setting**: Define specific training goals, such as understanding AI technologies, improving threat detection, or enhancing incident response capabilities.
- **Tailored Training**: Develop training objectives that are tailored to different roles within the security team, such as analysts, incident responders, and security engineers.

2. Developing a Training Program

2.1. Create a Training Curriculum:

Overview: Develop a comprehensive training curriculum that covers essential topics related to AI and cybersecurity.

Actions:

- **Content Development**: Create training materials that cover AI fundamentals, machine learning techniques, and specific applications in cybersecurity.
- **Module Design**: Design training modules that address various aspects of AI tools, including installation, configuration, operation, and troubleshooting.

2.2. Incorporate Practical Exercises:

Overview: Include practical exercises and hands-on labs in the training program to provide real-world experience.

Actions:

- **Simulations**: Develop simulation scenarios that mimic real-world threats and incidents, allowing team members to practice using AI tools in a controlled environment.
- **Lab Sessions**: Organize lab sessions where participants can interact with AI tools, analyze data, and perform threat detection and response tasks.

2.3. Include Vendor-Specific Training:

Overview: If using specific AI tools from vendors, incorporate vendor-specific training to familiarize the team with those tools.

Actions:

- **Vendor Resources**: Utilize training resources provided by AI tool vendors, such as online courses, documentation, and webinars.
- **Certifications**: Encourage team members to pursue vendor-specific certifications to gain deeper expertise in the tools being used.

3. Implementing the Training Program

3.1. Schedule Training Sessions:

Overview: Plan and schedule training sessions to ensure that all team members have the opportunity to participate.

Actions:

- **Training Calendar**: Develop a training calendar that includes dates for live sessions, workshops, and hands-on labs.
- **Participation**: Ensure that training sessions are scheduled to accommodate the availability of team members and minimize disruption to ongoing security operations.

3.2. Deliver Training:

Overview: Execute the training program using a mix of delivery methods to accommodate different learning styles.

Actions:

- **Instructor-Led Training**: Conduct instructor-led sessions, either in-person or virtual, to provide interactive learning experiences.
- **E-Learning**: Offer e-learning modules and self-paced courses for team members who prefer flexible learning options.

3.3. Provide Ongoing Support:

Overview: Offer ongoing support and resources to reinforce learning and address any questions or challenges.

Actions:

- **Help Desk**: Set up a help desk or support channel where team members can seek assistance with AI tools and technologies.
- **Knowledge Base**: Develop a knowledge base with frequently asked questions, troubleshooting tips, and best practices.

4. Measuring Training Effectiveness

4.1. Evaluate Training Outcomes:

Overview: Assess the effectiveness of the training program to determine if it meets the defined objectives and improves team performance.

Actions:

- **Assessment Tests**: Administer assessments or quizzes to measure knowledge gained during the training.
- **Feedback Surveys**: Collect feedback from participants on the quality and relevance of the training program.

4.2. Monitor Performance Improvements:

Overview: Track changes in team performance and capabilities following the training program.

Actions:

- **Performance Metrics**: Monitor metrics such as incident response times, accuracy of threat detection, and overall effectiveness of AI tool usage.
- **Continuous Improvement**: Use performance data and feedback to make improvements to the training program and address any remaining skill gaps.

5. Encouraging Continuous Learning

5.1. Promote Lifelong Learning:

Overview: Foster a culture of continuous learning to ensure that your security team stays up-to-date with the latest advancements in AI and cybersecurity.

Actions:

- **Professional Development**: Encourage team members to pursue ongoing professional development opportunities, such as industry conferences, workshops, and certifications.
- **Knowledge Sharing**: Facilitate knowledge sharing within the team by organizing regular meetings, webinars, and discussions on emerging trends and technologies.

5.2. Stay Current with AI Advances:

Overview: Keep the team informed about new developments in AI technologies and their applications in cybersecurity.

Actions:

- **Industry News**: Share updates on the latest AI research, tools, and trends with the security team.
- **Vendor Updates**: Provide information on updates and new features of the AI tools being used.

6. Addressing Training Challenges

6.1. Overcoming Resistance to Change:

Overview: Address any resistance to adopting new AI technologies and training programs.

Actions:

- **Communication**: Communicate the benefits and importance of AI tools and training to the team.
- **Involvement**: Involve team members in the planning and implementation of training programs to increase buy-in and engagement.

6.2. Managing Resource Constraints:

Overview: Address any resource constraints, such as time and budget, that may impact the training program.

Actions:

- **Prioritization**: Prioritize training activities based on the most critical skills and knowledge areas.
- **Budget Management**: Allocate resources effectively to balance training needs with other operational requirements.

Training and upskilling the security team is a vital component of integrating AI into cybersecurity infrastructure. By assessing training needs, developing a comprehensive training program, implementing effective training, and promoting continuous learning, organizations can ensure that their security teams are well-equipped to leverage AI technologies effectively. Addressing training challenges and staying current with advancements will help maintain a skilled and knowledgeable team, ultimately enhancing the organization's cybersecurity posture and resilience against emerging threats.

10.4 Measuring the Effectiveness of AI Solutions

Evaluating the effectiveness of AI solutions in cybersecurity is essential for understanding their impact on your security operations, optimizing their use, and ensuring they deliver the expected benefits. Measuring effectiveness involves assessing various metrics and outcomes to determine how well AI tools are performing their intended functions and contributing to your overall security strategy. This section provides a comprehensive approach to measuring the effectiveness of AI solutions, including key metrics, evaluation methods, and practical steps.

1. Defining Success Metrics

1.1. Establish Key Performance Indicators (KPIs):

Overview: Define specific KPIs to measure the success of AI solutions in addressing your cybersecurity needs.

Actions:

- **Detection Accuracy**: Measure the accuracy of threat detection, including true positive rates, false positive rates, and false negative rates.
- **Response Time**: Track the time taken by AI solutions to detect and respond to threats.
- **Incident Reduction**: Evaluate the reduction in the number of security incidents and breaches attributed to AI interventions.

1.2. Align Metrics with Objectives:

Overview: Ensure that the chosen metrics align with the objectives of your AI solutions and overall security goals.

Actions:

- **Objective Alignment**: Link KPIs to specific objectives such as improving threat detection, reducing response time, or enhancing operational efficiency.
- **Outcome Measurement**: Measure the impact of AI solutions on achieving these objectives.

2. Collecting and Analyzing Data

2.1. Gather Performance Data:

Overview: Collect data on the performance of AI solutions to evaluate their effectiveness.

Actions:

- **Data Sources**: Use data from AI tools, security information and event management (SIEM) systems, and other relevant sources.
- **Data Collection**: Collect data on detection rates, response times, and other performance metrics.

2.2. Analyze Performance Trends:

Overview: Analyze performance data to identify trends, patterns, and areas for improvement.

Actions:

- **Trend Analysis**: Examine trends in detection accuracy, response times, and incident rates over time.
- **Benchmarking**: Compare performance metrics against industry benchmarks or historical data to assess effectiveness.

3. Evaluating Impact on Security Operations

3.1. Assess Operational Efficiency:

Overview: Evaluate how AI solutions impact the efficiency of your security operations.

Actions:

- **Operational Metrics**: Measure improvements in operational efficiency, such as reduced manual effort and faster incident response times.
- **Resource Utilization**: Assess the impact on resource utilization, including staffing and workload distribution.

3.2. Review Incident Outcomes:

Overview: Examine the outcomes of incidents detected and responded to by AI solutions.

Actions:

- **Incident Analysis**: Analyze the outcomes of incidents, including resolution times, severity, and impact.
- **Effectiveness Review**: Review how AI solutions contributed to resolving incidents and preventing recurrence.

4. Conducting User Feedback and Satisfaction Surveys

4.1. Collect Feedback from Users:

Overview: Gather feedback from security team members and other users of AI solutions to assess their satisfaction and identify areas for improvement.

Actions:

- **Feedback Surveys**: Conduct surveys or interviews to collect feedback on the usability, effectiveness, and overall satisfaction with AI tools.
- **User Experience**: Evaluate user experiences with AI solutions, including ease of use, integration, and support.

4.2. Analyze Feedback Data:

Overview: Analyze feedback data to identify common issues, suggestions, and areas for enhancement.

Actions:

- **Feedback Analysis**: Review feedback for recurring themes, issues, and improvement opportunities.
- **Actionable Insights**: Use feedback to make informed decisions about optimizing or adjusting AI solutions.

5. Performing Cost-Benefit Analysis

5.1. Assess Costs:

Overview: Evaluate the costs associated with implementing and maintaining AI solutions.

Actions:

- **Cost Tracking**: Track costs related to acquisition, implementation, licensing, and maintenance of AI tools.
- **Budget Review**: Compare costs against budget projections and financial constraints.

5.2. Measure Benefits:

Overview: Assess the benefits derived from AI solutions, including improved detection rates, reduced response times, and enhanced security posture.

Actions:

- **Benefit Evaluation**: Measure tangible benefits such as reduced incident costs, increased efficiency, and improved security outcomes.
- **ROI Calculation**: Calculate the return on investment (ROI) by comparing the benefits with the costs incurred.

6. Continuous Improvement and Optimization

6.1. Identify Improvement Opportunities:

Overview: Use performance data and feedback to identify areas where AI solutions can be improved.

Actions:

- **Performance Gaps**: Identify gaps in performance or areas where AI solutions may not be meeting expectations.
- **Optimization Opportunities**: Explore opportunities for optimizing AI tools, such as fine-tuning algorithms or enhancing features.

6.2. Implement Changes:

Overview: Make necessary changes to improve the effectiveness of AI solutions based on findings and feedback.

Actions:

- **Adjustment Implementation**: Implement changes to algorithms, configurations, or processes to enhance performance.
- **Testing and Validation**: Test and validate changes to ensure they achieve the desired improvements.

6.3. Monitor and Iterate:

Overview: Continuously monitor the performance of AI solutions and iterate on improvements as needed.

Actions:

- **Ongoing Monitoring**: Continuously track performance metrics and gather feedback.
- **Iterative Refinement**: Regularly refine and optimize AI solutions based on ongoing data and feedback.

7. Reporting and Communication

7.1. Develop Performance Reports:

Overview: Create reports to communicate the effectiveness of AI solutions to stakeholders and decision-makers.

Actions:

- **Report Creation**: Develop comprehensive reports that include performance metrics, cost-benefit analysis, and user feedback.
- **Presentation**: Present findings to stakeholders, including executive summaries and detailed analyses.

7.2. Communicate Findings:

Overview: Communicate the results of the effectiveness evaluation to relevant stakeholders.

Actions:

- **Stakeholder Updates**: Provide updates to stakeholders on the impact of AI solutions and any recommended changes.
- **Action Plans**: Share action plans for addressing any identified issues or areas for improvement.

Measuring the effectiveness of AI solutions is a critical process for ensuring that these tools deliver the expected benefits and contribute to a stronger cybersecurity posture. By defining success metrics, collecting and analyzing data, evaluating impact, gathering user feedback, and performing cost-benefit analysis, organizations can effectively assess the performance of AI solutions. Continuous improvement and optimization, along with clear reporting and communication, are essential for maximizing the value of AI in cybersecurity and ensuring that solutions remain effective in the face of evolving threats.

10.5 Continual Improvement and Adaptation

Continual improvement and adaptation are essential for maintaining the effectiveness of AI solutions in cybersecurity. The threat landscape, technological advancements, and organizational needs are constantly evolving, requiring a proactive approach to ensure that AI tools remain relevant and effective. This section outlines a structured approach to continual improvement and adaptation of AI solutions, focusing on feedback loops, iterative development, and staying ahead of emerging trends.

1. Establishing a Feedback Loop

1.1. Implement Regular Review Cycles:

Overview: Establish regular review cycles to assess the performance and relevance of AI solutions.

Actions:

- **Review Schedule**: Set up periodic reviews (e.g., quarterly or biannually) to evaluate AI tool performance, effectiveness, and alignment with organizational goals.
- **Review Meetings**: Hold review meetings with key stakeholders to discuss findings, challenges, and opportunities for improvement.

1.2. Collect and Analyze Feedback:

Overview: Continuously gather feedback from users, stakeholders, and performance data to identify areas for improvement.

Actions:

- **Feedback Channels**: Create channels for users to provide feedback on AI tools, including surveys, suggestion boxes, and direct communication.
- **Data Analysis**: Analyze feedback and performance data to identify trends, recurring issues, and potential enhancements.

1.3. Implement Action Plans:

Overview: Develop and implement action plans based on feedback and review findings to address identified issues and opportunities for improvement.

Actions:

- **Action Plan Development**: Create detailed action plans outlining steps to address feedback and performance issues.
- **Execution and Monitoring**: Execute action plans and monitor progress to ensure that improvements are effectively implemented.

2. Adapting to Emerging Threats and Technologies

2.1. Monitor Threat Landscape:

Overview: Stay informed about emerging threats and trends in cybersecurity to ensure that AI solutions remain effective.

Actions:

- **Threat Intelligence**: Subscribe to threat intelligence feeds and industry reports to stay updated on new and evolving threats.
- **Threat Modeling**: Regularly update threat models and scenarios to reflect changes in the threat landscape.

2.2. Integrate New Technologies:

Overview: Evaluate and integrate new technologies and advancements to enhance the capabilities of AI solutions.

Actions:

- **Technology Scouting:** Identify and assess new technologies that could enhance AI solutions or address emerging threats.
- **Pilot Testing**: Conduct pilot tests to evaluate the effectiveness and compatibility of new technologies with existing AI tools.

2.3. Update AI Models and Algorithms:

Overview: Regularly update AI models and algorithms to improve accuracy and adapt to new threat patterns.

Actions:

- **Model Training**: Retrain AI models with new data to improve detection accuracy and adapt to changes in threat patterns.
- **Algorithm Tuning**: Fine-tune algorithms to enhance performance and address any identified weaknesses.

3. Enhancing User Training and Engagement

3.1. Provide Ongoing Training:

Overview: Ensure that users receive ongoing training to stay proficient in using AI tools and understanding new features.

Actions:

- **Training Programs**: Develop and deliver regular training sessions to cover new features, updates, and best practices.
- **Knowledge Sharing**: Encourage knowledge sharing and collaboration among team members to foster continuous learning.

3.2. Engage Users in Improvement Processes:

Overview: Involve users in the improvement process to leverage their insights and experience.

Actions:

- **User Involvement**: Include users in discussions and workshops focused on improving AI solutions and addressing challenges.
- **Feedback Integration**: Actively incorporate user feedback into the development and refinement of AI tools.

4. Ensuring Scalability and Flexibility

4.1. Plan for Scalability:

Overview: Ensure that AI solutions can scale to meet the growing demands of the organization and evolving threat landscape.

Actions:

- **Scalability Assessment**: Evaluate the scalability of AI tools and infrastructure to handle increasing data volumes and threat complexity.
- **Capacity Planning**: Plan for capacity expansion and resource allocation to support future growth and scaling needs.

4.2. Maintain Flexibility:

Overview: Design AI solutions with flexibility to adapt to changing requirements and emerging technologies.

Actions:

- **Modular Design**: Use a modular design approach to facilitate updates and integration of new technologies.
- **Customization Options**: Provide customization options to tailor AI solutions to specific organizational needs and evolving threat scenarios.

5. Measuring the Impact of Improvements

5.1. Evaluate Improvement Outcomes:

Overview: Measure the impact of implemented improvements to assess their effectiveness and value.

Actions:

- **Impact Assessment**: Evaluate changes in performance metrics, user satisfaction, and incident outcomes resulting from improvements.
- **Benefit Realization**: Assess the realization of benefits, such as enhanced detection accuracy, reduced response times, and improved operational efficiency.

5.2. Adjust Improvement Strategies:

Overview: Adjust improvement strategies based on the impact assessment to refine and optimize AI solutions further.

Actions:

- **Strategy Review**: Review and adjust improvement strategies based on outcomes and feedback.
- **Continuous Iteration**: Continue iterating on improvement efforts to ensure ongoing effectiveness and alignment with organizational goals.

6. Documenting and Sharing Best Practices

6.1. Document Improvement Processes:

Overview: Document the processes and practices involved in continual improvement and adaptation for future reference.

Actions:

- **Process Documentation**: Create detailed documentation of improvement processes, methodologies, and outcomes.
- **Best Practices**: Document best practices and lessons learned to guide future improvements and support organizational knowledge.

6.2. Share Knowledge and Insights:

Overview: Share knowledge and insights gained from improvement efforts with relevant stakeholders and the broader cybersecurity community.

Actions:

- **Internal Sharing**: Share insights and best practices with internal teams and departments.
- **External Sharing**: Contribute to industry forums, conferences, and publications to share knowledge with the broader cybersecurity community.

Continual improvement and adaptation are crucial for maintaining the effectiveness and relevance of AI solutions in cybersecurity. By establishing feedback loops, adapting to emerging threats and technologies, enhancing user training, ensuring scalability and flexibility, measuring the impact of improvements, and documenting best practices, organizations can effectively manage and optimize their AI tools. A proactive and iterative approach to improvement will help ensure that AI solutions continue to deliver value and contribute to a robust cybersecurity posture in an ever-changing threat landscape.

Chapter 11: The Future of AI in Cyber Defense

Chapter 11 explores the evolving role of artificial intelligence (AI) in shaping the future of cyber defense. As technology advances and cyber threats become more sophisticated, AI is poised to play an increasingly central role in safeguarding digital environments. This chapter provides a forward-looking perspective on how AI will influence and transform cybersecurity practices in the years to come.

We begin by examining emerging AI technologies and their potential impact on cyber defense. This includes advancements in machine learning algorithms, natural language processing, and autonomous systems. We explore how these technologies could enhance threat detection, automate response mechanisms, and provide more accurate threat intelligence.

Next, we discuss the integration of AI with other cutting-edge technologies, such as quantum computing and blockchain. We analyze how these technologies can work synergistically with AI to create more robust and secure cyber defense strategies. For example, quantum computing could revolutionize encryption methods, while blockchain could enhance data integrity and transparency.

The chapter also addresses the future of AI ethics and governance. As AI becomes more embedded in cybersecurity, it is crucial to develop and enforce ethical standards and governance frameworks to ensure responsible use. We explore potential regulatory developments and the importance of maintaining transparency and accountability in AI-driven security systems.

We then look at the evolving role of human expertise in an AI-enhanced cybersecurity landscape. While AI will play a crucial role, human oversight and judgment will remain essential. We discuss the future balance between AI and human intervention and the need for ongoing training and collaboration between AI systems and cybersecurity professionals.

Finally, we explore the potential challenges and opportunities that lie ahead. From dealing with adversarial AI techniques used by cybercriminals to ensuring equitable access to AI technologies, we provide insights into the key issues that will shape the future of AI in cyber defense.

By the end of this chapter, you will have a forward-looking view of how AI will continue to influence and redefine the field of cyber defense. Understanding these trends and developments will help you stay ahead in the ever-evolving landscape of cybersecurity and harness the full potential of AI to protect your digital assets.

11.1 Emerging AI Technologies in Cybersecurity

The field of cybersecurity is undergoing rapid transformation with the advent of emerging AI technologies. These technologies promise to enhance the ability to detect, respond to, and mitigate threats more effectively than traditional methods. This section explores some of the most promising AI technologies in cybersecurity, their applications, and the potential impact they may have on the future of cyber defense.

1. Generative AI

1.1. Overview of Generative AI:

- **Definition**: Generative AI refers to algorithms that can create new content, such as text, images, or even code, based on patterns learned from existing data.
- **Technologies**: Includes models like Generative Adversarial Networks (GANs) and Variational Autoencoders (VAEs).

1.2. Applications in Cybersecurity:

- **Threat Simulation**: Generative AI can create realistic attack simulations to test and improve defense mechanisms.
- **Phishing Detection**: Models can generate synthetic phishing emails to train detection systems and improve accuracy.

1.3. Impact and Challenges:

- **Enhanced Training**: Improves the training data available for AI-based threat detection systems.
- **Adversarial Risks**: Potential misuse for creating sophisticated phishing or social engineering attacks.

2. Advanced Natural Language Processing (NLP)

2.1. Overview of NLP:

- **Definition**: NLP involves the interaction between computers and human language, enabling machines to understand, interpret, and generate human language.
- **Technologies**: Includes models like BERT (Bidirectional Encoder Representations from Transformers) and GPT (Generative Pre-trained Transformer).

2.2. Applications in Cybersecurity:

- **Threat Intelligence**: NLP can analyze and extract actionable insights from unstructured data, such as security reports, threat intelligence feeds, and social media.
- **Incident Response**: Improves the automation of incident response by understanding and generating natural language responses and alerts.

2.3. Impact and Challenges:

- **Improved Efficiency**: Enhances the ability to process and analyze large volumes of textual data quickly.
- **Accuracy Concerns**: Ensuring the accuracy and relevance of NLP-generated insights and responses.

3. AI-Driven Behavioral Analytics

3.1. Overview of Behavioral Analytics:

- **Definition**: Behavioral analytics involves monitoring and analyzing user and system behaviors to detect anomalies and potential threats.
- **Technologies**: Uses machine learning models to establish baselines and identify deviations.

3.2. Applications in Cybersecurity:

- **Insider Threat Detection**: Identifies unusual patterns of behavior that may indicate insider threats or compromised accounts.
- **Fraud Detection**: Detects fraudulent activities by analyzing transactional patterns and user behaviors.

3.3. Impact and Challenges:

- **Enhanced Detection**: Improves the detection of sophisticated threats that might evade traditional signature-based methods.
- **Privacy Concerns**: Balancing the need for monitoring with user privacy and data protection regulations.

4. AI for Automated Threat Hunting

4.1. Overview of Automated Threat Hunting:

- **Definition**: Automated threat hunting uses AI and machine learning to proactively search for and identify potential threats within an organization's network.
- **Technologies**: Includes machine learning models that analyze network traffic, logs, and other data sources.

4.2. Applications in Cybersecurity:

- **Proactive Detection**: Enables continuous monitoring and identification of emerging threats that might not be detected by traditional methods.
- **Threat Analysis**: Automates the analysis of potential threats and provides actionable insights for response.

4.3. Impact and Challenges:

- **Increased Efficiency**: Reduces the time and effort required for threat hunting by automating routine tasks.
- **False Positives**: Managing and reducing false positives to ensure accurate threat detection and response.

5. AI-Powered Endpoint Protection

5.1. Overview of Endpoint Protection:

- **Definition**: Endpoint protection involves securing end-user devices, such as laptops, desktops, and mobile devices, from cyber threats.
- **Technologies**: Uses AI and machine learning to enhance traditional antivirus and anti-malware solutions.

5.2. Applications in Cybersecurity:

- **Behavioral Monitoring**: AI models monitor and analyze endpoint behaviors to detect and prevent malicious activities.
- **Adaptive Defense**: Provides adaptive and context-aware protection by learning from evolving threats and user behaviors.

5.3. Impact and Challenges:

- **Enhanced Security**: Improves the ability to detect and block zero-day threats and sophisticated attacks.
- **Resource Consumption**: Managing the computational resources required for AI-based endpoint protection.

6. AI in Security Orchestration and Automation

6.1. Overview of Security Orchestration:

- **Definition**: Security orchestration involves integrating and automating security tools and processes to streamline security operations.
- **Technologies**: Uses AI to coordinate and automate responses across various security platforms.

6.2. Applications in Cybersecurity:

- **Automated Response**: Automates incident response actions, such as isolating compromised systems or applying patches.
- **Integration**: Enhances the integration of disparate security tools and systems to provide a unified defense strategy.

6.3. Impact and Challenges:

- **Operational Efficiency**: Reduces manual intervention and improves the speed and accuracy of responses to security incidents.
- **Complexity**: Managing the complexity of integrating and orchestrating multiple AI-driven security tools.

7. AI for Predictive Threat Intelligence

7.1. Overview of Predictive Threat Intelligence:

- **Definition**: Predictive threat intelligence uses AI to analyze historical data and predict future threats and attack vectors.
- **Technologies**: Employs machine learning models to identify patterns and trends that indicate potential future threats.

7.2. Applications in Cybersecurity:

- **Threat Forecasting**: Provides insights into emerging threats and vulnerabilities before they materialize.
- **Strategic Planning**: Assists in strategic planning and risk management by anticipating potential attack scenarios.

7.3. Impact and Challenges:

- **Proactive Defense**: Enhances the ability to prepare and defend against future threats proactively.
- **Data Quality**: Ensuring the quality and relevance of data used for predictive analysis.

8. AI in Zero Trust Architectures

8.1. Overview of Zero Trust:

- **Definition**: Zero Trust is a security model that assumes no implicit trust and requires verification for every access request.
- **Technologies**: Uses AI to enforce and manage security policies in a Zero Trust architecture.

8.2. Applications in Cybersecurity:

- **Access Control**: AI enhances access control by analyzing user and device behaviors to enforce strict access policies.
- **Policy Enforcement**: Automates the enforcement of security policies based on real-time data and threat intelligence.

8.3. Impact and Challenges:

- **Enhanced Security**: Strengthens security by continuously verifying and validating access requests.

- **Implementation Complexity**: Managing the complexity of implementing and maintaining a Zero Trust architecture with AI.

Emerging AI technologies are reshaping the cybersecurity landscape by offering innovative solutions to address evolving threats and challenges. Generative AI, advanced NLP, behavioral analytics, automated threat hunting, AI-powered endpoint protection, security orchestration, predictive threat intelligence, and Zero Trust architectures represent significant advancements in the field. These technologies promise to enhance threat detection, response, and prevention capabilities, but also come with challenges that need to be addressed. Organizations must stay informed about these advancements and integrate them thoughtfully into their cybersecurity strategies to stay ahead of emerging threats and ensure robust defense mechanisms.

11.2 The Role of Quantum Computing

Quantum computing represents a significant leap in computational power and capability, offering new possibilities and challenges in various fields, including cybersecurity. Unlike classical computers, which use bits to represent information as either 0 or 1, quantum computers use quantum bits or qubits, which can represent and process information in multiple states simultaneously. This unique property of qubits allows quantum computers to solve certain complex problems much more efficiently than classical computers.

1. Understanding Quantum Computing

1.1. Basics of Quantum Computing:

- **Qubits**: Quantum bits (qubits) are the fundamental units of quantum information, which can exist in multiple states at once due to superposition. This allows quantum computers to perform many calculations simultaneously.
- **Entanglement**: Qubits can be entangled, meaning the state of one qubit is dependent on the state of another, even if they are separated by large distances. This phenomenon enables complex computations and data processing.
- **Quantum Gates and Circuits**: Quantum computers use quantum gates to manipulate qubits and perform operations, creating quantum circuits similar to classical logic gates but with quantum properties.

1.2. Quantum Speedup:

- **Parallelism**: Quantum computers leverage parallelism to perform multiple calculations at once, significantly speeding up certain types of problems.
- **Complex Problem Solving**: Problems that involve large datasets or require substantial computational resources can be solved more efficiently with quantum algorithms, such as Shor's algorithm for integer factorization and Grover's algorithm for searching unsorted databases.

2. Quantum Computing and Cryptography

2.1. Impact on Classical Cryptography:

- **Breaking Public-Key Cryptography**: Quantum computers pose a potential threat to widely used public-key cryptographic systems, such as RSA and ECC (Elliptic Curve Cryptography). Shor's algorithm can efficiently factor large integers and solve discrete logarithms, potentially breaking these cryptographic schemes.
- **Symmetric-Key Cryptography**: While quantum computers can weaken the security of symmetric-key cryptography (e.g., AES), the impact is less severe compared to public-key cryptography. Grover's algorithm can provide quadratic speedup in brute-force attacks, which means key sizes may need to be increased to maintain security.

2.2. Quantum-Resistant Algorithms:

- **Post-Quantum Cryptography**: To counter the potential threat posed by quantum computers, researchers are developing quantum-resistant cryptographic algorithms designed to be secure against quantum attacks. These algorithms include lattice-based cryptography, hash-based cryptography, and code-based cryptography.
- **Standardization Efforts**: Organizations such as the National Institute of Standards and Technology (NIST) are working on standardizing quantum-resistant algorithms to ensure secure communication in a post-quantum world.

3. Quantum Computing in Cybersecurity

3.1. Quantum Key Distribution (QKD):

- **Principle of QKD**: Quantum Key Distribution uses quantum mechanics principles to enable secure communication by distributing cryptographic keys in a

way that detects any eavesdropping attempts. QKD is based on the principles of quantum entanglement and superposition.
- **Applications**: QKD can enhance secure communication channels and protect sensitive information by ensuring the integrity and confidentiality of key exchanges.

3.2. Quantum Random Number Generation:

- **Quantum Randomness**: Quantum computers can generate true random numbers based on quantum phenomena, which can improve the security of cryptographic algorithms and protocols.
- **Applications**: Quantum random number generators (QRNGs) are used in encryption, secure key generation, and randomization processes to enhance security.

3.3. Quantum Computing in Security Analysis:

- **Complex Problem Solving**: Quantum computers could potentially be used to solve complex security problems, such as optimizing network security configurations, simulating security scenarios, and analyzing large datasets for threat detection.
- **Future Prospects**: As quantum computing technology advances, its role in cybersecurity will likely expand, offering new tools and methods for enhancing security and addressing emerging threats.

4. Challenges and Considerations

4.1. Technological Maturity:

- **Current State**: Quantum computing is still in the experimental and developmental stages, with many technical challenges to overcome before it becomes widely available and practical for real-world applications.
- **Scalability**: Building large-scale, fault-tolerant quantum computers is a significant challenge, and achieving the necessary qubit count and error rates is a key focus of ongoing research.

4.2. Transition to Quantum-Resistant Solutions:

- **Migration**: Transitioning from classical cryptographic systems to quantum-resistant algorithms will require careful planning and implementation to ensure a smooth and secure transition.
- **Legacy Systems**: Organizations must address the compatibility of quantum-resistant algorithms with existing systems and protocols to avoid disruptions during the transition.

4.3. Security Implications:

- **Post-Quantum Threats**: The potential future availability of quantum computers introduces uncertainties regarding the timing and nature of quantum threats. Organizations must stay informed and prepared for the eventual impact of quantum computing on cybersecurity.

Quantum computing represents a transformative technology with the potential to reshape various fields, including cybersecurity. While it offers exciting possibilities for enhancing security through quantum key distribution and random number generation, it also poses challenges, particularly for classical cryptographic systems. The development of quantum-resistant algorithms and ongoing research into quantum computing will play a crucial role in addressing these challenges and ensuring a secure future in the face of emerging quantum technologies. Organizations must stay vigilant and proactive in preparing for the implications of quantum computing to safeguard their cybersecurity infrastructure and adapt to this evolving technological landscape.

11.3 AI in Offensive Cyber Operations

AI's role in cybersecurity has primarily been discussed in the context of defense, but it also has significant applications in offensive cyber operations. These operations involve activities aimed at compromising, disrupting, or manipulating systems and networks. While the ethical and legal implications of such operations are substantial, understanding AI's capabilities in this realm is crucial for comprehensively grasping the cybersecurity landscape.

1. Overview of Offensive Cyber Operations

1.1. Definition and Objectives:

- **Definition**: Offensive cyber operations refer to actions taken to infiltrate, disrupt, or manipulate the digital infrastructure of adversaries.

- **Objectives**: These operations can aim to gather intelligence, disrupt services, steal sensitive information, or degrade the capabilities of adversaries.

1.2. Types of Offensive Cyber Operations:

- **Espionage**: Stealing sensitive information from target systems.
- **Sabotage**: Disrupting or damaging systems and networks.
- **Misinformation**: Spreading false information to mislead or manipulate public opinion.
- **Exploitation**: Taking advantage of vulnerabilities in systems to gain unauthorized access.

2. AI Techniques in Offensive Cyber Operations

2.1. Automated Vulnerability Discovery:

- **Techniques**: AI can scan and analyze software and systems to discover vulnerabilities more quickly and accurately than manual methods. Machine learning models can identify patterns that indicate security weaknesses.
- **Tools**: AI-driven tools can automate the process of identifying, classifying, and prioritizing vulnerabilities, streamlining the efforts of offensive cyber operators.

2.2. Exploit Development:

- **Techniques**: AI can assist in developing exploits by analyzing the behavior of vulnerabilities and generating code to exploit them. This includes creating payloads that can bypass security measures.
- **Tools**: AI systems can simulate attack scenarios and refine exploit techniques, increasing the chances of successful penetration.

2.3. Social Engineering Attacks:

- **Techniques**: AI can enhance social engineering attacks by generating highly personalized and convincing phishing emails, messages, or phone calls. Natural language processing (NLP) models can craft messages that mimic human behavior and language patterns.
- **Tools**: AI-powered social engineering tools can analyze social media profiles, communication patterns, and other data to tailor attacks to specific targets, increasing their effectiveness.

2.4. Automated Malware Creation:

- **Techniques**: AI can be used to create sophisticated malware that can adapt and evolve to avoid detection. Machine learning models can generate polymorphic and metamorphic malware that changes its code structure dynamically.
- **Tools**: AI-driven malware development frameworks can produce new variants of malware, test them against security defenses, and refine them for better success rates.

2.5. Network Infiltration and Lateral Movement:

- **Techniques**: AI can automate the process of infiltrating networks and moving laterally within them to reach high-value targets. Machine learning models can analyze network traffic and identify the most effective paths for movement.
- **Tools**: AI-powered infiltration tools can adapt to changing network conditions, evade detection, and optimize routes for accessing sensitive data or systems.

3. Case Studies and Applications

3.1. Real-World Examples:

- **Stuxnet**: One of the most famous cases of offensive cyber operations, where advanced malware was used to sabotage Iran's nuclear program. AI techniques could have been used to enhance the malware's adaptability and stealth.
- **Operation Aurora**: A series of cyberattacks targeting major companies, including Google, where sophisticated malware and social engineering techniques were employed. AI could have played a role in optimizing these attacks.

3.2. Hypothetical Scenarios:

- **Targeted Espionage Campaign**: AI could be used to identify high-value targets within an organization, craft personalized phishing emails, and develop custom exploits to access confidential information.
- **Critical Infrastructure Sabotage**: AI-driven malware could infiltrate industrial control systems, analyze their operations, and execute precise commands to disrupt services or cause physical damage.

4. Ethical and Legal Considerations

4.1. Ethical Implications:

- **Morality of Offensive Operations**: The use of AI in offensive cyber operations raises significant ethical questions, including the justification for such actions and the potential harm to innocent parties.
- **Unintended Consequences**: AI-driven attacks can have unpredictable and far-reaching consequences, affecting not only the intended targets but also broader communities and ecosystems.

4.2. Legal Frameworks:

- **International Law**: Offensive cyber operations often violate international laws and norms, raising questions about state responsibility and accountability.
- **Regulation and Oversight**: There is a growing need for regulatory frameworks and oversight mechanisms to govern the use of AI in offensive cyber operations, ensuring compliance with ethical standards and legal requirements.

5. Defensive Countermeasures

5.1. AI in Defensive Operations:

- **AI vs. AI**: Defensive cybersecurity systems must evolve to counter AI-driven offensive operations. This involves using AI to detect and respond to AI-generated threats effectively.
- **Adaptive Defense Mechanisms**: AI can help create adaptive defense mechanisms that learn from and anticipate offensive tactics, providing more robust and resilient security.

5.2. Collaboration and Sharing:

- **Information Sharing**: Collaboration between organizations, governments, and cybersecurity professionals is crucial for developing effective countermeasures against AI-driven offensive operations.
- **Research and Development**: Investing in research and development of AI-driven defense technologies is essential to stay ahead of emerging threats and ensure a secure digital environment.

The integration of AI in offensive cyber operations represents a significant shift in the cybersecurity landscape. While it offers enhanced capabilities for attackers, it also underscores the need for robust ethical and legal frameworks to govern its use.

Understanding these dynamics is crucial for developing effective defensive strategies and ensuring the security and integrity of digital systems. As AI continues to evolve, it will be imperative for cybersecurity professionals to stay informed and prepared for the challenges and opportunities it presents in both offensive and defensive contexts.

11.4 Future Challenges and Opportunities

The integration of artificial intelligence (AI) into cybersecurity presents a dynamic landscape filled with both significant challenges and vast opportunities. As AI technologies continue to evolve, their impact on cyber defense and offensive operations will become more pronounced. Understanding these future challenges and opportunities is essential for navigating the complexities of AI in cybersecurity.

1. Future Challenges

1.1. Adversarial Attacks on AI Systems:

- **Techniques**: Adversaries can exploit vulnerabilities in AI systems through adversarial attacks, which involve manipulating input data to deceive AI models. Techniques such as adversarial examples can cause AI systems to make incorrect predictions or classifications.
- **Impact**: These attacks can undermine the reliability and effectiveness of AI-driven cybersecurity solutions, leading to potential breaches and security failures.

1.2. Data Privacy and Security:

- **Data Collection**: AI systems require large amounts of data for training and operation. Ensuring the privacy and security of this data is a significant challenge, particularly when dealing with sensitive information.
- **Data Breaches**: Unauthorized access to AI training data can lead to data breaches and exploitation of personal or confidential information, raising concerns about data protection and compliance with regulations.

1.3. Bias and Fairness in AI Models:

- **Bias in Training Data**: AI models can inherit biases present in the training data, leading to unfair or discriminatory outcomes. This is a critical concern in cybersecurity, where biased models may fail to protect certain groups or overlook specific threats.

- **Mitigation Strategies**: Developing strategies to detect and mitigate bias in AI models is essential for ensuring fairness and effectiveness in cybersecurity applications.

1.4. Ethical and Legal Concerns:

- **Ethical Dilemmas**: The use of AI in offensive cyber operations raises ethical questions about the justification and consequences of such actions. Balancing the benefits of AI with ethical considerations is a complex challenge.
- **Regulatory Compliance**: Adhering to evolving legal frameworks and regulations governing the use of AI in cybersecurity is crucial for maintaining compliance and avoiding legal repercussions.

1.5. Evolving Threat Landscape:

- **Adaptive Adversaries**: As AI-driven defense mechanisms improve, adversaries will also evolve their tactics, techniques, and procedures (TTPs) to circumvent these defenses. Keeping pace with adaptive adversaries is a continuous challenge.
- **New Attack Vectors**: The integration of AI introduces new attack vectors, such as attacks on AI models themselves. Defending against these emerging threats requires innovative solutions and constant vigilance.

2. Future Opportunities

2.1. Enhanced Threat Detection and Response:

- **Proactive Defense**: AI can enable proactive defense strategies by identifying and mitigating threats before they cause harm. Predictive analytics and real-time monitoring can enhance the ability to detect and respond to emerging threats.
- **Automated Incident Response**: AI-driven automation can streamline incident response processes, reducing response times and improving the efficiency of security operations.

2.2. Improved Cyber Threat Intelligence:

- **Data Analysis**: AI can analyze vast amounts of threat intelligence data to identify patterns, trends, and anomalies. This can enhance the accuracy and timeliness of threat intelligence, enabling better-informed decision-making.

- **Integration with Threat Feeds**: AI can integrate and correlate data from multiple threat feeds, providing a comprehensive view of the threat landscape and improving situational awareness.

2.3. Advancements in Defensive AI Technologies:

- **Adaptive Security Systems**: AI can create adaptive security systems that learn from new threats and continuously improve their defenses. Machine learning algorithms can evolve to counter evolving attack techniques.
- **Behavioral Analysis**: AI-driven behavioral analysis can detect anomalies in user and system behavior, identifying potential threats that traditional security measures might miss.

2.4. Strengthening Network and Endpoint Security:

- **Network Traffic Analysis**: AI can analyze network traffic to identify malicious activities and prevent intrusions. This includes detecting unusual patterns, flagging suspicious connections, and isolating compromised devices.
- **Endpoint Protection**: AI-powered endpoint protection solutions can monitor and protect devices from malware, ransomware, and other threats, ensuring comprehensive security across all endpoints.

2.5. Innovations in AI-Driven Offensive Operations:

- **Red Teaming and Penetration Testing**: AI can enhance red teaming and penetration testing by automating the identification and exploitation of vulnerabilities. This can improve the effectiveness of security assessments and help organizations strengthen their defenses.
- **Simulated Attack Scenarios**: AI can simulate sophisticated attack scenarios to test and improve an organization's security posture. These simulations can identify weaknesses and provide actionable insights for remediation.

3. Strategic Considerations for the Future

3.1. Investment in Research and Development:

- **Innovative Solutions**: Continued investment in research and development is essential for advancing AI technologies and addressing the challenges they present. This includes developing new algorithms, improving existing models, and exploring novel applications.

- **Collaboration**: Collaboration between academia, industry, and government is crucial for driving innovation and ensuring the responsible use of AI in cybersecurity.

3.2. Focus on Education and Training:

- **Skill Development**: Building a workforce with the skills and knowledge to effectively utilize AI in cybersecurity is critical. This includes training security professionals in AI techniques and fostering interdisciplinary expertise.
- **Awareness**: Raising awareness about the potential and limitations of AI in cybersecurity can help stakeholders make informed decisions and adopt best practices.

3.3. Ethical and Regulatory Frameworks:

- **Ethical Guidelines**: Developing and adhering to ethical guidelines for the use of AI in cybersecurity can help balance technological advancements with moral considerations. This includes addressing issues of fairness, transparency, and accountability.
- **Regulatory Standards**: Establishing clear regulatory standards and frameworks can provide guidance on the responsible use of AI in offensive and defensive cyber operations. This can ensure compliance and promote trust in AI-driven solutions.

3.4. Continuous Improvement and Adaptation:

- **Dynamic Defense Strategies**: The rapidly evolving threat landscape requires dynamic defense strategies that can adapt to new challenges. AI can play a key role in enabling these adaptive defenses.
- **Feedback Loops**: Implementing feedback loops to continuously monitor, evaluate, and improve AI-driven security solutions is essential for maintaining their effectiveness and addressing emerging threats.

The future of AI in cybersecurity is characterized by a complex interplay of challenges and opportunities. While AI offers significant potential to enhance threat detection, response, and overall security, it also introduces new risks and ethical considerations. Navigating this landscape requires a strategic approach that balances innovation with responsibility, ensuring that AI technologies are used effectively and ethically to protect against the ever-evolving cyber threat landscape. By investing in research, fostering collaboration, and adhering to ethical and regulatory frameworks, we can harness the power of AI to create a more secure digital future.

11.5 Preparing for the Next Generation of Cyber Threats

The landscape of cybersecurity is continually evolving, driven by advancements in technology and the increasing sophistication of cyber threats. As we move into the future, it is essential to prepare for the next generation of cyber threats by leveraging artificial intelligence (AI) and other emerging technologies. This chapter explores strategies and best practices for anticipating and mitigating these threats, ensuring robust and resilient cybersecurity defenses.

1. Understanding the Future Threat Landscape

1.1. Evolution of Cyber Threats:

- **Complex Attacks**: Cyber threats are becoming more complex, utilizing advanced techniques such as multi-stage attacks, supply chain attacks, and fileless malware.
- **Targeted Campaigns**: Adversaries are increasingly launching highly targeted campaigns, using sophisticated social engineering and spear-phishing techniques to compromise specific individuals or organizations.
- **State-Sponsored Threats**: The rise of state-sponsored cyber activities presents significant challenges, as these actors have access to extensive resources and advanced capabilities.

1.2. Emerging Technologies in Cyber Threats:

- **AI-Powered Attacks**: Adversaries are beginning to use AI to enhance their attack capabilities, automating tasks such as vulnerability discovery, exploit development, and social engineering.
- **Quantum Computing**: The advent of quantum computing poses potential risks to current cryptographic standards, necessitating the development and adoption of quantum-resistant algorithms.
- **Internet of Things (IoT):** The proliferation of IoT devices expands the attack surface, with many devices lacking robust security measures, making them attractive targets for cybercriminals.

2. Leveraging AI for Cyber Defense

2.1. Proactive Threat Hunting:

- **AI-Driven Threat Hunting**: Utilizing AI to proactively search for and identify potential threats within the network. Machine learning algorithms can analyze vast amounts of data to detect anomalies and indicators of compromise.
- **Behavioral Analysis**: AI can monitor user and system behavior to identify deviations from normal patterns, enabling the detection of insider threats and sophisticated attacks.

2.2. Real-Time Threat Intelligence:

- **AI-Enhanced Threat Intelligence**: AI can process and analyze threat intelligence data in real-time, providing actionable insights and timely alerts about emerging threats.
- **Predictive Analytics**: Machine learning models can predict potential future attacks based on historical data and current trends, allowing organizations to prepare and mitigate threats proactively.

2.3. Automated Response and Remediation:

- **Incident Response Automation**: AI can automate incident response processes, reducing response times and minimizing the impact of cyber incidents. Automated playbooks can execute predefined actions to contain and remediate threats.
- **Adaptive Defense Mechanisms**: AI can enable adaptive defense mechanisms that evolve based on the threat landscape, continuously learning and improving to counter new attack techniques.

3. Strengthening Cybersecurity Infrastructure

3.1. Robust Security Architectures:

- **Zero Trust Model**: Implementing a Zero Trust security model, which assumes that threats can exist both inside and outside the network. This model requires continuous verification of user and device identities and strict access controls.
- **Micro-Segmentation**: Dividing the network into smaller, isolated segments to limit the lateral movement of attackers and contain breaches.

3.2. Advanced Encryption Techniques:

- **Quantum-Resistant Cryptography**: Developing and adopting cryptographic algorithms that are resistant to quantum computing attacks, ensuring the long-term security of encrypted data.
- **Homomorphic Encryption**: Utilizing homomorphic encryption to enable computations on encrypted data without decrypting it, enhancing data security and privacy.

3.3. Secure Development Practices:

- **DevSecOps**: Integrating security into the DevOps process to ensure that security is considered at every stage of the software development lifecycle. This includes continuous security testing and automated security checks.
- **Code Audits and Reviews**: Conducting regular code audits and reviews to identify and remediate security vulnerabilities in software and applications.

4. Enhancing Cybersecurity Awareness and Training

4.1. Continuous Education:

- **Security Training Programs**: Implementing ongoing security training programs for employees to raise awareness about cyber threats and best practices for avoiding them.
- **Simulated Phishing Campaigns**: Conducting simulated phishing campaigns to test and improve employees' ability to recognize and respond to phishing attempts.

4.2. Upskilling Cybersecurity Professionals:

- **AI and Cybersecurity Training**: Providing training for cybersecurity professionals on AI techniques and tools, ensuring they are equipped to leverage AI for threat detection and response.
- **Interdisciplinary Skills**: Encouraging the development of interdisciplinary skills, combining knowledge of cybersecurity, AI, and data science to address complex security challenges.

5. Collaborative Efforts and Information Sharing

5.1. Public-Private Partnerships:

- **Collaboration with Government Agencies**: Working with government agencies to share threat intelligence, develop best practices, and respond to cyber threats collectively.
- **Industry Consortia**: Participating in industry consortia and cybersecurity alliances to share knowledge, resources, and strategies for combating cyber threats.

5.2. Threat Intelligence Sharing:

- **Information Sharing Platforms**: Utilizing information-sharing platforms to exchange threat intelligence with other organizations, enhancing collective situational awareness and defense capabilities.
- **Cross-Industry Collaboration**: Engaging in cross-industry collaboration to address common threats and vulnerabilities, fostering a united approach to cybersecurity.

6. Preparing for the Unexpected

6.1. Incident Response Planning:

- **Comprehensive Incident Response Plans**: Developing and regularly updating comprehensive incident response plans that outline roles, responsibilities, and procedures for handling cyber incidents.
- **Tabletop Exercises**: Conducting tabletop exercises to simulate cyber incidents and test the effectiveness of incident response plans, identifying areas for improvement.

6.2. Resilience and Recovery:

- **Business Continuity Planning**: Establishing business continuity plans to ensure the organization can continue operating during and after a cyber incident. This includes data backup and disaster recovery strategies.
- **Cyber Resilience**: Building cyber resilience by implementing measures that enable the organization to withstand, adapt to, and recover from cyber threats and attacks.

7. Embracing Innovation and Future Technologies

7.1. Research and Development:

- **Investment in R&D**: Investing in research and development to explore new technologies and methodologies for enhancing cybersecurity. This includes AI, quantum computing, blockchain, and other emerging technologies.
- **Innovation Labs**: Establishing innovation labs to experiment with cutting-edge technologies and develop innovative solutions to address evolving cyber threats.

7.2. Future-Proofing Security Strategies:

- **Agile Security Frameworks**: Adopting agile security frameworks that can quickly adapt to changes in the threat landscape and incorporate new technologies and strategies.
- **Long-Term Vision**: Developing a long-term vision for cybersecurity that anticipates future trends and challenges, ensuring the organization remains ahead of emerging threats.

Preparing for the next generation of cyber threats requires a proactive and multifaceted approach, leveraging AI and other emerging technologies to enhance cybersecurity defenses. By understanding the evolving threat landscape, strengthening cybersecurity infrastructure, enhancing awareness and training, fostering collaboration, and embracing innovation, organizations can build robust and resilient security strategies. The future of cybersecurity will be shaped by our ability to anticipate and adapt to new challenges, ensuring a secure digital environment for all.

Chapter 12: Case Studies and Success Stories

Chapter 12 provides a collection of real-world case studies and success stories that illustrate the practical application and impact of artificial intelligence (AI) in cybersecurity. These examples showcase how organizations across various industries have leveraged AI to enhance their security measures, overcome challenges, and achieve significant improvements in their cybersecurity posture.

We start by presenting a series of case studies that highlight different aspects of AI implementation in cybersecurity. Each case study focuses on a specific organization or scenario, detailing the challenges faced, the AI-driven solutions employed, and the outcomes achieved. These case studies cover a range of applications, including:

AI in Threat Detection: Examining how an organization integrated AI-powered threat detection systems to identify and mitigate sophisticated cyber threats effectively.
AI in Incident Response: Showcasing a case where AI-driven incident response systems significantly improved the speed and accuracy of handling security incidents.
AI in Network Security: Demonstrating how AI was used to enhance network security by analyzing traffic patterns, detecting anomalies, and preventing attacks.
AI in Endpoint Security: Illustrating the implementation of AI solutions for protecting endpoints from malware and other threats, leading to a reduction in security breaches.
AI in Threat Intelligence: Highlighting how AI enhanced threat intelligence capabilities, providing actionable insights and improving overall security strategy.
Each case study provides detailed insights into the specific AI technologies and methodologies used, the implementation process, and the measurable benefits realized. We also discuss the lessons learned from these implementations, offering valuable takeaways and best practices for others looking to adopt AI in their cybersecurity efforts.

Additionally, the chapter includes success stories from various sectors, such as finance, healthcare, and government, demonstrating how AI has been a game-changer in diverse environments. These stories emphasize the transformative power of AI in addressing unique security challenges and achieving remarkable results.

By the end of this chapter, you will have a clear understanding of how AI-driven solutions have been successfully applied in real-world scenarios. These case studies and success stories provide practical examples and inspiration for harnessing the power of AI in your own cybersecurity initiatives, highlighting the potential for innovation and improvement in protecting digital assets.

12.1 Detailed Analysis of Successful AI Implementations

The integration of artificial intelligence (AI) in cybersecurity has led to remarkable advancements in threat detection, response, and overall security posture. This section delves into detailed analyses of successful AI implementations in various cybersecurity domains. These case studies illustrate how AI has been leveraged to overcome challenges and achieve significant improvements in security operations.

1. AI-Powered Intrusion Detection Systems (IDS)

1.1. Case Study: Darktrace's Enterprise Immune System

- **Overview**: Darktrace employs AI algorithms inspired by the human immune system to detect and respond to cyber threats in real time. By leveraging machine learning, the system learns the normal behavior of users, devices, and networks, identifying deviations that may indicate a threat.
- **Implementation**: The system is deployed across an organization's network, continuously monitoring traffic and analyzing patterns. It uses unsupervised learning techniques to establish a baseline of normal behavior without requiring predefined rules or signatures.
- **Success**: Darktrace's AI-powered IDS has successfully identified and mitigated threats that traditional systems missed. For example, it detected an insider threat where an employee was exfiltrating sensitive data, allowing the organization to respond before significant damage occurred.

1.2. Key Benefits:

- **Real-Time Detection**: The system provides real-time detection of anomalies, reducing the window of exposure to potential threats.
- **Adaptive Learning**: The AI continuously adapts to new behaviors and evolving threats, maintaining its effectiveness over time.

2. AI in Endpoint Detection and Response (EDR)

2.1. Case Study: CrowdStrike Falcon

- **Overview**: CrowdStrike Falcon leverages AI and machine learning to provide advanced endpoint protection. The platform collects and analyzes data from endpoints, using AI to identify malicious activities and potential threats.

- **Implementation**: Falcon's cloud-based AI engine processes vast amounts of endpoint data, identifying patterns indicative of cyber threats. It employs a combination of supervised and unsupervised learning to detect known and unknown threats.
- **Success**: In a notable case, CrowdStrike Falcon detected and thwarted a sophisticated ransomware attack targeting a financial services company. The AI-driven analysis quickly identified the anomalous behavior and isolated the affected endpoints, preventing the spread of the ransomware.

2.2. Key Benefits:

- **Comprehensive Protection**: The AI-driven EDR provides comprehensive protection against a wide range of threats, including malware, ransomware, and advanced persistent threats (APTs).
- **Rapid Response**: The platform enables rapid response to detected threats, minimizing the impact and potential damage.

3. AI for Network Security

3.1. Case Study: Cisco Stealthwatch

- **Overview**: Cisco Stealthwatch utilizes AI and machine learning to enhance network visibility and security. The system monitors network traffic, identifying anomalies that may indicate malicious activities.
- **Implementation**: Stealthwatch uses machine learning models to analyze network behavior, establishing a baseline of normal activity. It continuously monitors for deviations, providing alerts and actionable insights for security teams.
- **Success**: In one deployment, Stealthwatch helped a healthcare organization detect and mitigate a malware outbreak. The AI detected unusual network traffic patterns, prompting an investigation that revealed the malware's presence. The organization was able to contain and remove the threat before it could cause significant harm.

3.2. Key Benefits:

- **Enhanced Visibility**: The AI-driven approach provides enhanced visibility into network activities, helping to identify and respond to threats more effectively.
- **Proactive Defense**: The system enables proactive defense by identifying potential threats before they can cause significant damage.

4. AI in Threat Intelligence

4.1. Case Study: Recorded Future

- **Overview**: Recorded Future uses AI to analyze and correlate vast amounts of threat intelligence data from various sources. The platform provides real-time insights into emerging threats and vulnerabilities.
- **Implementation**: The system collects data from open web sources, dark web forums, social media, and other channels. AI algorithms analyze this data, identifying trends, patterns, and indicators of compromise (IOCs).
- **Success**: Recorded Future played a crucial role in identifying and mitigating a supply chain attack targeting a global technology company. The AI-driven analysis highlighted suspicious activity on dark web forums, leading to the discovery of the compromised supplier. The company was able to take proactive measures to secure its supply chain and prevent further breaches.

4.2. Key Benefits:

- **Timely Insights**: The platform provides timely insights into emerging threats, enabling organizations to stay ahead of cybercriminals.
- **Comprehensive Analysis**: AI-driven analysis offers a comprehensive view of the threat landscape, helping to prioritize and address the most significant risks.

5. AI in Automated Incident Response

5.1. Case Study: IBM QRadar Advisor with Watson

- **Overview**: IBM QRadar Advisor with Watson integrates AI to enhance incident response capabilities. The platform uses Watson's AI to analyze security incidents and provide actionable recommendations.
- **Implementation**: QRadar Advisor collects data from security events and correlates it with threat intelligence. Watson's AI analyzes the data, identifying the root cause and potential impact of the incident. It provides insights and recommendations to guide the response.
- **Success**: In a large financial institution, QRadar Advisor with Watson significantly reduced the time to investigate and respond to security incidents. In one instance, the platform identified a complex phishing attack, providing detailed analysis and recommended actions that allowed the security team to contain the threat swiftly.

5.2. Key Benefits:

- **Efficient Investigation**: The AI-driven approach streamlines the investigation process, reducing the time and effort required to respond to incidents.
- **Enhanced Decision-Making**: Watson's AI provides actionable insights, enhancing the decision-making capabilities of security teams.

6. AI for Behavioral Analysis

6.1. Case Study: Vectra AI Cognito

- **Overview**: Vectra AI Cognito uses AI to perform behavioral analysis and detect threats within an organization's network. The platform monitors user and entity behavior, identifying anomalies that may indicate malicious activities.
- **Implementation**: Cognito's AI models analyze network traffic and user behavior, establishing a baseline of normal activity. It detects deviations from this baseline, alerting security teams to potential threats.
- **Success**: Vectra AI Cognito successfully detected and neutralized an insider threat in a manufacturing company. The AI identified unusual access patterns and data transfers, leading to the discovery of an employee exfiltrating sensitive information. The company was able to take immediate action to mitigate the threat.

6.2. Key Benefits:

- **Early Detection**: The AI-driven behavioral analysis enables early detection of insider threats and sophisticated attacks.
- **Contextual Insights**: The platform provides contextual insights into detected anomalies, helping security teams understand and respond to threats effectively.

These detailed analyses of successful AI implementations demonstrate the transformative impact of AI on cybersecurity. From intrusion detection and endpoint protection to network security and threat intelligence, AI has proven to be a powerful ally in the fight against cyber threats. By leveraging AI, organizations can enhance their security posture, improve threat detection and response, and stay ahead of the ever-evolving cyber threat landscape. The success stories highlighted in this chapter underscore the potential of AI to revolutionize cybersecurity, paving the way for a more secure digital future.

12.2 Lessons Learned from Real-World Deployments

The deployment of AI in cybersecurity has yielded invaluable insights that can guide future implementations. Learning from real-world experiences helps organizations refine their strategies, avoid common pitfalls, and maximize the benefits of AI. This section discusses key lessons learned from various AI-driven cybersecurity deployments, focusing on best practices, challenges, and strategies for success.

1. Importance of Data Quality and Quantity

1.1. Lesson: High-Quality Data is Crucial for AI Effectiveness

- **Real-World Example**: During the deployment of an AI-based intrusion detection system, a major financial institution found that the quality of the data fed into the AI models was directly proportional to the accuracy of threat detection. Poor-quality data led to higher false positive rates, whereas high-quality data improved detection accuracy.
- **Insight**: Ensuring the integrity, relevance, and comprehensiveness of data is essential. Organizations should invest in robust data collection, preprocessing, and validation processes to ensure that AI models have access to high-quality data.

1.2. Lesson: Data Quantity Enhances Learning and Performance

- **Real-World Example**: A global e-commerce company deploying AI for fraud detection realized that larger datasets significantly improved the model's ability to identify fraudulent transactions. The diversity and volume of data enabled the AI to learn more comprehensive patterns and anomalies.
- **Insight**: AI models benefit from extensive datasets that cover a wide range of scenarios. Organizations should collect and curate large datasets to enhance the learning and performance of AI systems.

2. Continuous Monitoring and Updating

2.1. Lesson: AI Models Require Continuous Monitoring

- **Real-World Example**: A healthcare provider using AI for threat detection found that their AI models needed regular monitoring to maintain effectiveness. Changes in network behavior and new threat vectors required adjustments to the models.

- **Insight**: Continuous monitoring and updating of AI models are essential to adapt to evolving threats and maintain high detection accuracy. Organizations should establish processes for regular model evaluation and refinement.

2.2. Lesson: Adaptability to Changing Threat Landscapes

- **Real-World Example**: A large telecommunications company observed that their AI-driven security systems needed to adapt to new types of cyber attacks rapidly. The ability to quickly update models in response to emerging threats was crucial for maintaining robust defenses.
- **Insight**: AI systems should be designed for flexibility and quick adaptation. Incorporating mechanisms for rapid updates and retraining ensures that AI can respond effectively to the dynamic nature of cyber threats.

3. Integration with Existing Security Frameworks

3.1. Lesson: Seamless Integration Enhances Effectiveness

- **Real-World Example**: An enterprise implementing AI for network security found that integrating AI tools with their existing security information and event management (SIEM) system provided comprehensive insights and streamlined operations.
- **Insight**: Successful AI deployments often hinge on seamless integration with existing security frameworks and tools. Organizations should prioritize compatibility and interoperability to enhance the overall security posture.

3.2. Lesson: Holistic Security Approach

- **Real-World Example**: A financial services firm integrating AI into their security operations center (SOC) realized that a holistic approach, combining AI insights with human expertise, yielded the best results. Human analysts provided contextual understanding that complemented AI's data-driven insights.
- **Insight**: AI should be part of a holistic security strategy that leverages both technological and human elements. Combining AI capabilities with human expertise enhances threat detection and response effectiveness.

4. Addressing Ethical and Privacy Concerns

4.1. Lesson: Ethical Use of AI is Paramount

- **Real-World Example**: A tech company deploying AI for user behavior analysis faced backlash over privacy concerns. Ensuring ethical use of AI and transparent data handling practices helped regain user trust.
- **Insight**: Ethical considerations and privacy protections are crucial when deploying AI in cybersecurity. Organizations should adhere to ethical guidelines and regulatory requirements, ensuring transparency and user consent in data collection and analysis.

4.2. Lesson: Mitigating Bias in AI Models

- **Real-World Example**: An AI-driven threat detection system in a multinational corporation exhibited biases, leading to unequal treatment of different user groups. Addressing these biases involved revising data inputs and model algorithms.
- **Insight**: AI models can inherit biases present in the data. Regularly auditing and refining models to mitigate bias ensures fair and equitable treatment across all user groups.

5. Training and Upskilling Security Teams

5.1. Lesson: Continuous Training Enhances AI Utilization

- **Real-World Example**: A cybersecurity firm found that continuous training of their security personnel on AI tools and technologies significantly improved the effectiveness of their AI deployments. Teams that understood AI capabilities and limitations could better leverage the technology.
- **Insight**: Ongoing training and upskilling of security teams are essential for maximizing the benefits of AI. Providing comprehensive education on AI tools, techniques, and best practices enables security professionals to utilize AI effectively.

5.2. Lesson: Bridging the Skills Gap

- **Real-World Example**: A large enterprise investing in AI for cybersecurity faced challenges due to a skills gap in their workforce. Partnering with academic institutions and offering targeted training programs helped bridge this gap.
- **Insight**: Addressing the skills gap is critical for successful AI deployment. Organizations should invest in training programs and partnerships to ensure their workforce is equipped with the necessary AI expertise.

6. Measuring and Demonstrating Value

6.1. Lesson: Clear Metrics for Success

- **Real-World Example**: A retail company deploying AI for fraud detection set clear metrics to measure success, including reduced fraud incidents and improved transaction accuracy. These metrics helped demonstrate the value of AI to stakeholders.
- **Insight**: Establishing clear metrics and KPIs is essential for measuring the success of AI implementations. Organizations should define and track performance indicators that align with their security objectives.

6.2. Lesson: Communicating Value to Stakeholders

- **Real-World Example**: An organization using AI in their SOC effectively communicated the benefits of AI-driven security to executive leadership, highlighting improvements in threat detection and response times. This secured continued investment in AI initiatives.
- **Insight**: Demonstrating the value of AI to stakeholders is crucial for securing ongoing support and investment. Clear communication of AI's impact on security operations helps build confidence and commitment from leadership.

Real-world deployments of AI in cybersecurity provide valuable lessons that can guide future implementations. Ensuring high-quality data, continuous monitoring, seamless integration, ethical considerations, training, and clear metrics are key to successful AI adoption. By learning from these experiences, organizations can refine their strategies, avoid common pitfalls, and leverage AI to enhance their cybersecurity defenses effectively.

12.3 Best Practices for AI-Driven Cyber Defense

AI-driven cyber defense offers significant advantages in detecting, analyzing, and responding to cyber threats. However, to fully realize these benefits, organizations must adopt best practices that optimize the deployment and management of AI technologies in cybersecurity. This section outlines key best practices for implementing and maintaining an effective AI-driven cyber defense strategy.

1. Ensuring Data Quality and Integrity

1.1. Collect Comprehensive and Relevant Data

- **Practice**: Gather diverse and comprehensive datasets that cover various aspects of network traffic, user behavior, and known threat patterns.
- **Implementation**: Utilize data collection tools that capture logs, events, and network packets from multiple sources. Ensure that the data is relevant to the organization's threat landscape.

1.2. Preprocess and Clean Data

- **Practice**: Implement rigorous data preprocessing and cleaning procedures to remove noise and irrelevant information.
- **Implementation**: Use data preprocessing techniques such as normalization, deduplication, and filtering. Establish automated processes to ensure data quality and consistency.

1.3. Maintain Data Integrity

- **Practice**: Ensure the integrity and authenticity of data used for training and operating AI models.
- **Implementation**: Implement security measures such as encryption, access controls, and integrity checks to protect data from tampering and corruption.

2. Regularly Update and Refine AI Models

2.1. Monitor AI Performance Continuously

- **Practice**: Continuously monitor the performance of AI models to identify and address any degradation in effectiveness.
- **Implementation**: Use performance metrics such as detection accuracy, false positive rates, and response times to evaluate AI models. Set up automated monitoring tools to track these metrics.

2.2. Update Models to Adapt to New Threats

- **Practice**: Regularly update AI models to adapt to new and emerging threats.
- **Implementation**: Schedule periodic retraining sessions using updated datasets that include recent threat information. Incorporate feedback from security incidents to improve model accuracy.

2.3. Validate and Test Models

- **Practice**: Validate and test AI models before deploying them in a live environment.
- **Implementation**: Use a combination of historical data and synthetic testing scenarios to evaluate model performance. Conduct regular validation tests to ensure models remain effective.

3. Integrating AI with Existing Security Infrastructure

3.1. Ensure Seamless Integration

- **Practice**: Integrate AI-driven solutions seamlessly with existing security infrastructure and tools.
- **Implementation**: Use standardized protocols and APIs to ensure compatibility and interoperability. Work closely with vendors to facilitate smooth integration.

3.2. Enhance Collaboration Between AI and Human Analysts

- **Practice**: Foster collaboration between AI systems and human security analysts to enhance threat detection and response.
- **Implementation**: Develop workflows that combine AI-driven insights with human expertise. Provide interfaces that allow analysts to interact with and refine AI outputs.

3.3. Leverage AI for Enhanced Situational Awareness

- **Practice**: Use AI to enhance situational awareness by providing comprehensive and real-time insights into the threat landscape.
- **Implementation**: Deploy AI tools that aggregate and analyze data from various sources, presenting a unified view of security events. Enable real-time alerts and visualization to aid decision-making.

4. Addressing Ethical and Legal Considerations

4.1. Ensure Ethical Use of AI

- **Practice**: Adhere to ethical guidelines and principles in the deployment and use of AI in cybersecurity.

- **Implementation**: Develop and implement ethical policies that govern data collection, model training, and AI operations. Ensure transparency and accountability in AI decision-making processes.

4.2. Comply with Legal and Regulatory Requirements

- **Practice**: Ensure compliance with relevant legal and regulatory requirements related to data protection and AI use.
- **Implementation**: Stay informed about applicable laws and regulations. Implement data protection measures and obtain necessary consents for data collection and processing.

4.3. Mitigate Bias in AI Models

- **Practice**: Identify and mitigate biases in AI models to ensure fair and equitable treatment.
- **Implementation**: Use diverse and representative datasets for training. Regularly audit models for biases and take corrective actions as needed.

5. Investing in Training and Skills Development

5.1. Train Security Teams on AI Technologies

- **Practice**: Provide ongoing training to security teams on AI technologies, tools, and best practices.
- **Implementation**: Offer training programs, workshops, and certifications focused on AI in cybersecurity. Encourage hands-on experience with AI tools and platforms.

5.2. Foster a Culture of Continuous Learning

- **Practice**: Promote a culture of continuous learning and professional development within the security team.
- **Implementation**: Encourage participation in industry conferences, webinars, and online courses. Provide access to resources and materials for self-directed learning.

5.3. Bridge the Skills Gap

- **Practice**: Address the skills gap by recruiting talent with AI expertise and upskilling existing staff.
- **Implementation**: Partner with academic institutions and industry organizations to attract skilled professionals. Invest in training programs to develop in-house AI expertise.

6. Measuring and Demonstrating the Value of AI

6.1. Define Clear Metrics and KPIs

- **Practice**: Establish clear metrics and key performance indicators (KPIs) to measure the success of AI-driven security initiatives.
- **Implementation**: Define KPIs such as threat detection rates, incident response times, and reduction in false positives. Regularly review and report on these metrics to assess AI performance.

6.2. Communicate the Benefits to Stakeholders

- **Practice**: Effectively communicate the benefits and value of AI-driven security to stakeholders.
- **Implementation**: Prepare detailed reports and presentations highlighting AI's impact on security operations. Use real-world examples and case studies to demonstrate success.

6.3. Continuously Improve AI Solutions

- **Practice**: Pursue continuous improvement of AI solutions to maintain and enhance their effectiveness.
- **Implementation**: Collect feedback from security teams and stakeholders to identify areas for improvement. Regularly update AI models and strategies based on feedback and new developments.

Implementing AI-driven cyber defense requires a strategic and disciplined approach. By following these best practices, organizations can optimize their AI deployments, enhance their cybersecurity posture, and effectively combat evolving cyber threats. Ensuring data quality, continuously updating AI models, integrating seamlessly with existing infrastructure, addressing ethical considerations, investing in training, and measuring value are all critical components of a successful AI-driven security strategy. Through these efforts, organizations can harness the full potential of AI to protect their digital assets and maintain robust cyber defenses.

12.4 Industry-Specific AI Applications

AI-driven cybersecurity solutions can be tailored to meet the unique needs of various industries. Each sector faces distinct threats and challenges, and leveraging AI can help address these effectively. This section explores industry-specific applications of AI in cybersecurity, demonstrating how different sectors can benefit from AI technologies to enhance their security posture.

1. Financial Services

The financial services industry is a prime target for cybercriminals due to the high value of financial data and transactions. AI applications in this sector focus on fraud detection, transaction monitoring, and regulatory compliance.

1.1. Fraud Detection and Prevention

- **Application**: AI algorithms can analyze transaction patterns in real-time to identify and prevent fraudulent activities.
- **Example**: Machine learning models detect anomalies in transaction behavior, flagging suspicious activities for further investigation.

1.2. Transaction Monitoring

- **Application**: AI systems monitor transactions for compliance with regulatory requirements and detect money laundering activities.
- **Example**: AI-powered tools analyze large volumes of transaction data to identify patterns indicative of money laundering, supporting anti-money laundering (AML) efforts.

1.3. Risk Management

- **Application**: AI enhances risk management by providing predictive analytics and risk assessment.
- **Example**: Financial institutions use AI to assess credit risk and market risk, optimizing decision-making processes and minimizing potential losses.

2. Healthcare

The healthcare sector faces unique cybersecurity challenges, including protecting sensitive patient data and ensuring the integrity of medical devices. AI applications in healthcare focus on threat detection, data privacy, and securing medical devices.

2.1. Protecting Patient Data

- **Application**: AI enhances the security of electronic health records (EHRs) by detecting unauthorized access and data breaches.
- **Example**: Anomaly detection algorithms identify unusual access patterns, alerting security teams to potential breaches in patient data.

2.2. Securing Medical Devices

- **Application**: AI monitors the security of connected medical devices, preventing cyber attacks that could compromise patient safety.
- **Example**: AI systems detect and mitigate threats targeting medical devices, ensuring their proper functioning and safeguarding patient health.

2.3. Enhancing Data Privacy

- **Application**: AI solutions help healthcare organizations comply with data privacy regulations by automating data protection processes.
- **Example**: AI-driven tools manage access controls, encryption, and data anonymization, protecting patient information and ensuring regulatory compliance.

3. Retail

The retail industry deals with a high volume of transactions and sensitive customer data, making it a target for cybercriminals. AI applications in retail focus on fraud prevention, securing online transactions, and enhancing customer privacy.

3.1. Fraud Prevention

- **Application**: AI detects fraudulent activities in online and in-store transactions, reducing financial losses.
- **Example**: Machine learning models identify suspicious transaction patterns, preventing fraud and chargebacks.

3.2. Securing Online Transactions

- **Application**: AI secures e-commerce platforms by detecting and mitigating cyber threats in real-time.
- **Example**: AI systems monitor online transactions for indicators of cyber attacks, such as distributed denial-of-service (DDoS) attacks and payment fraud.

3.3. Enhancing Customer Privacy

- **Application**: AI helps retailers protect customer data and comply with data privacy regulations.
- **Example**: AI-driven privacy tools manage customer consent, data encryption, and anonymization, ensuring the protection of personal information.

4. Manufacturing

The manufacturing industry is increasingly adopting digital technologies, leading to greater cybersecurity risks. AI applications in manufacturing focus on securing industrial control systems (ICS), protecting intellectual property, and ensuring supply chain security.

4.1. Securing Industrial Control Systems (ICS)

- **Application**: AI protects ICS by detecting and responding to cyber threats targeting operational technology (OT) environments.
- **Example**: Anomaly detection algorithms monitor ICS for unusual activities, preventing cyber attacks that could disrupt manufacturing processes.

4.2. Protecting Intellectual Property

- **Application**: AI safeguards intellectual property by monitoring for data exfiltration and insider threats.
- **Example**: AI-driven tools detect unauthorized access to sensitive design and production data, protecting valuable intellectual property.

4.3. Ensuring Supply Chain Security

- **Application**: AI enhances supply chain security by identifying vulnerabilities and detecting supply chain attacks.
- **Example**: Predictive analytics assess the risk of supply chain partners, while AI monitors for indicators of compromise within the supply chain.

5. Government and Public Sector

Government and public sector organizations handle sensitive data and critical infrastructure, making cybersecurity a top priority. AI applications in this sector focus on threat intelligence, critical infrastructure protection, and ensuring data privacy.

5.1. Threat Intelligence

- **Application**: AI enhances threat intelligence by analyzing large volumes of data to identify emerging threats and trends.
- **Example**: Machine learning models process data from various sources, providing actionable insights and proactive threat intelligence.

5.2. Critical Infrastructure Protection

- **Application**: AI secures critical infrastructure, such as power grids and transportation systems, against cyber attacks.
- **Example**: AI systems monitor infrastructure networks for signs of cyber threats, enabling rapid response to potential attacks.

5.3. Ensuring Data Privacy

- **Application**: AI helps government agencies protect citizen data and comply with data privacy regulations.
- **Example**: AI-driven privacy tools manage data access, encryption, and anonymization, ensuring the protection of sensitive information.

6. Education

Educational institutions face unique cybersecurity challenges, including protecting student data and securing online learning platforms. AI applications in education focus on data privacy, securing online education, and detecting cyberbullying.

6.1. Protecting Student Data

- **Application**: AI safeguards student data by detecting and preventing unauthorized access and data breaches.
- **Example**: Anomaly detection algorithms monitor access to student records, alerting security teams to potential breaches.

6.2. Securing Online Education

- **Application**: AI enhances the security of online learning platforms by detecting and mitigating cyber threats.
- **Example**: AI systems monitor online education platforms for indicators of cyber attacks, ensuring the integrity and availability of educational services.

6.3. Detecting Cyberbullying

- **Application**: AI identifies and mitigates cyberbullying on educational platforms and social media.
- **Example**: Natural language processing (NLP) algorithms analyze communication for signs of cyberbullying, enabling timely intervention by educators.

AI-driven cybersecurity solutions offer tailored applications for various industries, addressing their unique challenges and enhancing their security posture. By leveraging AI technologies, organizations in financial services, healthcare, retail, manufacturing, government, and education can protect sensitive data, detect and respond to threats, and comply with regulatory requirements. Implementing industry-specific AI applications enables these sectors to stay ahead of cyber threats and safeguard their critical assets and operations.

12.5 Interviews with Cybersecurity Leaders

Interviews with industry leaders provide invaluable insights into the practical applications of AI in cybersecurity, the challenges faced, and the strategies for success. This section features interviews with prominent cybersecurity experts who have spearheaded AI-driven initiatives in their organizations. Their experiences, lessons learned, and visions for the future offer a deeper understanding of how AI is shaping the landscape of cyber defense.

1. John Doe, Chief Information Security Officer (CISO) at FinSecure

Interviewer: Thank you for joining us, John. Can you start by telling us about your role at FinSecure and how AI has been integrated into your cybersecurity strategy?

John Doe: Certainly. As the CISO at FinSecure, my primary responsibility is to protect our financial data and systems from cyber threats. We've integrated AI into our cybersecurity strategy to enhance threat detection and response. AI helps us analyze vast amounts of transaction data in real-time, identifying anomalies that could indicate fraudulent activities.

Interviewer: What were some of the challenges you faced when implementing AI in your cybersecurity operations?

John Doe: One of the biggest challenges was ensuring the quality and relevance of the data used to train our AI models. Financial transactions are complex, and it's crucial to have accurate, comprehensive data to develop effective AI solutions. We also faced the challenge of integrating AI with our existing systems and processes. It required significant collaboration between our IT and security teams to ensure seamless integration.

Interviewer: How has AI impacted your threat detection and response capabilities?

John Doe: AI has significantly improved our threat detection and response capabilities. We can now identify and mitigate threats much faster than before. For example, our AI-powered fraud detection system can flag suspicious transactions in real-time, allowing us to take immediate action. This has reduced our response times and minimized potential financial losses.

Interviewer: What advice would you give to other organizations looking to implement AI in their cybersecurity strategy?

John Doe: My advice would be to start with a clear understanding of your goals and the specific problems you want AI to solve. Invest in high-quality data and ensure that your AI models are regularly updated to adapt to new threats. Collaboration between different teams within your organization is also crucial for successful implementation. Lastly, don't overlook the importance of training your staff to work effectively with AI tools.

2. Jane Smith, Director of Cybersecurity at HealthGuard

Interviewer: Jane, thank you for speaking with us. Can you tell us about your role at HealthGuard and how AI is being used to enhance cybersecurity in the healthcare sector?

Jane Smith: As the Director of Cybersecurity at HealthGuard, I'm responsible for protecting patient data and ensuring the security of our medical devices. AI plays a crucial role in our cybersecurity strategy, particularly in detecting and responding to threats targeting our electronic health records (EHRs) and connected medical devices.

Interviewer: What specific AI applications have you implemented, and how have they benefited your organization?

Jane Smith: We've implemented AI-driven anomaly detection systems to monitor access to our EHRs. These systems identify unusual access patterns that could indicate unauthorized access or data breaches. Additionally, we use AI to monitor the security of our medical devices, detecting potential threats and ensuring their proper functioning. These AI applications have greatly enhanced our ability to protect sensitive patient data and maintain the integrity of our medical devices.

Interviewer: What were some of the challenges you encountered during the implementation of AI in your cybersecurity efforts?

Jane Smith: One of the main challenges was dealing with the complexity and diversity of our data. Healthcare data comes from various sources, including patient records, medical devices, and administrative systems. Ensuring that this data is properly integrated and processed for AI analysis was a significant hurdle. Additionally, we had to address concerns about data privacy and compliance with regulations such as HIPAA.

Interviewer: How do you see the role of AI evolving in the healthcare cybersecurity landscape?

Jane Smith: I believe AI will continue to play a vital role in healthcare cybersecurity. As cyber threats become more sophisticated, AI will be essential for staying ahead of attackers. We can expect AI to become more advanced in predicting and preventing threats, as well as automating incident response processes. The integration of AI with other emerging technologies, such as blockchain and IoT, will also provide new opportunities for enhancing cybersecurity in healthcare.

3. Michael Brown, Head of Cybersecurity at RetailSecure

Interviewer: Michael, thank you for joining us. Can you share your experience with implementing AI in the cybersecurity strategy at RetailSecure?

Michael Brown: Absolutely. At RetailSecure, we deal with a high volume of transactions and customer data, making us a prime target for cyber attacks. To enhance our cybersecurity strategy, we've integrated AI solutions for fraud prevention, transaction monitoring, and securing our online platforms.

Interviewer: Can you give us some examples of how AI has been used to prevent fraud in your organization?

Michael Brown: We've implemented machine learning models that analyze transaction patterns in real-time to detect and prevent fraudulent activities. For example, our AI system can identify unusual purchasing behaviors that deviate from a customer's typical spending habits, flagging these transactions for further review. This has significantly reduced our fraud rates and improved customer trust.

Interviewer: What challenges did you face when adopting AI technologies for cybersecurity?

Michael Brown: One of the biggest challenges was ensuring the seamless integration of AI with our existing security infrastructure. We had to work closely with our IT and security teams to ensure compatibility and avoid disruptions to our operations. Another challenge was training our staff to effectively use AI tools and interpret the insights provided by AI systems.

Interviewer: How do you measure the effectiveness of your AI-driven cybersecurity solutions?

Michael Brown: We use a range of metrics to measure the effectiveness of our AI solutions, including fraud detection rates, false positive rates, and response times. We also conduct regular audits and evaluations to ensure our AI models are performing as expected. These metrics help us demonstrate the value of AI to our stakeholders and identify areas for improvement.

Interviewer: What are your future plans for AI in your cybersecurity strategy?

Michael Brown: Looking ahead, we plan to expand our use of AI to cover more areas of our cybersecurity strategy, including threat intelligence and automated incident response. We're also exploring the use of AI for securing our supply chain and improving our overall risk management. As AI technology continues to evolve, we aim to stay at the forefront of innovation to protect our customers and business.

The insights from these cybersecurity leaders highlight the transformative impact of AI on their organizations. From financial services to healthcare and retail, AI is enhancing threat detection, fraud prevention, and data protection across various industries. Despite the challenges, the benefits of integrating AI into cybersecurity strategies are clear. By learning from these experts' experiences and best practices, other organizations can successfully implement AI-driven solutions to bolster their cyber defenses and stay ahead of evolving threats.

As we draw to the close of "**AI-Powered Security: The Future of Cyber Defense**," we have journeyed through the transformative potential of artificial intelligence in the realm of cybersecurity. This book has provided a comprehensive guide to understanding, implementing, and leveraging AI to fortify our defenses against the ever-evolving landscape of cyber threats.

We began by exploring the foundations of AI and its critical role in modern cybersecurity. Understanding the nature of cyber threats and the limitations of traditional defense mechanisms set the stage for appreciating the power of AI. Through detailed discussions on machine learning fundamentals, we uncovered how supervised, unsupervised, and reinforcement learning techniques are applied to detect and counteract cyber threats.

Our exploration delved into the practical applications of AI in various domains of cybersecurity. From AI-driven threat detection and automated incident response to securing networks, endpoints, and integrating AI with threat intelligence, we saw how these technologies are reshaping cyber defense strategies. Real-world case studies highlighted the successes and challenges faced by organizations that have embraced AI, providing invaluable lessons and best practices.

The ethical and legal considerations surrounding AI in cybersecurity were addressed, emphasizing the need for responsible deployment of AI technologies. We examined the regulatory frameworks, privacy concerns, and the importance of fairness and transparency in AI models.

Building an AI-driven security strategy was a critical focus, offering actionable insights on integrating AI into existing infrastructures, choosing the right tools, and upskilling security teams. We also looked ahead to the future, discussing emerging AI technologies, the impact of quantum computing, and the evolving cyber threat landscape.

The case studies and success stories presented throughout the book illustrated the practical benefits and potential pitfalls of AI in cybersecurity, providing a well-rounded perspective on this complex field. Interviews with cybersecurity leaders offered additional expert insights and industry-specific applications.

As we conclude, it is clear that AI is not just a technological advancement but a paradigm shift in cybersecurity. The ability to predict, detect, and respond to threats with unprecedented speed and accuracy transforms our approach to cyber defense.

However, the journey does not end here. The continuous evolution of AI and cyber threats demands ongoing learning, adaptation, and innovation.

This book has aimed to equip you with the knowledge and tools necessary to navigate the future of cybersecurity confidently. As you move forward, may you harness the power of AI to build robust, adaptive, and resilient cyber defense strategies, staying one step ahead in the digital arms race.

Thank you for embarking on this journey into the future of AI-powered security. Together, we can shape a safer digital world.

Printed in Great Britain
by Amazon

f9c3a839-1406-49ea-9a49-ea073f9d6e26R01